Toward a Well-Fed World

Toward a Well-Fed World

DON PAARLBERG

THE HENRY A. WALLACE SERIES
ON AGRICULTURAL HISTORY AND RURAL STUDIES

IOWA STATE UNIVERSITY PRESS • AMES

Don Paarlberg, former Professor and Distinguished Professor at Purdue University, has farmed, performed agricultural research, and served as the first coordinator of the Food-For-Peace Program. He has been appointed to agriculture-related positions by three presidents and four secretaries of agriculture. His extensive travels have familiarized him with the food problems of all five continents and further prepared him for the consulting, speaking, and writing that occupy him today.

© 1988 Iowa State University Press, Ames, Iowa 50010
All rights reserved

Composed by Iowa State University Press
Printed in the United States of America

First edition, 1988

Library of Congress Cataloging-in-Publication Data

Paarlberg, Don, 1911–
　　Toward a well-fed world.

　　(The Henry A. Wallace series on agricultural history and rural studies)
　　Includes index.
　　1. Food supply.　　2. Famines.　　3. Food relief.　　4. Birth control.　　I. Title.
II. Series.
HD9000.5.P215　　1988　　　　　　　　363.8　　　　　　　87-36152
ISBN 0-8138-1729-3

This book is dedicated to the memory of my teacher of more than forty years ago,

Dr. Frank A. Pearson,

Professor of Agricultural Economics at the New York State College of Agriculture, Cornell University, who introduced me to the study of world hunger.

CONTENTS

EDITOR'S INTRODUCTION

THE HENRY A. WALLACE SERIES on Agricultural History and Rural Studies is designed to enlarge publishing opportunities in agricultural history and thereby to expand public understanding of the development of agriculture and rural society. The Series will be composed of volumes that explore the many aspects of agriculture and rural life within historical perspectives. It will evolve as the field evolves. The press and the editor will solicit and welcome the submission of manuscripts that illustrate, in good and fresh ways, that evolution. Our interests are broad. They do not stop with Iowa and U.S. agriculture but extend to all other parts of the world. They encompass the social, intellectual, scientific, and technological aspects of the subject as well as the economic and political. The emphasis of the Series is on the scholarly monograph, but historically significant memoirs of people involved in and with agriculture and rural life and major sources for research in the field will also be included.

Most appropriately, this Iowa-based Series is dedicated to a highly significant agriculturist who began in Iowa, developed a large, well-informed interest in its rural life, and expanded the scope of his interests beyond the state to the nation and the world. An Iowa native and son of an agricultural scientist, journalist, and secretary of agriculture, Henry A. Wallace was a 1910 graduate of Iowa State College, a frequent participant in its scientific activities, editor of *Wallaces' Farmer* from 1921 to 1933, founder in 1926 of the Hi-Bred Corn Company (now Pioneer Hi-Bred International, Inc.), secretary of agriculture from 1933 to 1940, and vice president of the United States from 1941 to 1945. In the agricultural phases of his wide-ranging career, he was both a person of large importance in the development of America's agriculture and the leading policymaker during the most creative period in the history of American farm policy.

In his distinguished career, the author of the present addition to the Wallace Series has represented a development that Wallace as secretary of agriculture, like his father before him, promoted in major ways. This is the move into government of persons with professional training in agricultural economics. Hoping to enlarge the role of that discipline in American thinking about farm matters, Henry C. Wallace, while serving as secretary of agriculture in the Harding administration, established a Bureau of Agricultural Economics (BAE). Then, a decade later, Secretary Henry A. Wallace drew heavily on agricultural economists to assist in the shaping of the New Deal for agriculture, even making the BAE in 1938 the central planning agency for the Department of Agriculture.

A critic of rather than a participant in the New Deal, Don Paarlberg nevertheless continued the practice among agricultural economists of moving into government service, doing so in Republican administrations during the 1950s and 1970s. Born in 1911 and raised on an Illinois farm, he was educated at Purdue and Cornell, earning the Ph.D. from the latter in 1947. Joining the Purdue faculty, he rose to the rank of professor before moving to Washington in 1953 to become economic adviser to the secretary of agriculture. After playing that role for four years, he became assistant secretary of agriculture and then special assistant to the president and food-for-peace coordinator, staying on until 1961. Returning to Purdue as Hillenbrand professor of agricultural economics, he remained there until 1969. In that year, he began seven years of work as director of agricultural economics in the USDA. In 1976 he became professor emeritus at Purdue.

In this volume Paarlberg focuses on a problem that greatly concerned Henry A. Wallace: how to serve the food needs of the world's people. In fact, in this biographical approach to the problem, Paarlberg devotes one chapter to Wallace. He is one of the heroes of the story, one of the famine fighters "who waged the age-old battle against hunger" and provided leadership "toward a well-fed world." According to the author's conception here, Wallace represented science, one of the three groups waging the battle. Paarlberg emphasizes Wallace's contribution to the development and use of hybrid corn. On that contribution, the author writes: "The national average of corn yield per acre has increased more than four times since Wallace began his work. Perhaps half of that increase is attributable to genetics, expressed in large part through hybridization. This is a massive increase in the production of food and feed and a significant step in the conquest of hunger." Finding even more to be said of Wallace's work on food, Paarlberg concludes that Wallace "helped improve world food production, actual and potential. He assisted in bridging the gap between the laboratory and the farmer's field. He helped lay the foundation for institutionalized food aid."

In the book as a whole, the author pursues a theme that has been central to his own work as both an academic and a government official. In Washington he provided leadership in the Food-For-Peace Program; as an academic, he wrote frequently about the battle against hunger. His first book, published in 1944 and written with his major professor, Frank A. Pearson of Cornell, was entitled simply *Food*. "Hunger is playing a dominant role in human history," the book began. "Conquest, Plague, Famine, and Death, the Four Horsemen of the Apocalypse, are riding in this war as they rode in others." And the author's most recent work prior to the present volume, *Farmers of Five Continents*, published in 1984, begins with this challenging historical interpretation: "Food is man's most ancient problem." Based on interviews with farmers conducted in eleven countries by Professor Paarlberg and his wife, Eva, the book also asserts early on: "Most notable among the famine-fighters are the farmers, who man the front-line trenches."

For those interested in Wallace, *Toward a Well-Fed World* supplies perspective. For those concerned about an even larger subject—the solution to the problem of hunger in the world—the book has much to offer.

RICHARD S. KIRKENDALL
Henry A. Wallace Professor of
Agricultural History and Rural Studies
Iowa State University

ACKNOWLEDGMENTS

HONOR IS PAID to the some forty people whose battles against hunger are here recounted. The achievements of these people stand as memorials, far eclipsing any words of mine. Ten of them are still living as this is written, most of them personally known to me. The following people have reviewed preliminary drafts of their respective chapters: Norman Borlaug, Anthony Dias, Bob Mills, Yuan Long Ping, T. W. Schultz, Pastor Stumpf, and M. S. Swaminathan.

Various parts of early drafts were read and commented on by William Brown, M. A. Hermodson, Bernard Liska, Don Paarlberg, Jr., S. R. Sen, Fred Warren, and Sylvan Wittwer. Betsy Schuhmann read, helpfully, the entire manuscript. Thanks to them and to Lowell Hardin, who organized a series of seminars on international agricultural development at Purdue on which I have drawn. Thanks to three persons, unknown to me, who reviewed a preliminary draft for the publisher, helping to correct errors and shorten the work.

And thanks especially to my wife, Eva, who typed repeated drafts of the manuscript.

Much of the material is taken from the various libraries of Purdue University, the National Agricultural Library, and the Library of Congress. Thanks are extended to the authors and publishers from whom I have drawn and to those persons who were interviewed.

I am in debt to many people for the material that has gone into this book. The theme that holds it together, however, is my own.

INTRODUCTION

HUNGER IS HUMANITY'S OLDEST ENEMY. From the time when humankind first became an identifiable species, perhaps 4 million years ago, the food supply has been the prime concern. Biologists rank the acquisition of food first among the motivations of human beings. "Give us this day our daily bread" is the first request of the Lord's Prayer. An old Byzantine proverb has it thus: "He who has bread has many problems; he who lacks bread has only one problem."

The exception to this generalized condition is the developed world of the twentieth century. Most of the people who read this book never missed a meal except by choice. For the majority of us the prevalence of hunger in human history is a fact forgotten if ever learned.

First to escape the shadow of hunger were those young countries, the United States and Canada, with their vast agricultural resources and sparse populations. Next came Western Europe, where industrial exports made possible the importation of huge amounts of food. Then, one by one, other countries improved their agriculture, helped their needy to escape hunger, and restrained population growth.

Even in these favored countries deprivation and want continue for limited numbers of people. But in the Western world, hunger as a general condition is a thing of the past. Elsewhere, hunger on the part of particular individuals and groups is much more prevalent and the threat of widespread famine is an authentic fear if not an actual fact.

The fight against hunger has been waged by three groups, with the troops unequally deployed. (1) *Science:* This is the sector in which the researchers, the educators, and the agribusiness people have made astounding advances. But the triumphs in this sector, however noteworthy, can be helpful only if put into use on farms. (2) *Food aid:* Flood, drought, earthquake, and war can jeopardize the food supply, particularly in a country close to the border of want. In any country, even a wealthy one, there are unfortunate individuals who are unable to care for themselves. If hunger is to be overcome, the needs of these disadvantaged people must be met. (3) *Family planning:* Birth control addresses the human side of the food-people equation; in that respect it differs profoundly from the food production sector. It is the newest of the salients. Fewer resources have been committed to this sector than to the others, and we know least about it.

Food aid is short-run, agricultural production is intermediate, and family planning is long-run. If the still-hungry nations are to escape widespread hunger they must, in their own ways, press the attack on all three fronts. They are doing so, in uneven fashion, as this book will show. This three-pronged attack is needful both for free nations and for countries that are centrally directed; the forces that relate food to people have little regard for political systems.

What is the prospect that people for whom famine remains a threat may escape this ancient enemy? For the first time in history there can be hope that this may occur. In much of the world previous to our day, intermittent famine was accepted as an ugly but natural and unavoidable condition. This need no longer be so. The necessary scientific knowledge with which to overcome hunger exists or is in prospect. The needed institutional framework has been conceived and is partly in place. Required are commitment and political will.

How did we in our battle against hunger reach a position such that conquest of the ancient enemy is a conceivable goal? It was not an accident, the result of some benign force. It was the work of heroes, less known and less celebrated than our military leaders but heroes nevertheless. The successful famine fighters were scientists, farmers, educators, welfare workers, family planners, institution builders, experimenters, tradesmen, and political leaders. They were men and women, primitive and modern, spanning the ages. Some succeeded and some, by their failures, demonstrated what should not be done. They came from various social classes. Some of them are among us today. They are so many that they cannot be numbered.

Famine fighters have been as diverse as any other fighters. Some were brawlers and some boxers. While some have been perceived as heroes, others have been cast as villains, and on still others history has not yet passed judgment. Many of the most effective famine fighters have not been perceived as battlers at all, even by themselves. Some hunger fighters were strategists, others were tacticians. Some fought for the cause and others for love of the battle. Many were bystanders, drawn into the fight. Some were mercenaries, interested in the paycheck. Most of them were from the Western world but some came from the developing countries. Some prodigious battles produced nothing of consequence while in other cases enormous results flowed from what seemed trivial causes. This book examines the triumph and the tragedy of those who waged the age-old battle against hunger.

Famine fighters who have borne arms in each of these sectors will be portrayed in this book. Whenever possible the fight against famine is personalized, the better to elicit the drama therefrom. Little is said about institutions, an institution being, as Emerson stated, "the lengthened shadow of one man."

No one is capable of singling out those most worthy of notice. Symbolism will therefore be employed; a named individual will stand for an unnamed host.

There is the well-known story about various people, all working at the same building site, being asked the question: "What are you doing?" One says, "Hauling stone," another "Shaping this block," another "Mixing mortar," another "Laying a wall." All were in fact building a cathedral. In similar fashion one might ask the people in this book what they were doing. James Watson (Chapter 17) might answer, "Discovering new knowledge." Bob Mills (Chapter 21) might say, "Growing crops and livestock." Pastor Stumpf (Chapter 26) might respond, "Doing the Lord's work." Chiang Mon Lin (Chapter 31) might say, "Bringing down the birthrate." Actually all were working to overcome hunger, to lead toward a well-fed world. That is the theme which holds the book together.

A NOTE ON REFERENCES

THE LAY READER IS REPELLED by citations, footnotes, and references; the expert is maddened by their absence. I wish to reach both groups, so I have compromised by giving references when the results seem surprising or little known or when a source is used heavily.

I have read or scanned innumerable books, journals, reports, articles, and papers. At the end of most chapters is a short list of those references that have been most helpful.

I have kept the first draft of this manuscript, which contains full documentation. It can be drawn upon on request if the reader wishes to go beyond the references offered in the book.

The Heritage

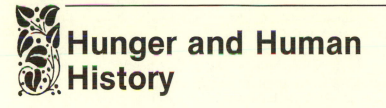

CHAPTER 1

Hunger and Human History

THOMAS HOBBES, writing in the seventeenth century, said that in a state of nature the life of man is "solitary, poor, nasty, brutish, and short." Part of this bleakness arose from hunger. Present causes of hunger are crop failure, war, civil disorder, inept economic systems, and burgeoning population growth. Some causes are man-made.

W. S. Thompson reports that between A.D. 10 and 1846 there were 201 famines in the British Isles. A study at Nanking University revealed that from 108 B.C. to A.D. 1911 there were 1,828 famines in China, or nearly one somewhere every year. The 1958 to 1961 famine in China, the largest in history, is said to have cost the lives of from 16 to 30 million people. In the middle of the nineteenth century crop failures in Ireland are reputed to have reduced the population by 2.5 million. For centuries famines were an important factor in limiting the population in Russia. There have been two major famines in the Soviet Union since the Revolution, one from 1921 to 1923 and one in the Ukraine from 1932 to 1934. Estimates of death vary but for each the assessment ranges around 5 million. The Bengal famine of 1943 is reported to have cost the lives of 1.5 million people. Some years ago northeastern Brazil experienced famine or near famine, a result of poor crops. War and civil disorder have caused famine in Biafra, Kampuchea, Ethiopia, Ogaden, and Timor. The famine of the mid-1980s in sub-Sahara Africa took an unnumbered toll. In 1985 the World Bank estimated that about 9 million African people faced a serious nutritional threat.

These major famines are of course dramatic. Less sensational but perhaps larger in toll of human lives is the year-after-year attrition that never reaches the headlines: here an infant dies because his malnourished mother is unable to nurse him; there a weanling child is lost, having a low priority on a limited food supply; elsewhere a mother perishes, worn out from too much work, too much childbearing, and too little food. All of this happens with a food supply that appears basically no different from what is customary. A remote village may experience local crop failure, resulting in a fearful death toll that never gets reported. Nobody knows how many deaths result from this dispersed form of famine, which is harder to cope with than the dramatic episodes that are sufficiently great and concentrated to alert the government and generate relief efforts.

Famines are seasonal, for human beings as well as other species. In the temperate zones, wildlife numbers are reduced during the winter, when food supplies are short. The rest of the year food supplies are relatively abundant; the birds and the deer do not then ordinarily experience hunger. The same is true of human beings, most of whom live in regions where some seasonal change occurs. Famine often strikes in the spring after a meager harvest has been consumed and before the new crop comes in. The duration of most famines is likely to be brief. With people as with other species, the population shrinks to the size of the food supply; usually this time of agonizing adjustment is mercifully short. Sometimes, however, bad years come in clusters, so that the dearth of food is prolonged.

When famine strikes, the reduced intake of food lowers the body's resistance. The conventional diseases then increase in incidence and severity. Rarely will death be officially attributed to starvation; pride and public reaction forbid. Famine watchers measure the severity of the food situation by the increase in the death rate attributed to the conventional diseases. This is why it is so hard to get an accurate count of deaths resulting from starvation.

The manner in which the population is adjusted to a short food supply is grim and best told briefly. First to die are the ill, the aged, the very young, and the very poor. Best able to survive are the wealthy and the strong. Whether males or females survive in larger proportion depends on the relative social status of the sexes prior to the famine.

The first manifestation of hunger is the gnawing desire for food, accompanied by surliness, aggression, and frenzied activity. With the passage of time, if food is not supplied, energy diminishes, strength wanes, and activity is reduced. Before death there comes lassitude, listlessness, weakness, and exhaustion. Thus, toward the end, nature eases the ordeal. The best popular writing on this subject, for empathy and accuracy, is in Pearl Buck's classic on China of an earlier day, *The Good Earth*.

Efforts of afflicted people to cope with famine take many forms. Reduced rations are one such adjustment. A healthy human being can go for six weeks without any food at all, as we know from hunger strikes. There is the well-authenticated case of Terrence MacSwiney, an Irish revolutionist who in 1920 went seventy-four days without food in a British prison before dying of starvation. Reduced intake coupled with diminished physical activity and lowered body weight can stretch out a short food supply. During the sometimes short rations of the hunting and gathering period the body developed adaptations to improve metabolic efficiency for coping with a dearth of food.

The slaughter of livestock is another potent means of coping with famine. When food is in short supply the people kill and eat their animals and then eat what the animals would otherwise have eaten. The potency of this adjuster is enormous where the animal population is large. Killing off grain-eating cattle will expand the food supply at least ten times. For hogs the factor is about five; for poultry it is perhaps three. When crops again are good the livestock population is rebuilt. The time required for repopulation of animals depends on the severity of the reduction, the strength of the recovery, and the length of the life cycle – generally about eighteen months for chickens, four years for hogs, and six years for cattle. The dietary changes associated with downward adjustments in the supply of meat, milk, and eggs are strongly resisted because of the persistent nature of food habits. But there is little evidence that these changes are seriously hurtful to health. Nations with large livestock populations, like the United States and Western Europe, have excellent built-in shock absorbers and are unlikely to experience famine. Some of the nations of Asia have relatively few domestic animals and so have no real cushion in their food supplies.

Storage has historically been used to cope with famine. When crops are seasonal and storable there must be, and long have been, ways of carrying part of the crop until the next harvest. Some is ordinarily carried over into the next season as insurance against famine. Danger of spoilage, insect pests, and the characteristic human discount for potential future problems usually keep this carryover at a modest level. Wealthy people store silver and gold instead of food; in time of famine they have thus been able to bid food away from the poor, many of whom then starve. The biblical story of Joseph in Egypt, storing the excess grain of seven good years against the needs of the predicted seven poor years is noteworthy because it is an exception. To build up a reserve means withholding some food from current consumption, which is difficult in a poor country. And storage is costly; even under good conditions, in about six years the cost of storage equals the value of the product.

Increased crop production, achieved by better cultural practices, is a way of warding off famine and has been most effective in alleviating hunger, as we shall learn throughout this book. If it is available, new land is brought into cultivation. But these are longer-term solutions and are of little value when famine looms or has already struck.

Another way of coping with famine is to intensify the cropping system. This adjuster, too, works gradually over a period of time. If the population presses heavily on the food supply and land is limited, more intensive crops are cultivated. Potatoes, rice, and corn produce about twice as much food per acre as wheat, whereas rye produces only about half as much. Carrots and onions yield about twice as much as wheat, while beets and celery yield about the same as wheat. Tomatoes, peas, lettuce, and asparagus yield one-fifth to one-third as much as wheat. As has been said, livestock are notoriously inefficient producers of food. However, if land is too rough or too dry for cultivated crops and can be used for grazing or if there are crop residues that can be eaten by animals, then livestock can add to the food supply.

In more recent times trade has been an important way of coping with famine. If the stricken nation has the means with which to buy, the trade is commercial, as with purchase of food from the United States by the Soviet Union in 1972–73. If there is not money with which to buy, if food is available in the donor country, and if diplomatic relationships accommodate, there may be international food aid, as was provided to India by the United States in 1966–67. These unrequited transfers are recent developments, with almost no precedent in remote times.

Migration is a means of meeting the threat of famine. In China, people historically moved from famine-stricken lands to areas with surplus food. In primitive societies, lacking good transportation, it was easier to move the human population to the food supply than to move the food to the people. The great migration of the Irish to the United States during the mid-nineteenth century was in part a famine-induced movement. Sometimes migrations are temporary and the people move back to their original homes, as was often true in China. Sometimes they are permanent, as with the Irish in the United States.

Famines can contribute to revolution and to plunder. Food riots preceded both the French and the Russian revolutions. Famines are redistributors of wealth and power. Those who are rich and those who hold political responsibility have good reasons to fear the unrest that accompanies famine.

War is both a cause of famine and a means employed to overcome it. Throughout history hunger has known no law. The pressure of population on the food supply caused the more powerful groups to raid or seize the fertile valleys and plains from their better-fed neighbors. Many different peoples raided the fertile valleys of the Euphrates, the Nile, the Danube, the Rhine, the Volga, the Indus, the Ganges, and the Yangtze. The Scottish Highlanders raided the Lowlands to the south. The Pilgrims, driven by hunger, raided the food supplies of the Indians. Sometimes raiders were small groups and sometimes they were armies of millions.

The equation of food and people must be brought into balance. Every effort is made to bring about adjustment on the food side. But after all such efforts have been exhausted, the people side of the equation is adjusted. The means of doing so include delayed marriage, abstaining from sexual intercourse, and various forms of contraception, including onanism and prolonged lactation with its associated reduction of the conception rate. These failing there are abortion, infanticide, and euthanasia. Occasionally and in the extreme, cannibalism occurs. Death resulting from famine is the ultimate adjuster.

How has humankind been able to survive when the dodo, the dinosaur, and countless other species have become extinct? The handicaps were great. Formidable fangs and claws were lacking, as was protection against cold of winter. The birthrate was among the lowest of the animal kingdom. The proportion of life spent in infancy, dependent on others, was greater than for almost any other species.

People have two organs that assist in survival. One is the brain; ability to think has given our name, *Homo sapiens,* the thinking animal. The other remarkable organ is the stomach; we can eat almost anything. We can eat, digest, and draw strength from meat in all its forms, fish, cereal grains, fruits, vegetables, nuts, herbs, insects, crustaceans, invertebrates, and other substances which out of respect for the reader's sensibility are best omitted. In time of famine hungry people will eat roots, the bark of trees, and even the earth itself, which contains some nutritious substances from which a starving man, in his desperation, can draw a limited amount of nourishment. We cannot live on grass as can the ruminants — cattle, sheep, goats, deer, and some other animals. Our digestive apparatus will not permit us to draw sustenance from cellulose as they can.

The koala bear eats nothing but eucalyptus and so has staked its existence on the continued availability of that species. The monarch butterfly is limited to the milkweed. But we, fortunately, have the teeth, the taste buds, the stomach, and the digestive appartus that permit us to be omnivorous. In much of Asia the staple is rice, in the Arctic it is fish, and in the tropics it is mandioca. Each of these staples is accompanied by a wide range of supplemental foods, mostly indigenous to the area. To the amazement of modern Americans with their varied, palatable, and expensive food, Asians, Africans, and Latin Americans work, fight, and reproduce effectively on what seem strange diets.

The flexibility in our capability to thrive on a variety of foods has enormous advantages. Maize is a high-yielding crop, but it was unknown to the Old World until Columbus brought it from America in the fifteenth century. It was accepted as a food and now is widely consumed in Asia and Africa. During the three hundred years since 1650, following the introduction of the potato from the New World to Europe, the population of the continent increased fivefold. When the buffalo were gone the Sioux shifted to other foods. These changes come slowly and are strongly resisted but with time do occur.

How are these adjustments made? Historically, before the emergence of the exchange economy, they were made by individual persons, families, and tribes, making direct disposition of their own resources. When the exchange economy developed, adjustments were brought about through the price system. When food was scarce the price increased, simultaneously inhibiting consumption and stimulating production. Thus the short supply was rationed and augmented. When grain supplies were short in England relative to the continent the Liverpool price was high relative to the Rotterdam price; grain was attracted to England's deficit areas. When drought cut the U.S. grain supply in 1934, 1936, and 1974 people bid the grain away from the animals. The livestock population declined and the people had the necessary food. When crops are disappointing and the market is free to fluctuate prices rise early in the season, giving the signal to all users that food is precious and is to be used sparingly. When famine looms rising prices provide the necessary but unwelcome information that food is scarce and should be conserved.

In much of the world the price system is seen as inequitable; the adjustment it provides permits the wealthy to eat well while the poor do the adjusting and the starving. Consequently central decision making has, to a degree, replaced the market system. The tools are allocations, priorities, rationing, price ceilings, food aid, fair price shops, requisitions, government-held food reserves, subsidies, and embargoes. These techniques can help avert famine or reduce its severity. We shall examine them in the chapters on food aid.

The short-time adjusters, brought into play when famine is a visible danger, are rising prices to facilitate conservation of food, slaughter of livestock, commercial trade if money is available and food aid if it is not, drawdown of stocks, and rationing. The long-term adjusters are rising prices to stimulate production and conserve supplies, better agricultural technology, bringing new land into tillage, intensification of agricultural systems, increased emphasis on agricultural research and education, and family planning. In either case, the maintenance of effective governance is essential; no system of food production and distribution can operate effectively in a setting of civil disorder.

What share of human history is significantly affected by hunger and a dearth of food? It would take a bold man indeed to venture an answer. But one can say with confidence that over the centuries famine has been a major force limiting the numbers of people. The quest for additional food has outfitted armies and launched ships. Empires have risen and thrones toppled in the struggle to control the food supply.

Saint John the Divine, writing from the Isle of Patmos around the close of the first century of the Christian era, produced his visionary work, the Revelation, last book of the New Testament. In it he described the Four Horsemen of the Apocalypse: Pestilence, War, Famine, and Death. The Horsemen rode together. It would be difficult to judge which was the greatest scourge.

REFERENCES

Bhatia, B. M. 1963. *Famines in India: A Study in Some Aspects of the Economic History of India, 1800–1845.* Bombay: Asia Publishing House.

Cahill, K. M. 1982. *Famine.* Maryknoll, N.Y.: Orbis.

Cohen, Mark N. 1977. *The Food Crisis in Pre-History: Overpopulation and the Origins of Agriculture.* New Haven: Yale Univ. Press.

Dando, William A. 1977. *Man-Made Famines: Past, Present, Future.* U.S. Department of Agriculture, Washington: Graduate School Press.

George, Susan. 1977. *How the Other Half Dies.* Montclair, N.J.: Allenheld, Osmun.

Hunger Project. 1985. *Ending Hunger: An Idea Whose Time Has Come.* New York: Praeger.

Lappé, Frances Moore, and Joseph Collins. 1977. *Food First.* Boston: Houghton Mifflin.

Pearson, F. A., and Don Paarlberg. 1946. *Starvation Truths, Half-Truths, Untruths.* Ithaca: New York State College of Agriculture.

Sen, Amartya. 1981. *Poverty and Famines: An Essay on Entitlement and Deprivation.* Oxford: Clarenden Press.

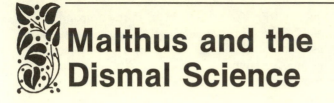

CHAPTER 2

Malthus and the Dismal Science

UNTIL FAIRLY RECENT TIMES the curse of famine was explainable largely in mythical or spiritual terms. Did the crops fail? If so, it must be punishment for some offense to the deity. Did famine stalk the land? If it did, some evil spirit was afoot. Such were the dominant explanations until about two hundred years ago.

The Reverend Thomas Robert Malthus corrected the misperceptions but replaced them with gloom. He was born in Rockery, County Surrey, England, in 1766 and came of a respectable family. Young Malthus studied philosophy and theology at Cambridge, graduating with honors in 1788, and was made a Fellow of Jesus College not long after. Upon leaving Cambridge he took charge of a small parish in his native county.

The Reverend Mr. Malthus, a keen observer and a sensitive man, was influenced by conditions in England just prior to and during the time he wrote. English historian Thorold Rogers comments thus on the last thirty years of the eighteenth century: "This country was at war with nearly the whole civilized world; the nation well-nigh suffered the horrors of famine." The historian John Richard Green writes of Ireland in his *Short History of the English People:* "Poverty was added to the curse of misgovernment and poverty deepened with the rapid growth of the native population till famine turned the country into a Hell."

Malthus brooded about these things. He sought to learn the underlying principles which explained hunger. He found the explanation in the tendency of the population to outrun the food supply. He was not the first to lay hold of the principle but he was the most effective in presenting it. In 1751 that remarkable American, Benjamin Franklin, wrote an *Essay on the Increase of Mankind* bearing this cogent statement:

There is, in short, no bound to the prolific nature of plants or animals, but what is made by their crowding and interfering with each other's means of subsistence. Was the face of the earth vacant of other plants, it might be gradually sowed and overspread with one kind only, as, for instance, with fennel; and were it empty of other inhabitants, it might in a few ages be replenished with one nation only, as, for instance, with Englishmen.

Malthus made use of the works of Wallace, Hume, Smith, and Price. In the revised edition of his famous essay he noted with some surprise that much had been done by Montesquieu, Franklin, Stewart, Young, and Townsend.

The first edition of his controversial work, published anonymously in 1798, was little more than a pamphlet. It was titled simply *Essay on Population.* Malthus's unwillingness to put his name to it arose from the fact that he was attacking two popular and well-entrenched ideas. One was the mercantilist notion that a high birthrate and a dense population were desirable. The other stemmed from Rousseau, the philosophical father of the French Revolution. Rousseau's idea, very popular at the time, was that the natural state of man was happiness, that misery came from conditions unwisely imposed by government. The idea of "The Noble Savage," which pervaded art and letters during the late eighteenth and early nineteenth centuries, stemmed from Rousseau. In 1793 an Englishman, William Godwin, supported Rousseau's idea of the Noble Savage. He wrote a sensational work titled *Enquiry Concerning Political Justice and Its Influence on Morals and Happiness.* Its thesis was the perfectability of man.

Malthus disagreed deeply with both Godwin's thesis and the mercantile pronatal bias. He held that human institutions, far from aggravating misery, had tended to mitigate it though they never could remove it entirely. His thought was conditioned by two assumptions: (1) "that food is necessary for the existence of man" and (2) "that the passion between the sexes is necessary and will remain nearly in its present state."

In 1803 Malthus revised, modified, and extended his essay. He courageously put his name to the work, which bore the imposing title *Essay on the Principle of Population; or A View of Its Past and Present Effects on Human Happiness; With an Enquiry into Our Prospects Respecting the Future Removal or Mitigation of the Evils which it Occasions.* Regarding population, Malthus says: "It may safely be pronounced therefore, that population, when unchecked, goes on doubling itself every twenty-five years, or increases at a geometric rate." As to food production, "It may be fairly pronounced therefore, that, considering the present state of the earth, the means of subsistence, under conditions most favorable to human industry, could not possibly be made to increase faster than an arithmetical ratio."

There you have it. Population tends to increase by a geometric ratio: 2, 4, 8, 16, 32. Food production tends to increase by an arithmetic ratio: 2, 4, 6, 8, 10. No mathematical genius is required to discern that if this is indeed the case, want, hunger, famine, and starvation are the natural lot of man. The Reverend Mr. Malthus so reasoned. A clergyman and an economist, he had come up with a profoundly pessimistic conclusion.

Malthus considered various kinds of "checks" to population. The ultimate check, he said, was always to be found in limitations on the food supply. This ultimate check never operates directly except in time of famine. The intermediate checks include all diseases due to scarcity of subsistence and all causes prematurely weakening the body.

Malthus's essay set off a storm of controversy that echoes to the present day. Opposing him were most of his fellow clergymen, who resented this secularization of things previously thought to be spiritual. Also opposed were many people of good will and optimism who recoiled from the implications of his conclusion. Opposing him, too, were political revolutionaries who contended that the central problem was bad governance, not a limited food supply. Traditionalists, who were strongly pronatal, were likewise opposed. Supporting him were the biologists and the economists, the latter with their seeming affinity for any gloomy proposition. It is the economists' support for Malthus's position that, as much as anything else, caused Thomas Carlyle to describe economics as "the dismal science."

Shortly after Malthus wrote, profound changes occurred in the Western world. England and then the Continent industrialized, greatly improving efficiency and increasing production. The American Midwest opened up, supplying a flood of farm products that increased at more than "an arithmetic ratio." A revolution in agricultural technology increased the yield per acre and reduced the per unit cost of producing farm products. The dearth of food was alleviated, the death rate fell, and the population increased. From 1820 to 1920 the population of the United Kingdom trebled. These things were not foreseen by Malthus. Nor did he foresee the new life-style and the new methods of contraception that would cut the birthrate. It became popular in the Western world to belittle Malthus and his gloomy "principles."

With the passage of time the growing population laid increasing demands on land and water resources. Cultivation was pushed onto fragile lands, inviting erosion. Forest lands were denuded for firewood and for tillage, leaving watersheds unprotected. People crowded together in enormous cities; the civil disturbance associated with excessive numbers became a threat. Resources were depleted, raising a question as to whether science and technology could develop needed substitutes.

If population continues to grow at rapid rates and if these trends continue unabated, grave problems may ensue. It is indeed possible that even if food problems are solved, unrestrained population growth may plunge us into other difficulties. Maybe, in identifying the food supply as the ultimate restraint on population growth, Malthus was in error.

When poor crops reduce per capita food supplies, "neo-Malthusians" break into print in Western journals. This has happened four times since World War II: 1946–47, 1966–67, 1972–75, and 1980–81. Prominent among these writers are Ehrlich, the Paddocks, and Garrett Hardin. At other times Malthus's ideas are either ignored or are viewed by many as antiquated and irrelevant.

The present writing provides an opportunity for yet another of the many appraisals of Malthus's work. Malthus introduced factual, scientific, theoretical, and secular ideas into an area from which they had been largely excluded. His depiction of the relationship between food and people, written almost two centuries ago, described with insight the circumstances that had generally governed human existence up to that time, no small achievement. Furthermore, his work directed attention to the population side of the food-people equation, which had not occurred previously. It helped reshape thinking and so assisted the Western world to escape famine. It provided a theoretical concept of this profound subject which had been lacking. Malthus helped undermine the romanticism associated with Rousseau's concept of man's perfectability.

Malthus's work extended beyond his intended audience. It was instrumental in leading Charles Darwin to his doctrine of natural selection. Darwin himself has said that his theory of the struggle for existence was only "the doctrine of Malthus applied with manifold force to the whole animal kingdom."

Karl Marx saw in Malthus's work the competitive system at its worst, rationalizing hunger, accepting a subsistence level of wages, and conceding all economic gains to the landlord class. According to Marx, hunger was caused by private ownership of the means of production. We shall see these issues joined clearly in Chapter 30 when we consider family planning in China. Part of Marx's zeal for overthrowing the competitive system was a reaction to Malthus's work.

Controversial, innovative, and dramatic, this philosopher-clergyman-economist-demographer-pamphleteer produced one of the world's profoundly influential writings. All the remainder of this book will relate, somehow, to his thought.

Malthus was a famine fighter in that he described the nature of the enemy. He was not a fighter in the trenches; he was a man of ideas. This man produced a profoundly pessimistic theory. But he helped explain misery and set in motion forces that assisted in overcoming it. If other parts of the world are to escape misery they will have to take his principles into account. Many are now doing so, as we shall see. Malthus, perhaps the most controversial member of a profession noted for contentiousness, is fittingly the first listed of our famine fighters.

REFERENCES

Green, John Richard. 1898. *Short History of The English People.* London: Cooperative Publication Society.

Haney, Lewis H. 1949. *History of Economic Thought.* New York: Macmillan.

Malthus, Thomas R. 1800. *An Investigation of the Cause of the Present High Price of Provisions, Containing an Illustration of the Nature and Limits of Fair Price in Times of Scarcity.* London: J. Johnson.

_____. 1803. *Essay on the Principle of Population; or A View of Its Past and Present Effects on Human Happiness; With an Enquiry into Our Prospects Respecting the Future Removal or Mitigation of the Evils which it Occasions.* London: J. Johnson.

_____. 1820. *Definitions in Political Economy.* London: J. Murray.

Whittaker, Edmund. 1940. *A History of Economic Ideas.* New York: Longmans, Green.

Science

THE AGE OF REASON is commonly dated from the publication in 1620 of the great work *Novum Organum* by Francis Bacon of England. Before Bacon, knowledge was commonly sought by uncritical study of the acknowledged authorities of the past, chiefly Aristotle and received religious doctrine. The Aristotelian method implicit in his great work *Organon* (Instrument), written four hundred years before Christ, was deductive reasoning. The elements were generalization, categorization, and logic. The process moved from the general to the particular. "All Greeks have beards. Zeno is a Greek. Therefore Zeno has a beard." If the generalization was correct, the categorization accurate, and the logic true, the method was faultless.

Bacon broke with the past. His method was to set up hypotheses, to test these by experiment, and to reject those that failed the test. Unlike Aristotle, he advocated moving from the particular to the general. For example, scurvy had long been thought to result from the will of God. James Lind, a scientifically minded Scottish doctor, doubted this. He had another hypothesis, that scurvy resulted from a deficiency in the diet. Following the Baconian method, he set up in 1747 an experiment to test his hypothesis. He took a group of men sick with scurvy, fed them various diets, and discovered that the individuals fed oranges and lemons recovered while the others did not. In the precise but quaint language of statistics, his hypothesis could not be rejected. Thus Lind came to the general proposition, based on study of individual cases, that if people who had scurvy were fed oranges and lemons they would be cured. A scourge was banished. Deductive reasoning could not have produced this finding.

To our generation, living in a scientific age, Bacon's method is so sensible that we wonder at its late emergence. But to the people who first heard it the method was audacious and sacrilegious. The title chosen by Bacon, *Novum Organum* (New instrument), was an overt challenge to Aristotle's *Organon*. Bacon's choice of title was warranted. The "new instrument" came to dominate the years since Bacon as Aristotle's "instrument" had dominated the years before it. Bacon's method was comprehensive. He said, "I have taken all knowledge to be my province."

But in agriculture some two hundred years elapsed before his method caught on. What were the reasons for agriculture's lag? One can only speculate. Perhaps tradition was stronger in agriculture than elsewhere. Clearly production agriculture commanded little esteem, though the lifestyle of the big landholder was greatly admired. Farming practices were not much questioned. The new science pressed its inquiries elsewhere. This neglect of agriculture, from which the Western world has now escaped, lingers on in the developing nations.

In this section of nineteen chapters we trace the evolution of agricultural science, which began in Western Europe, spread to the New World, and is being diffused throughout the globe.

CHAPTER 3

Jethro Tull:
The Great Innovator

EIGHTEENTH-CENTURY ENGLAND desperately needed someone to break tradition's grip on agriculture, to ask the troublesome questions, to challenge things as they had long been. That man appeared. His name was Jethro Tull. He was a most irascible man, original and abrasive. He was an inventor, author, polemicist, musician, and lawyer. Though of urban upbringing he became a farmer.

Jethro Tull was born at Basildon, Berks, England on March 30, 1674, of the "gentry"; his family was an ancient one, possessing a "competent paternal estate." As a young man Tull left the city for the country, probably for reasons of health. In his farming Tull made abrupt changes from the standard practices. City raised, he was without traditional farm practice predispositions. He developed original theories about tillage and plant nutrition to go with his practice. Following are the major features of his system.

The long-established seeding method was broadcasting, with heavy rates of application. Tull planted in rows, at reduced rates, and designed a seed drill to do the job. He allowed space between his rows so that horse-drawn tillage tools could pass. The spacing he prescribed persisted for two hundred years, until the advent of the tractor.

Standard practice was farming with the land as level as it could be; Tull furroughed his land, raised ridges, and placed his plant rows thereon. It was his tillage system together with his theory of plant nutrition that made him controversial. Tillage traditionally had been minimal—enough to make a bed for the seed, with some hand hoeing to keep down the weeds. Tull advocated plowings that were deep and frequent, four or more. While conventional tillage had scratched the surface, Tull culti-

17

vated close, deep, and often. Tillage as Tull prescribed it was terribly hard work for man and beast. Tull had need of all his persuasive powers to get his tenants to follow his orders.

The long-established method of maintaining fertility had been fallow, rotation, and manuring. Tull said manure was not needed, that fallowing was a waste, and that with his form of tillage growing the same species of crop year after year was good practice.

Tull believed that "the roots are the guts of the plants and the leaves are their lungs." Tull's theory, in his own words, was this: "The roots take fine particles of earth from the Superfices of the Pores or Cavities wherein the Roots are included. . . . These Particles . . . are the Pabulum of Plants." Therefore hoeing and plowing, which reduce the soil to fine particles, increase the food supply for the plant. Tillage substituted for fallowing and manuring. Tull put his practices into use on his two estates west of London, Prosperous Farm and Howberry Farm. He kept crude records of his yields and claimed superior results.

Where did Tull get his ideas, so much at variance with those of his neighbors? Some of them came from his visit to southern France and to Italy, where he saw vineyards that had been productive over many decades without rotation, planted in wide rows and intensively tilled. Some of his ideas came from experimentation of which he practiced a crude sort, more to confirm his ideas than to test them; he preceded Rothamstead, the first agricultural experiment station, by one hundred years. A large share of his ideas came from reflective thought. Tull was an observer with a keen but selective eye. He was an original thinker and an experimenter of less than Baconian objectivity.

Few of Tull's ideas came from such limited agricultural science as existed in his day. John Woodward, who lived at the end of the seventeenth century, had done some work that cast doubt on the ability of tillage to substitute for soil organic matter. He had published his findings in 1699. Here is Tull's comment on Woodward: "Dr. Woodward seems to have no good Eyes and as strong an Imagination as the Old Woman Who saw the Needle upon the Barn, but could not see the Barn. I will by no means call in Question the Veracity of so learned and good a Man; and therefore am willing to believe that he made this extraordinary Observation in his sleep."

In 1731 Tull published *The New Horse-Ploughing Husbandry or an Essay on the Principles of Tillage and Vegetation.* This was an unsigned treatise, followed by a further and expanded but poorly organized work, *The Horse-Hoeing Husbandry or an Essay on the Principles of Tillage and Vegetation,* printed in 1733. This turgid collection was assembled and put in excellent order by William Cobbett and republished in London in 1829, almost a century after Tull produced his tome. It is the definitive statement and interpretation of Tull. A copy rests on the shelves of the Life Science Library at Purdue, the pages still uncut after 150 years. Thus do the echoes of earlier battles grow dim with time.

A number of Tull's ideas had merit. Drilling the seed, planting in rows, spacing to permit use of draft animals, furrowing the land, use of legumes – all of these were worthy and continue in various places to this day. It was his tillage ideas that were controversial, were proved wrong, and became the symbol by which he is known.

Deep and frequent tillage was hard work. This had seeming merit in a country where rewards were expected to come only with real deserving and where medicine was thought to be good only if it was bitter. There were those who were intensely loyal to Tull. One John Mills wrote of Tull in 1762: "England may boast of having given rise to one of the greatest improvements that any Age has hitherto made in agriculture." In 1891 Earl Cathcart said, "Tull was the first Englishman, perhaps the first writer, ancient or modern, who has attempted with any tolerable degree of success, to reduce the art of agriculture to certain and uniform principles."

While some praised the work others were sharply critical. One Stephen Switzer made a virulent attack in 1733. T. H. Marshall, writing of Tull in 1929, nearly two centuries after the controversy had reached its zenith, gave this appraisal:

Scientific exploration was in fact an excrescence upon his work. He had been an accurate observer of facts but he guessed wildly at their interpretation . . . and was not disturbed to find himself in glorious isolation, battling against the collective wisdom of his age. . . . He had, apparently, first evolved his system of husbandry, then invented a scientific theory to explain it . . . and finally began to study the literature of the subject. In view of the state of scientific knowledge of the time it is surprising that anyone could publish such childish absurdities.

Perhaps the most cogent comment on Tull's farming system is that when he died in 1741 the tenants on his two farms abandoned horse-hoe husbandry and reverted to their earlier ways. An admirable account of the battle over Tull's ideas was supplied by the historian G. E. Fussell.

Tull gave enormous encouragement to the cult of the hoe and the plow. With what result? Millions of tons of soil, loosened in accordance with his prescription, washed down the slopes with the rain and blew through the air with the wind. A considerable portion of the topsoil, the most fertile layer of earth, was kept in a state of continual agitation and thus inhospitable to the roots. When tillage was done with draft animals, the roots were chopped off with prodigious toil and rivers of sweat. When the horses were replaced by tractors, the soil was punished with huge machines, drinking up great tanks of motor fuel.

My father, like most farmers of his day, was in the grip of the Tullian tradition, though he had never heard the man's name. He admonished me when I was a boy to "cultivate deep and keep the top soil loose." I remember pulling up at the end of the row, seeing the mangled corn roots dangling from the shovels. How could it be good to make the horses sweat in order to prune off the roots? Four offenses: against the land, the corn, the horses, and the cultivator.

The cult of plowing took on great prestige. Plowing matches were held, attracting tens of thousands of people. The prize went to the man who plowed straight and deep, covering all plant growth. Now we know that if we plow at all it should be on the contour, and we know that trash should be left on the surface to break the fall of the rain, trap the winter snows, and hold the soil against erosion by wind and water. The moldboard plow may someday be retired to the museum. It may even be removed from the emblem of the United States Department of Agriculture, where Tullian tradition placed it. We shall read more about tillage and soil conservation in Chapter 19, when we consider the life and work of Hugh Bennett.

What can we say of Jethro Tull? Does he belong in our list of hunger fighters? Probably Tull, if asked this question, would have returned a blank stare or published something crisp, his leading nouns capitalized. He wasn't consciously fighting hunger; he was trying to learn about crops and soils, trying to change long-established practices, to increase yields, to help farmers make money. If he had broader purposes, they did not appear in his writings.

If a famine fighter, was he a loser? In terms of recommended tillage practices the answer must be "yes." His proposals, judged scientifically, were, as Marshall said, "childish absurdities." They had serious adverse consequences, erosion being the greatest. Some mistakes, such as Tull's, are so great that they are almost magnificent.

But in a larger sense one cannot so easily charge Tull with failure. The modern era of agricultural change began during his lifetime and owes much to his audacity. Before Tull the established practice reigned unchallenged. With Tull and after the traditional wisdom was more frequently challenged. Changes, even inept ones, could more readily be proposed. The resulting gain for the overcoming of hunger was enormous. The escape from the Malthusian dilemma which the Western world experienced was based on the legitimacy of innovation, and not all innovation can turn out well. Tull was a great innovator. He broke with custom.

Challenge to the status quo has been the essential ingredient of every agricultural advance beginning with the domestication of plants and animals. The audacity which was Tull's prime attribute and of which he was in a sense the pioneer has been enormously important in the fight against famine.

Here we have a dilemma. The traditionalists, fearful of men like Tull, want to close the gate to new ideas. But this would also keep out Liebig, Pasteur, and Mendel. The innovators are ready to open the gate and risk a Tull in the hope of getting a Pasteur. When you open the gate there is no telling who will come through. By the eighteenth century the Enlightenment had advanced to the point that the agricultural gate could no longer be kept shut. And the first man through was Jethro Tull. The fortunate thing is that agricultural innovation survived this difficult man.

REFERENCES

Batie, Sandra, and Robert G. Healy, eds. 1980. *The Future of American Agriculture as a Strategic Resource.* Washington: The Conservation Foundation.

Fussell, G. E. 1973. *Jethro Tull: His Influence on Mechanized Agriculture.* Reading: Osprey.

Tull, Jethro. 1731. *The New Horse-Ploughing Husbandry or an Essay on the Principles of Tillage and Vegetation.* London: I.T. Published for the author.

_____. 1733. *The Horse-Hoeing Husbandry or an Essay on the Principles of Tillage and Vegetation.* London: I.T.

_____. 1829. *The Horse-Hoeing Husbandry.* Introduction by William Cobbett. London: Mills, Jowett and Mills.

CHAPTER 4

Justus von Liebig and Plant Nutrition

JETHRO TULL GAVE FAULTY ANSWERS but he did raise the right questions. How do plants feed? How can yields be increased?

No one has done more to help provide good answers to these questions than Justus von Liebig. Liebig was the first of the big four famine fighters of the nineteenth century. These were Justus von Liebig, the German chemist; Louis Pasteur, the French pathologist; Cyrus McCormick, the American inventor; and Gregor Mendel, the Austrian geneticist.

In the early nineteenth century, as a result of centuries of exploitive husbandry, European yields per acre had stabilized at a low level. In the eastern United States, the only part of the country then in major production, the early fertility had been drawn down and yields were declining. The static or declining yields placed a constraint on the number of people who could be fed. Malthus formulated his views during the time when agriculture was stagnant or nearly so; it is not difficult to understand his pessimism.

The processes by which plants obtained their nutrients were poorly understood. One theory, Jethro Tull's view, was that plants ingested the materials of the soil much as animals were observed to take in their food. A rival concept (the humus theory) was that soil minerals had only a minor role in plant growth, that of simply supporting the plant so that the roots could absorb their true food, dissolved organic matter. Liebig's theory, later confirmed by experiment, was that the humus had to disintegrate into its chemical components before it could be assimilated. There were disputes as to how much of the plant's growth came from the air. What was the role of sunlight in plant growth? And water—was it a nutrient or simply a conveyance for nutrients?

To these questions on plant growth were added many issues regarding animals. Why did animals prosper on certain rations and languish on others? How did animals divide the potential of ingested feeds between growth on the one hand and energy on the other? What was the chemistry of the digestive process? What were the original materials that entered into metabolism, what was the process itself, and what were the products and the by-products? Agriculture could make little real progress until there were better answers to these basic questions.

Eclipsing these straightforward questions was a deeper issue. Did plants have a vital force, going beyond the province of science? If plants had a life force their study would have to be shared with metaphysics. If there was no life force then questions related to plant growth were wholly within the realm of physical science, specifically chemistry, responsive to the methods of study prescribed by Bacon two hundred years earlier. This issue continued prominent until well into the nineteenth century, when the consensus arose that questions related to plant growth were in the realm of physical science. But the issue is not wholly closed. The gardener who talks to plants and considers them responsive to human moods is at heart a vitalist.

As inquiry proceeded in the biological area, a related disciplinary battle arose. The physiologists, who studied living things, claimed the field for their own, which indeed it had been during the two millennia since Aristotle, though they had advanced learning but little during that long span. The chemists were the upstarts, the challengers, and ultimately the winners.

Chemistry was the first scientific discipline to focus on agriculture. The long years spent in alchemy had developed laboratory techniques and analytical methods in addition to a body of factual knowledge. The other agriculturally related disciplines such as microbiology, pathology, and genetics were not in a like state of readiness when the Age of Reason struck off the chains of the past. The chemists, the physicists, the mathematicians, and the biologists eventually joined hands to probe for the mysteries of life, as we shall see in Chapter 17.

From the many early chemists the name of Justus von Liebig is singled out. Selman Waksman, discoverer of streptomycin, says of Liebig: "Liebig's place in agricultural science is not that of a great experimenter and discoverer, but of a brilliant coordinator and popularizer, who clearly summarized the existing knowledge, and who pointed the way to new discoveries."

This, then, is the story of Justus von Liebig, moody, contentious, arrogant, impulsive, given to error as well as to insight, inspired teacher, eloquent with tongue and pen, immensely gifted, dedicated to the discovery of knowledge and the alleviation of hunger.

Justus von Liebig was born in Darmstadt, Germany in 1803, one of ten children. His father was a pharmacist and a merchant of dyes. The boy had an intense interest in his father's laboratory and books. He says in his autobiography, "I became indifferent to every other thing that ordinarily attracts children." His avid reading developed his naturally keen mind: "Everything I saw remained intentionally or unintentionally fixed in my memory with equal photographic fidelity. . . . My position at school was very deplorable; I had no ear memory, and retained nothing or very little of what is learned through this sense."

One day the despairing rector asked his student what he thought would become of him. "When I answered that I would be a chemist, the whole school and the good old man himself broke into an uncontrollable fit of laughter, for no one at the time had any idea that chemistry was a thing that could be studied."

As a boy Liebig became apprenticed to a druggist. He learned fast but wanted to be a chemist rather than a druggist. He experimented with explosives and, according to his biographer, Jakob Volhard, blew off a piece of the roof, thereby terminating his apprenticeship.

At sixteen Liebig went to the University of Bonn and then to Erlanger as a student of a chemistry professor named Kastner. In his eighteenth year he went to Paris, where he studied at the Sorbonne with the brilliant French chemist Gay-Lussac. He met and impressed favorably the eminent German scientist and geographer Alexander von Humboldt, through whose patronage he was able to obtain a professorship at an early age in the tiny town of Giessen, in his native Hesse-Darmstadt.

At Giessen Liebig built, by hard work and astuteness, a substantial laboratory. He developed improved methods of quantitative and qualitative analysis. Students, including many from abroad, began coming to his laboratory, attracted by his growing fame. They performed experiments of their own and received personal direction, a form of learning then new and novel. Liebig's lectures were dramatic. He had presence and authority in the old German style. This from his student E. N. Horsford: "The hour of the lecture was on the point of striking – the murmur of conversation had subsided to a whisper – presently, the whole audience by one impulse rose, and I saw entering and bowing to the salutation, Dr. Liebig." When twenty-two years old Liebig became a full professor of chemistry. He had been married a few months earlier. The marriage, a happy one, produced five children.

Liebig worked with his friend Wöhler on organic, agricultural, and physiological chemistry. Together they discovered chloroform. With Wöhler he was editor of one of the major chemical journals of the day, a position at once influential and instructive.

By the decade of the 1830s Liebig, though young, was already a famous man. In 1837 the British Association for the Advancement of Science asked him to write a review of the state of organic chemistry. The chemistry of living or once-living material was then a new and amorphous subject, developing somewhat separate from inorganic chemistry. Liebig produced a book, *Organic Chemistry in its Applications to Agriculture and Physiology,* almost exclusively on agricultural chemistry. This endeared him to the agricultural community, then suffering from the twofold curse of inadequate knowledge and low status.

Why did Liebig, an urban man, choose to focus on agriculture? Perhaps the best explanation is that offered by Liebig himself in the foreword of his book: "agriculture is the true foundation of all trade and industry—it is the foundation of the riches of states."

Liebig's book, published in 1840, appeared when he was thirty-seven years old and at the height of his powers. It had enormous influence. Margaret Rossiter comments thus: "Liebig thus managed in less than two hundred pages to put together a wholly new synthesis of agricultural chemistry. It was probably one of the most important scientific books ever published and marks the beginning of a 'scientific revolution.'"

Setting aside what was peripheral, Liebig was able to pick out the principal issues and come immediately to the heart of his subject. He was concerned with what elements a plant needed, where it got them, and which farm practices helped most. He focused on three essential points: (1) the destruction of the humus theory; (2) elaboration of the nitrogen cycle; and (3) explanation of the role of minerals.

Here are major valid points in Liebig's book. He showed that the carbon dioxide in the atmosphere, rather than the carbon in the humus, contributed to the carbon found in plants. Advocates of the humus theory contended, in effect, that all life came from pre-existing life. With characteristic insight Liebig challenged the humus theory by asking, Where did the first plants get their humus? He showed, a century and a half ago, that the food of plants is of inorganic nature, taking this form before it can be ingested, a fact still not accepted by some proponents of organic farming. He showed that the nitrogen taken up by plants comes through the roots, and that certain amounts of it are carried into the soil from the air by rainfall. He identified phosphorus as an element of critical need, and considered both bones and mineral deposits as sources. Liebig discussed the practice of adding sulphuric acid to bones to make the phosphate more readily available, producing what came to be known as superphosphate. He emphasized the importance of potash as fertilizer. He provided the chemical explanation as to why the guano, lime, marl, and gypsum used by farmers were helpful in increasing crop yields. His work helped in the ascendancy of the chemists over the physiologists and the vitalists. He developed "the law of the minimum," which sets forth the following proposition: "Increasing the supply of the most deficient plant nutrient of a soil should be the first step toward improving its fertility."

Liebig accepted and promoted the views of previous chemists, notably Lavoisier, regarding the oxygen cycle: that plants take in carbon dioxide and give off oxygen while animals do the reverse. In short, he laid the foundation for an understanding of soil chemistry and plant nutrition. He is thus the father of the fertilizer industry, that formidable weapon against hunger.

Liebig made discoveries outside the realm of agriculture. These, being beyond the scope of this book, are not reported.

There were errors in Liebig's work. He viewed the soil as a bank; he thought that no more could be taken out than was put in. This oversimplification, as erroneous for banks as it is for soil, remains in the views of many people to the present day. He also underestimated the potential of nitrogen fertilizer, having convinced himself that sufficient quantities of nitrogen from the air got into the soil as ammonia. Such was the potency of his influence that the use of nitrogen fertilizer did not develop importantly until one hundred years after he wrote. He emphasized the role of the phosphates so strongly that the other elements were neglected. Liebig wrongly attributed fermentation to a "catalytic force" rather than to microbial action. He dismissed the germ theory with a shrug of his shoulders, regarding Pasteur's view that microbes caused fermentation as ridiculous and naive, likening it to the opinion of a child "who would explain the rapidity of the Rhine current by attributing it to the violent movement of the many millwheels at Mainz." He permitted inclusion in his 1852 book of an unscientific and erroneous cure for late blight in potatoes. But these errors, understandable as coming from a bold man pioneering in a new field, should not be permitted to eclipse his great contribution.

Liebig's style in both writing and speaking was crisp, sweeping, and simplified. He often was guilty of failing to credit the work of his predecessors, leaving the inference that the work was his own. He had keen insight, the result of an enormous stock of accumulated knowledge. But occasionally he enaged in intuitive leaps, presenting hypotheses as if they were demonstrated facts. He sometimes relied on the "photographic fidelity" of his mind when he might better have consulted his notes. He pushed his ideas very hard. J. Campbell Brown, who translated Liebig's autobiography from the German, says of him, "Probably no chemist has ever equalled Liebig as a propagandist. His talent for persuasive and polemic writing was not, however, an unmixed blessing for, while it enabled him to command wide recognition, his dogmatic tone of infallibility and his discourteous language involved him in countless disputes."

No sooner was his book in the public domain than two currents of comment arose. One, coming chiefly from practitioners, was effusive in praise for its originality, comprehensiveness, lucidity, and relevance. The other, mainly from his fellow chemists, was sharply critical of the book's errors, of its real or alleged plagiarism, and for representing as fact propositions that were as yet only hypotheses.

There began an exchange of polemics between Liebig and his many detractors. Brown says, "The attacks published against Liebig after 1840, if assembled, would exceed the space of President Eliot's famous 60 inch shelf." Liebig responded with the most abrasive words of his considerable vocabulary. Wöhler, Liebig's gentle friend, wrote him this wise, patient, humorous, and ineffective letter:

To make war upon Marchand (or anyone else for that matter) is of no use. You merely consume yourself, get angry, and ruin your liver and your nerves—finally with Morrison's Pills. Imagine yourself in the year 1900, when we shall both have been decomposed again into carbonic acid, water and ammonia, and the lime of our bones belongs perhaps to the very dog who then dishonors our grave. Who then will care whether we lived at peace or in strife? Who then will know anything about your scientific controversies—of your sacrifices of health and peace for science? No one: but your good ideas, the new facts you have discovered, these, purified from all that is unessential, will be known and recognized in the remotest times.

The major disappointments of Liebig's life were two. One was the criticism of his peers, which cut him to the quick. The other was an unfortunate commercial venture, precisely in the field of his expertise. In 1845, at the apex of his career, he and a student, James Muspratt of Liverpool, whose father owned a large industrial establishment there, took out a patent (number 10616) for a mineral fertilizer. The disastrous result is reported by Rossiter:

Liebig developed six kinds of fertilizer suitable for different crops. . . . They were sold for the growing seasons of 1846 and 1847, but very little reached the United States. After great hopes had been aroused for this new and cheaper alternative to guano, the fertilizer turned out to be a fiasco. The theory was not wrong, as far as it went, but in his efforts to keep the minerals from being washed away by the rain, Liebig had made them too insoluble to enter the plants, and a crust (probably like plaster of Paris) developed on the fields. The whole episode caused a great stir in English agricultural circles, whose strong criticisms thoroughly embittered Liebig toward the British, with whom he had previously had fairly close relations. The British reaction caused Liebig to maintain his mineral theory all the more strongly and served to exacerbate the debates with his British critics in the 1850s.

Liebig's main contributions were in his early years. The criticisms of his fellow chemists and his catastrophic venture in commercial fertilizer

took something out of him. Other chemical laboratories, largely stimulated by Liebig's work, were springing up in Berlin, Leipzig, Göttingen,
and Heidelberg. These laboratories with the support of their larger and
richer universities soon began to eclipse the small laboratory at Giessen.
The new and younger chemists, including some trained by Liebig,
showed the flaws in the work of the master. Unfortunately Liebig looked
on these developments as a challenge to his leadership. More accurately
assessed, they were the building of a worthy structure on the good foundation he had laid. In 1852 Liebig closed his laboratory at Giessen, moved
to Munich, and gradually retreated from his chemical inquiries.

Liebig was both a theoretical chemist and a laboratory scientist. He
did not carry on field experiments. In fact, field experiments were little
known in his day. The first reputable ones were at Rothamstead in
England, the beginning date for which is commonly placed at 1834, six
years before Liebig's principal work. Rothamstead was a private farm,
managed by John Bennet Lawes, who later was joined by Joseph Henry
Gilbert, one of Liebig's students and occasionally one of his adversaries.
The names of Lawes and Gilbert are among the oldest and most famous
in agronomy.

The interest in improving agricultural knowledge, stemming from
Liebig's work, led to the establishment of the world's first publicly supported agricultural experiment station. This was at Möckern outside
Leipzig, founded in 1851. The effort was looked on as a combination of
laboratory and farm that would provide a middle way between the
theorizing of a university-based Liebig who did no fieldwork and the
undisciplined experimentation of assorted farmers who scorned theory.

Liebig's influence on his students was prodigious. After the man is
more than one hundred years in his grave and after all is reckoned up, his
influence over his students lives on into the present generation. Among
his American students three stand out. One was E. N. Horsford, who in
1847 became Rumford Professor at Harvard, with special responsibility
for building up the scientific work of the university, particularly in
chemistry. Another was S. W. Johnson, who was instrumental in setting
up agricultural experiment stations in the United States. Yet another was
C. M. Wetherill, the first scientist employed in 1862 by the new United
States Department of Agriculture. So strongly was chemistry identified
with agricultural science in the public mind that a chemist was chosen for
this practical and symbolic post.

In 1863, at sixty years of age, Liebig published *The Natural Laws of
Husbandry,* a product of his mature thought. In his preface he wrote: "As
for myself, I have reached the age when the elements of the mortal body
betray a certain tendency to commence a new circle of action, when we
begin to think about putting our house in order, and must defer to no later

period what we have still to say." He then proceeded in somewhat restrained language to reiterate positions stated in his earlier books, with refinements that came from the sixteen years that had elapsed since his last previous major writing. He still had some things to say and to repeat, but by then others, building on his work, had moved beyond him.

Liebig died of pneumonia in 1873, having attained his allotted three score years and ten, honored by many, reviled by some, known by all. He marked the transition of agriculture from tradition to science, a path that was both troublesome and rewarding. He was a fighter. Like many another campaigner, he lost some battles but won the war.

REFERENCES

Liebig, Justus. 1840. *Organic Chemistry in its Applications to Agriculture and Physiology.* Edited from the manuscript of the author by Lyon Playfair. London: Taylor and Walton.

_____. 1847. *Chemistry in its Applications to Agriculture and Physiology.* Edited by Lyon Playfair and William Gregory. 4th ed. London: Taylor and Walton.

_____. 1852a. *Animal Chemistry or Organic Chemistry in its Applications to Physiology and Pathology.* Edited from the author's manuscript by William Gregory. Philadelphia: T. B. Peterson.

_____. 1852b. *Familiar Letters on Chemistry and its Relation to Commerce, Physiology, and Agriculture.* From the last London edition by John Gardner. Philadelphia: T. B. Peterson.

_____. 1863. *The Natural Laws of Chemistry.* Edited by John Blyth. New York: Appleton and Company.

_____. 1891. *An Autobiographical Sketch.* Translated from the German by J. Campbell Brown. In *Annual Report of the Board of Regents of the Smithsonian Institution.* Washington, D.C.

Moulton, Forest Ray, ed. 1942. *Liebig and after Liebig: A Century of Progress in Agricultural Chemistry.* Publication of the American Association for the Advancement of Science, no. 16. Washington: Smithsonian Institution Building.

Rossiter, Margaret W. 1975. *The Emergence of Agricultural Science, Justus Liebig and the Americans.* New Haven: Yale Univ. Press.

Russell, Sir E. John. 1942. "Rothamstead and Its Experiment Station." *Agricultural History* 16, no. 4.

Volhard, Jakob. 1909. *Justus von Liebig.* Vols. 1 and 2 (in German). Leipzig: J. A. Barth.

CHAPTER 5

Louis Pasteur: The Microbe Hunter

THE HUMAN POPULATION HAS EXPERIENCED three distinct bursts in numbers since becoming a distinguishable species. The first occurred a million or more years ago when our progenitors learned to make tools, especially weapons for the hunt. With the resulting greater food supply they were able to increase their numbers from a very low to a substantially higher level. The second quantum jump in population numbers began about eleven thousand years ago with the increased food supply resulting from domestication of plants and animals. The third burst in numbers began about two hundred years ago, with the onset of the scientific revolution, resulting in what has been called the population explosion. The two earlier expansions probably produced relative increases comparable with that of recent times, though the current increase in absolute terms is vastly greater.

No single person bears more responsibility for the present upsurge in the world's population than does Louis Pasteur, microbe hunter and establisher of the germ theory. Immunization and sanitation, his contributions, increased population numbers and food production.

Consider first the food production side. His anthrax vaccine laid the basis for immunization of animals. His work on silkworms is fundamental to livestock sanitation. The control of plant diseases traces to his lifetime of labor in pathology.

On the people side, his principle of sterilization reduced the incidence of infectious disease and his dramatic innoculation to prevent rabies gave credibility to preventive medicine.

Pasteur was born in 1822 at Dole, in the eastern part of France. His early home was at Arbois, in the Jura region. His father was a tanner and a former soldier in Napoleon's army; his great-grandfather was a serf. Pasteur lived a long, active, ambitious, contentious, productive, brilliant, and reverent life. He died, seventy-three years old and ripe with honors, holding a crucifix in one hand and the hand of his wife in the other. I begin this chapter with pleasure. Of the many people whose careers are chronicled in this book, no other so warms the heart and lifts the spirit as does Louis Pasteur.

How stood the world of pathology before Pasteur? In agriculture, diseases of plants and animals were endemic, occasionally bursting out in epidemics. During the mid–nineteenth century, what we now know to be late blight of potatoes cut production in northern Europe to a fraction of its earlier level, reportedly causing 2.5 million deaths in Ireland alone. This potato disease helped persuade my great-grandfather to migrate from the Netherlands to the United States. Animal diseases such as cholera, anthrax, and tuberculosis took a terrible toll.

For the human population the death rate was high, about forty per thousand, approximating the birthrate, which also was high, so that total numbers changed little. Occasionally there came an epidemic like the bubonic plague of the mid-1300s, known as the Black Death, which killed about one-fourth of Europe's population, after which population numbers were restored to their former level. Infant mortality was frightfully high. Infectious diseases were rampant. During the Crimean War of 1854–56, the French army lost ten thousand men in battle and eight times as many on account of sickness or wounds. Among amputees during that war the mortality, 92 percent, was greater than for those who, having the same injury, were not operated on. There are still with us older people whose fear of hospitals is the legacy of those terrible times.

How explain such afflictions of plants, animals, and people before there was a germ theory? The will of God was the generally accepted explanation, leading to a search as to what had offended the deity. Bad air, poor food, the evil eye, and various kinds of witchery were all cited as causes of human illness. Chance and Providence, those great reservoirs of unexplained causes, accounted for a large share of life's events.

The story of the conquest of disease goes a long way back. Five thousand years ago the Chinese had a means of immunizing for smallpox; matter from smallpox sores would be dried, powdered, and blown into the nostrils. Anton van Leeuwenhoek, an eccentric Dutchman born in 1632, developed a lens that would magnify 200–fold, bringing bacteria into human awareness. Lazzaro Spallanzani, an eighteenth-century Italian, proved in a brilliant experiment that these bacteria were not generated spontaneously as was popularly believed.

Others of Pasteur's precursors must be reported. Every great man stands on the shoulders of those who have gone before. In 1796 Edward Jenner, a British physician, performed what was the first vaccination as we know it. In 1810 Nicolas Appert was able to preserve food by boiling it in air-tight containers. In 1837 a German doctor by the name of Schwann published a paper with the news that meat becomes putrid not from the air itself but only when subvisible animals get into it. Also in 1837 a Frenchman, Cagniard de la Tour, examined microscopically a few foamy drops from a vat of beer. He noticed tiny globules of yeast with buds bursting from their sides, buds like seeds sprouting. He wrote a short paper describing these tiny creatures and how they grew, observing that no brew of hops and barley ever changed into beer without the presence of these growing yeasts.

Pasteur began as a chemist. In the tradition of scientists then as now, the young Pasteur was attracted to basic research. He studied the crystals of tartaric acid and at the age of twenty-six discovered that there are four distinct kinds of tartaric acid instead of two, the then accepted number. A small triumph.

But soon he shifted his attention to other things. He went to Lille as professor and dean of the faculty of sciences. One of the French industries there was the making of alcohol from sugar beets. A distiller of alcohol, a Mr. Bigo, father to one of Pasteur's students, came for help. Some of Bigo's vats wouldn't make alcohol. Pasteur examined beet pulp from both healthy and sick vats and found, in the brew from the healthy vats, swarms of curious dancing specks, which he recognized as the yeasts described by Cagniard de la Tour. In the brew from the sick vats he found rodlike things, much smaller than the yeasts. He concluded that the differing microbial populations explained the differing behavior of the sick and the healthy vats. Pasteur's work on fermentation of beets brought his skills to the making of wine and vinegar. This work was successful both professionally and practically, winning him numerous honors. So his reputation grew. During the Prussian War of 1870–71, loyal Frenchman that he was, he sought to make French beer superior to the beer of the invading Germans. He wrote *Studies on Fermentation,* published in 1879, still a classic.

In 1865 Pasteur, at the request of his old professor, Dumas, turned to what may seem a strange enterprise – saving France's silkworm industry. Silkworm growers explained that a disease was killing their worms. *Pebrine* it was called, because the black spots which covered the sick worms looked like pepper. Pasteur traced the trouble to parasites that were infecting the silkworms and admonished the farmers to keep healthy worms from contact with leaves the sick worms had soiled. The silk industry was saved.

As he approached victory in his campaign to save the silkworm industry (an effort that took six years), Pasteur, aged forty-five, was stricken by a hemorrhage of the brain and nearly died. He was paralyzed on one side and never fully recovered. Resolutely, he set to work in spite of his handicap. By exercise and disciplined self-help he was able to bring himself back to full mental effectiveness, though thereafter he walked with a limp.

It was a time of intellectual ferment regarding the various manifestations of life. Darwin had published his *Origin of Species* in 1859. Talk of evolution was in the air. Theological explanations of the origin of life were on the defensive. The old issue of spontaneous generation rose again, phoenixlike, from the ashes to which Spallanzani thought he had consigned it. Pasteur plunged into the fight. He conducted a series of brilliant experiments, testing the occurrence of microbes in various settings: the cellar of the Observatory of Paris, outside in his yard, and on the slopes of the Alps. He was able to demonstrate that under strictly controlled conditions microbes did not appear spontaneously. Pasteur's prestige was sufficient to end the controversy for all who were open-minded enough to respect the facts.

The deeper question as to the origin of life itself—all life, not just microbes—was beyond the capability of scientists to answer. After all, Darwin had addressed himself to the origin of species, not to the origin of life. If there were to be answers to the deeper question of life's beginnings they had to come from the theologians, the philosophers, the metaphysicians, and the physiologists working along with the biologists. Pasteur answered the limited question. He showed that under experimental conditions and within the specified time frame, life did not develop spontaneously. Microbes had parents.

Pasteur turned his attention from the sickness of silkworms to the sorrows of people. From his experiments he had learned about contagion in silkworms and sugar beet fermentations. He now moved to check the ravages of microbes among the human population.

Child-bed fever was widespread. On the average, death took one of every nineteen women who went to the lying-in hospitals of Paris. Pasteur was able to show that this affliction was germ borne, the result of uncleanliness. He kept hammering away at the dangers of contagion, propagandist that he was, and he was heard overseas. Joseph Lister, the great British physician who founded antiseptic surgery, wrote Pasteur a letter bearing the following paragraph: "Permit me to thank you cordially for having shown me the truth of the theory of germs of putrefaction by your brilliant researches, and for having given me the simple principle that has made the antiseptic system a success. If you ever come to Edinburgh it will be a real recompense to you, I believe, to see in our hospital in how large a measure humanity has profited from your work."

All of this was preliminary to and eclipsed by the two triumphs for which Pasteur is best known: his vaccine for anthrax and his inoculation to prevent rabies.

Anthrax is a highly contagious disease of animals, the symptoms of which are chills, fever, dysentery, and convulsions. Typically the animals die suddenly. As a result of Pasteur's efforts the disease is now almost unknown, but a hundred years ago in France it attacked horses, cows, and sheep, causing great loss. The disease is contracted by eating contaminated food. Human beings can get the disease by exposure to infected animals or to animal products. The anthrax bacterium was first seen by the French scientist Casimir Davaine in 1850. In 1876 the great German physician Robert Koch established that this bacterium caused anthrax. It was the first germ known to cause a specific disease.

Pasteur had been working on anthrax. He had a bottle of boiled urine in which he had planted anthrax bacilli. One day he discovered, to his disgust, that the culture was swarming with unbidden guests; contaminating microbes from the air had sneaked in. The following day he observed that there were no anthrax germs left; they had been completely choked out by the bacilli from the air. He began to dream about turning beneficent living organisms against deadly disease-bearing microbes; in other words, immunization. Jenner had done it with smallpox, nearly a century earlier. Could it be done with anthrax?

Pasteur injected four cows with virulent anthrax microbes. All four developed large feverish swellings on their shoulders at the point of injection. Two of the animals died, but two somehow survived. Whether by whim or whether with experimental intent, Pasteur later injected the two surviving animals with an especially savage strain of anthrax bacilli. Nothing happened; the cows did not even develop swelling at the point of injection. Pasteur jumped to one of his quick but accurate conclusions: "Once a cow has had anthrax but gets better from it all the anthrax microbes in the world can not give her another attack—she is immune!" The cause of immunity was not yet clear. The multiplication of antibodies that resulted from the injection would await later discovery.

By 1881 Pasteur had his immunization technique for anthrax developed to the point that he had confidence in it and said so. Skepticism was widespread. A public test was proposed and carried out in the spring of 1881. It has become a landmark of agricultural research. The story is told by Paul DeKruif in his classic book *The Microbe Hunters* and by René

DuBos in his fine work *Pasteur and Modern Science*. Twenty-four sheep, one goat, and six cows were immunized with Pasteur's vaccine. They and twenty-nine other unvaccinated animals were then infected with a highly virulent anthrax culture. Two days later all the vaccinated sheep were well. Twenty-one of the control sheep were dead of anthrax and the three other control sheep died within the day. The six vaccinated cows were well whereas the four control cows had swellings at the site of inoculation and febrile reactions. The triumph was complete.

What the anthrax demonstration was to the agricultural community the rabies demonstration was for people. Rabies, sometimes called hydrophobia, was one of the most horrible and dreaded of all diseases, spread most often by the bite of a rabid dog. Pasteur set out to find an immunization for rabies. After much work he learned that it is the dog's nervous system that is affected—the brain and the spinal cord. He and his assistants learned to trephine a dog—drill a little hole in its skull—and inject the deadly rabid stuff directly into the brain. Dogs thus treated invariably developed rabies and died.

Needed was a rabies microbe that was attenuated so that when injected into an animal it would result in a mild case of rabies, followed by recovery and so immunity, as with Pasteur's inoculation for anthrax. As a result of painstaking effort, Pasteur and his assistants found how to do it. They took a little section of the spinal cord of a rabbit dead of rabies and hung this bit of deadly stuff up to dry in a germ-proof bottle for fourteen days. This shriveled bit of nervous tissue they shot into the brains of healthy dogs, and the dogs did not die. Successively, they injected the dogs with rabbit inoculum that had hung thirteen days, twelve days, eleven days, and so on to material one day old—fourteen injections in all. Then Pasteur and his assistants injected full-strength inoculum into the brains of two vaccinated dogs and two unvaccinated ones. The two that had been vaccinated were unaffected; the other two died.

But how apply this wondrous knowledge? There were two and a half-million dogs in France, in addition to other creatures susceptible to rabies. Which ones were likely to develop rabies? Pasteur couldn't tell. Vaccinate them all? Impossible.

Pasteur found the way out of the problem. Vaccinate the people instead of the dogs, and only those people who had been bitten. It is always weeks before the disease develops, plenty of time to administer the fourteen doses.

A woman named Mrs. Meister came from Meissengott in Alsace, leading her nine-year-old boy, Joseph, badly gashed two days before by a mad dog. She had heard that Pasteur had an inoculum for hydrophobia and begged to have her son vaccinated. Pasteur vaccinated the lad with his series of injections and the boy went home with no trace of the dread disease. Word of this marvelous event went out over France and abroad. It was one of the most dramatic and significant of the world's medical events.

In 1892, Pasteur's seventieth birthday, a medal was given to him at a great meeting in his honor at the Sorbonne in Paris. Joseph Lister, the British physician, was present and embraced the old man. Pasteur was too weak to give his speech; his son read it for him.

Do not let yourselves be tainted by a deprecating and barren skepticism, do not let yourselves be discouraged by the sadness of certain hours which pass over nations. Live in the serene peace of laboratories and libraries. Say to yourselves first: What have I done for my instruction? and, as you gradually advance, What have I done for my country? until the time comes when you may have the immense happiness of thinking that you have contributed in some way to the progress and good of humanity.

Pasteur, however ambitious and intense, was also warm and humble. His family life was filled with love and affection, a model of nineteenth-century role acceptance. He was scrupulous in his methods and honest in his reports. He was a very hard worker. Somewhere beneath his hard work and scientific attitude lay the poet and the artist. As a young man he painted portraits, rather good ones. He had worked out the relationship between the scientific and the reverent parts of his life. His biographer Vallery-Radot quotes him thus:

There are two men in each one of us: the scientist, he who starts with a clear field and desires to rise to the knowledge of Nature through observation, experimentation, and reasoning, and the man of sentiment, the man of belief, the man who mourns his dead children, and who cannot, alas, prove that he will see them again, but who believes that he will, and lives in that hope, the man who will not die like a vibrio, but who feels that the force that is within him cannot die. The two domains are distinct, and woe to him who tries to let them trespass on each other in the so imperfect state of human knowledge.

Pasteur died on September 28, 1895, at the age of seventy-three. His body was placed in a chapel in the Pasteur Institute at the request of the French government.

A century has passed since Pasteur labored among us. What has flowed from his work? He helped increase food production. We have the conquest of cholera in hogs, Newcastle disease in poultry, anthrax in sheep, and hoof-and-mouth disease in cattle and sanitation measures for all of these. The whole field of plant pathology is undergirded by Pasteur's work, so that crop diseases are now amenable to control. Pasteur's work was addressed primarily to agricultural animals and farm products:

silkworms, grapes, sugar beets, sheep, cattle, chickens. Even his work on hydrophobia began with the animal and was only in the last stage transferred to people. He was of country origin, from the common people of France, and he never forgot it.

For human beings the immunization and sanitation that stem from Pasteur have spread throughout the world. As a result, the death rate has dropped, setting off what Deevey calls the third wave of population growth. Population and food supply are now equated at a new, higher, and better level.

Pasteur brought to human awareness the world of microorganisms whose potential for good or ill had been unknown, whose influence on human life and food production had been only vaguely suspected.

REFERENCES

Deevey, E. S., Jr. 1960. "The Human Population." *Scientific American* (Sept.).

DeKruif, Paul. 1926. *The Microbe Hunters.* New York: Harcourt-Brace.

DuBos, René. 1960. *Pasteur and Modern Science.* New York: Doubleday.

Holmes, S. J. 1924. *Louis Pasteur.* New York: Harcourt-Brace.

Magner, Lois N. 1979. *A History of the Life Sciences.* New York and Basel: Marcel Dekker.

Metchnikoff, Elie. 1939. *The Founders of Modern Medicine: Pasteur, Koch, Lister.* New York: Walden. (Includes *Prevention of Rabies,* by Pasteur.)

Nicolle, Jacques. 1961. *Louis Pasteur, the Story of His Major Discoveries.* Greenwich: Fawcett-Crest.

Pasteur, Louis. 1879. *Studies on Fermentation.* London: Macmillan.

Vallery-Radot, Réne. 1901. *The Life of Pasteur.* Translated from the French by Mrs. R. L. Devonshire, 1919. London: Constable.

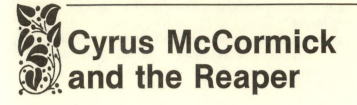

CHAPTER 6

Cyrus McCormick and the Reaper

THE YEAR 1776 WAS SIGNIFICANT in the battle against hunger, its importance best seen in retrospect. In 1776 Adam Smith, the Scotsman, laid out the scenario for the open competitive economy that, with modifications, was to serve the Western world for subsequent generations. In that same year James Watt, the Englishman, produced an operational steam engine, instrument and symbol of the mechanical age. And in colonial America Thomas Jefferson penned the Declaration of Independence, charter for political freedom.

These three great initiatives, economic, technical, and political, would come together to help a new country break through the Alleghenies and open up the largest and best-endowed agricultural area of the world. Whether measured in the physical volume of food production or in the precedent-setting pattern of agricultural development, this was a towering historic event. In the present chapter the agricultural engineering side of this advance is examined.

Any one of a number of persons could be named to symbolize the transformation. One could name George Washington, the farmer of Mount Vernon, who in the late 1700s experimented with new equipment, new crops, and new practices. Or C. Hoxie of Hudson, New York, who produced a threshing machine in 1806. Or John Deere, the blacksmith from Illinois, who in 1837 built a steel plow that would turn the sticky prairie soil cleanly, with reduced draft. Or J. S. Fawkes of Pennsylvania, who produced a successful self-propelling steam plow in 1858. Or John Froelich, who built the first gasoline tractor in 1892. Instead, the choice of this chapter is Cyrus Hall McCormick of Virginia, who in 1831 built the first successful reaper.

This then is the story of agriculture's mechanical breakthrough, as distinct from the chemical and the biological advances already discussed and the genetic progress to be considered in the next chapter. Mechanical pioneering occurred, logically, in the United States where labor was scarce, land abundant, competition open, and rewards generous.

McCormick's reaper cut harvest time by half. Subsequent improvements in the reaper, along with other mechanical innovations, would further cut the farm labor load. Seeding, tillage, transport, and processing were all transformed. To become an inventor was a driving urge for many of the youth of that time. In the single year 1860 the annual report of the commissioner of patents listed 917 agricultural discoveries or inventions. The mechanical revolution multiplied the output per farm worker by approximately a factor of 20.

The cost of food production was reduced by these labor-saving changes, coupled as they were with other innovations. Before the agricultural revolution the family spent half or more of its income on food. By 1985 food was taking 18 percent of personal consumption expenditures.

This enormous gain for the consumer came at the cost of wrenching changes in agriculture. Mechanization increased the number of acres a man could farm. Size of farms rose dramatically. As farms increased in size their number diminished. Farmers were squeezed off the land. In the middle of the nineteenth century, before the mechanical revolution took hold, farm people constituted the majority of the U.S. population. By 1986 the farm population had been reduced to a little more than 2 percent of the total. From 1930 to 1974, the period when farm leaving was at its peak, the out-migration from agriculture totaled 33 million people, the greatest vocational shift in history. Workers released from agriculture took jobs in agribusiness, in industry, in the service trades, and in a whole range of other activities. Each person's decision to leave the farm was intensely personal and meant a break with tradition. But the effect, given some time, was, on average, an improvement in living levels both for those who went and those who stayed. To put it briefly, the American agricultural revolution transformed what was once an agrarian culture into an urban economy. It will similarly transform any other agrarian country in which it takes hold. Obviously Cyrus McCormick and his fellow inventors were doing more than improve the technology of agricultural production. They were changing the face of America.

The reaper had subtle effects. It released men to fight in the Northern armies during the Civil War, thus speeding the end of slavery and the plantation system. It helped make agriculture capital-intensive, moving farming from subsistence to the exchange economy. It increased the comparative advantage of level land; the agricultural decline of rocky, hilly New England can thus in part be explained.

Before McCormick the standard method of harvest was the cradle, a hand-held tool with a sharp curved blade and small parallel strips of wood to gather the cut grain. The cradle was swung rhythmically by a man half-erect, half-bent, cleanly mowing the standing grain. It laid the grain straight in the swath, the heads all in the same direction. A man using a cradle needed two or three others to tie the grain and set it in shocks. Such a crew could harvest perhaps two acres a day if they all worked hard. The harvest had to be accomplished within about ten days, the span between immaturity and the shattering of over-ripe seed. The advantage of replacing the hand-harvest bottleneck with some mechanical device was plain to all.

William T. Hutchinson in his definitive biography of Cyrus Hall Mc-Cormick lists seventeen different inventors, British and American, who antedated McCormick, producing mechanical reapers between 1786 and 1831. None of these machines performed satisfactorily and none caught on.

Cyrus Hall McCormick's great-grandfather Thomas, a Covenanter, came to America from Ulster during the troublesome days of 1735. Our inventor was born in Rockbridge County, Virginia, on February 15, 1809, three days after the birth of Abraham Lincoln. Two younger brothers, Leander and William, were to figure prominently in the McCormick enterprises. Cyrus's father owned Walnut Grove, the home farm of 532 acres. He also owned four slaves and seven horses. Cyrus attended a log school where he learned his three Rs. Little is known of these early years; like Abraham Lincoln he was largely self-taught.

Robert McCormick, Cyrus's father, no doubt was the inspiration for his son. Robert invented a machine for processing hemp, a clover sheller, a blacksmith's bellows, a hydraulic machine, a threshing machine, and a hillside plow. As early as 1809 he began to work on a reaper, on which he labored intermittently for twenty years with little success. After a final discouraging test in the early harvest of 1831 he apparently abandoned the project.

In 1831 Cyrus, twenty-two years old, of inventive bent and no doubt tutored by his father, apparently produced his famous reaper. Reliable facts regarding this event are scarce indeed. The machine put together four vital elements, some of which had appeared individually in previous machines. All were combined by Cyrus for the first time and all were incorporated in later successful reapers produced by others:

1. A flexible grain deck with a master wheel at one end and a small grain wheel at the other.
2. A reciprocating knife with a serrated edge, operating in conjunc-

tion with fixed teeth, to shear off the standing stalks. (This was the chief improvement over his father's machine.)

3. A rotating reel, to push the stalks against the knife and drop them on the platform.

4. A divider, to separate the grain to be cut from the grain left standing.

The machine was pulled by one horse, in shafts, walking beside the standing grain. It was a two-man operation, one riding this horse and one walking alongside, raking the grain from the platform. This machine successfully cut about six acres of oats on the neighboring farm of John Steele in late July 1831. So far as is known, not more than three or four persons, besides members of the McCormick family, witnessed this first public trial.

Cyrus admitted that his first reaper did not cut perfectly and improvements were made. In 1832 50 acres were cut on the home farm and one or two public trials were held. In 1833 after further improvements a public exhibition was held near Lexington. McCormick built a larger reaper and in 1840 he made his first sale. In 1842 he sold 7 machines. The next year sales increased to 29 and in 1844 50 were sold. In 1847, with his eye on the growing midwestern market, McCormick moved his operations to Chicago, then a city of 17,000 people. He built 500 reapers for the 1848 harvest. He was joined by his two younger brothers, Leander having responsibility for building the reapers in what had become a factory operation, while William supervised sales, collections, and purchases of supplies. By 1856 the Chicago plant produced 4,000 reapers.

McCormick's success brought out a host of competitors who battled him in machine design, field trials, sales, litigation, and the press. The reaper went through a series of improvements, the product of competition. The McCormick firm and the rival Deering company were combined in 1890, the new firm being named McCormick-Deering. In 1902 the leading companies that produced reapers were combined into International Harvester under McCormick leadership. The fifty-year reaper war was abated. Two hundred harvester companies had been reduced to fourteen.

The binder, which tied the cut grain into bundles, was supreme for forty years with McCormick-Deering the leading manufacturer. This was the machine I knew as a young man on the home farm in Indiana during the 1930s. Then came the combine, which threshed the kernels from the standing grain. International Harvester began making combines in 1914 and by 1938 production of combines exceeded production of binders.

Mechanical improvements in grain harvesting came about through a flood of inventions, patents, new companies, and lawsuits. Cyrus McCormick was almost continually in the courts, winning some cases but losing more than he won. He lost to Obed Hussey, who sued him for infringement of patent rights. The banner court case was McCormick's 1855 suit against John H. Manny, the most successful of his competitors, for infringement of minor 1845 and 1847 patents. The case for Manny, the winner, was carried by a brilliant group of lawyers, including Abraham Lincoln, on his way to the presidency, and Edwin M. Stanton, who would become Lincoln's secretary of war. Though McCormick kept losing lawsuits concerned with patent rights for his reaper, such were the merits of his machine and the aggressiveness of his merchandising that his sales continued to increase. He hardly needed the protection of patents.

It is not only in the United States that McCormick sold his reaper. It took the world for its market. By 1980 one-third of International Harvester's sales consisted of foreign operations.

International Harvester became a full-line farm equipment company. In 1910 Harvester began operation of a new tractor factory. In 1923 the Farmall tractor was launched, a tricycle-type tractor made for row-crop operation, the prototype of equipment designed for horseless farming. Thereafter came the redesigning of the product line with the phasing out of horse-drawn machines.

Harvester ventured beyond the farm equipment field. Motor truck production started in Akron, Ohio, in 1907, and by 1980 accounted for 43 percent of total sales. In 1979 Harvester was manufacturing such industrial equipment as wheel loaders, crawler loaders, bulldozers, haulers, scrapers, excavators, skidders, loggers, forklifts, and backhoes. Its sales in fiscal 1978–79 were $6.3 billion.

Beginning in the late 1970s International Harvester began reeling from a number of setbacks. John Deere, the archrival, was making steady gains by good design and aggressive merchandising. In 1979 Harvester, long suffering from bad labor relations, held out against its striking labor force for six months; while Harvester shut down John Deere and other implement companies forged ahead. Management had been kept within the McCormick family; there were charges that this was unwise and in 1980 Brooks McCormick retired as chairman of the executive committee. A worldwide recession in the early eighties hurt both the farm and nonfarm equipment business; dividends were passed up in 1981, the first such omission since 1910. In 1983, under the federal commodity program, a deep cut was made in acreage of farm crops, further eroding a weak farm equipment market. Harvester's stock, which had sold at $45 a share in 1979, plunged to a small fraction of its earlier value.

In 1984 Harvester's farm machinery line was bought by its rival, J. I.

Case, a part of the Tenneco conglomerate. It was like the merger of 1902, when International Harvester was formed by taking over its leading rivals, except that this time the McCormick people themselves were swallowed. When the McCormick firm was efficient in meeting implement needs it was richly rewarded; when it lost the competitive edge it was penalized. A century and a half of distinguished service to agriculture and the nation counted for nothing in the bargaining terms of the takeover. Mercifully the inventor had passed on before these misfortunes befell the firm he had founded.

Cyrus Hall McCormick, inventor and business man, was above all financially successful. His fortune was estimated at $10 million, a huge sum for his day. He was a nineteenth-century industrial tycoon in the pattern of railroad, financial, and oil tycoons.

In the end poor health overtook him. He died at his Chicago home on May 13, 1884, at seventy-five years of age. His son took over presidency of the company and his wife, then forty-nine years old, full of vigor and thoroughly familiar with company affairs, took strong hold of the business.

Cyrus's two brothers, Leander and William, held important but subordinate posts in the McCormick enterprise. They believed that the 1831 reaper was invented by their father, Robert, not by their brother Cyrus. All four of Cyrus's siblings—Leander, William, Amanda, and Caroline—joined in this belief. Leander especially was deeply wounded by what he considered Cyrus's pretensions as the inventor. The family released a study, the purport of which was that the father, Robert, had "given" the reaper to his eldest son in the belief that the young man, who already displayed qualities of leadership and tenacity, would be successful in developing it. With the gift allegedly had gone responsibility for sharing its benefits with other members of the family. In 1885 Leander published *The Memorial to Robert McCormick,* attributing invention to the father rather than the son. This was the year after Cyrus had died. The issue was thus revived more than half a century after the event when memories had faded and after Cyrus's position as inventor had been widely accepted. Leander McCormick's tract added little hard information about the invention of the reaper but it revealed much about the feelings within the family. The recognized facts regarding the first successful use of the reaper in 1831 are scarce indeed. Hutchinson, Cyrus's friendly biographer, has this to say: "The story that Robert gave it [the invention] to his son at the time of the patent in 1834 can hardly be true."

Whatever the facts, there was a McCormick reaper and it helped transform world grain production. We are all in debt to its inventor. That we are uncertain as to the identity of our benefactor does not make the debt less real.

The system of enterprise, competition, incentive, and reward helped produce the reaper. No other country achieved agricultural development so rapidly as did the United States with its open system. The reward bestowed on Cyrus McCormick, measured in millions of dollars, was small in relation to the public benefits.

The enemy, hunger, is not a well-ordered foe, marshalled and massed in battle formation or fighting from a fixed position. Hunger fights like a guerilla, appearing sometimes in full and clear view, at other times seeming to withdraw or disappear. This enemy cannot be fought with a single strategy, frontal fashion. The fight against famine is a series of skirmishes, fought by different kinds of people on different fronts, with different motives. One such fighter was Cyrus McCormick, brave, aggressive, and effective. He was a mercenary, fighting for pay. The pay was good and he earned it. In nineteenth-century America that was accolade enough.

REFERENCES

Casson, H. N. 1909. *Cyrus McCormick, His Life and Work.* Chicago: McClurg.

Hutchinson, William T. 1930. *Cyrus Hall McCormick: Seed-Time, 1809–1856.* New York and London: Century.

———. 1935. *Cyrus Hall McCormick: Harvest, 1856–1884.* New York and London: D. Appleton-Century.

International Harvester. 1947. *Roots in Chicago a Hundred Years Deep, 1847–1947.* Chicago: International Harvester.

Lyons, Norbert. 1955. *The McCormick Reaper Legend: The True Story of a Great Invention.* New York: Exposition Press.

McCormick, Cyrus. 1931. *The Century of the Reaper.* Boston and New York: Houghton Mifflin, Riverside Press.

Marsh, Barbara. 1985. *A Corporate Tragedy: The Agony of International Harvester Company.* New York: Doubleday.

Ozanne, Robert. 1967. *A Century of Labor Management Relations at McCormick and International Harvester.* Madison, Milwaukee, and London: Univ. of Wisconsin Press.

Thwaites, Reuben Gold. 1909. "Cyrus Hall McCormick and the Reaper." From the *Proceedings of the State Historical Society of Wisconsin for 1908.* Published by the society.

USDA Yearbook. 1960. *The Power to Produce.* Washington, D.C.: Government Printing Office.

CHAPTER 7

Gregor Mendel and the Riddle of Heredity

BEFORE MENDEL THE CONTINUITY OF LIFE between parent and off-spring was a subject of awe, wonder, mystery, myth, riddle, or received doctrine—anything but science. In the breeding of animals the pure line was thought to be best. "Purebred" was a word of approval. An animal of mixed breeding was a "scrub," a term of derision. It is possible that biblical admonition, then very powerful, was influential in this attitude. The Book of Leviticus has it thus: "Thou shalt not let thy cattle gender with a diverse kind: thou shalt not sow thy field with mingled seed" (19:19).

In the human population, a "half-breed" was an inferior person. The male was thought to be the more important of the two parents, stamping his attributes on the offspring. Tracing the male parentage was for many years the accepted way of recording ancestry for human beings and for animals.

One sees here a reflection of the racism, sexism, and aristocratic pretensions that characterized human institutions throughout the ages. Mendel's work would destroy the basis for these beliefs, but the correction would be a long time coming. Farmers, under pressure to make their operations pay, would slough off these erroneous ideas sooner than would the leaders of the social system.

Darwin said that natural selection, carried out by nature, must be superior to artificial selection, carried out by man. However this may be, during the eleven millennia between the beginning of agriculture and the time of Mendel, artificial selection had changed the bovine animal from the wild auroch, standing seven feet high at the withers, to a tame cow, a little more than half as tall. The ear of corn had grown from the size of a man's thumb to as big as a pop bottle.

45

At Mendel's time a great error prevailed: the myth that acquired characters could be inherited. The belief was that if a species of plant experienced a change in environment it would take on a modified form appropriate to the new setting and transmit this new attribute to the next generation. A man who was injured and had developed a scar would, if he sired children thereafter, transmit this scar to his offspring. Lamarck, who wrote at the beginning of the nineteenth century, popularized the idea. Improvements of crops and livestock were held back by ignorance.

Everything about Gregor Mendel seems improbable. He twice failed examinations to qualify himself as a high school teacher but was successful in teaching without certification. He became a monk apparently not because of religious commitment but in order to continue his secular studies. He was declared unsuited for pastoral duties and so began his biological experiments. He undertook studies in genetics, probing into questions for which his church considered that it had already supplied satisfactory answers. By good fortune or by some undisclosed knowledge he chose to work with peas, which were well suited to testing his hypotheses. In advance of his time he devised an experimental method which evokes admiration more than a century later. He worked eight years on his experiment, discovering principles that would undergird all subsequent work in genetics. He produced a paper which he read in February 1865 to some forty members of a provincial scientific society, drawing from his audience neither comment nor question. The paper, "Experiments in Plant Hybridization," was printed in the proceedings of the society where it remained, little noticed, for thirty-four years. He sent a reprint of his paper to Nägeli, the Swiss botanist, who gave it scant attention. He sent another copy to Kerner, professor of botany at Munich, in whose library it was later found, the pages uncut. Discouraged, Mendel gave up his experiments, for which he was eminently qualified, and took over adminstrative duties of his monastery, for which his credentials were limited. He died, undistinguished and unknown. His scientific papers were burned. When the merits of his experiments became known, geneticists of the world sought to erect a statue in his hometown but encountered opposition from the local citizens; a statue, they said, would take space needed for amusement booths at fair time. If it were not for the diligent work of his biographer, Hugo Iltis, we would know little about this great man.

The main effect of Mendel's work was to lay the basis for plant and animal breeding, particularly the green revolution, which improved food production for the hungry people of the world and held off famine for millions. A side effect was that every scientist who delivers a paper that goes unnoticed dreams that its deep significance will ultimately be discovered.

Mendel was born July 22, 1822, in Heinzendorf, Austria (now Hyncice, Czechoslovakia, near Krnov). His given name was Johann. The additional name of Gregor, by which he became known, was bestowed when he became a member of the Augustinian order. Johann soon distinguished himself in school. The serious bent of the young scholar is demonstrated by a poem he wrote, a line of which reads thus: "As the Master willed, you shall dispel the gloomy power of superstition which now oppresses the world." He wrote a brief autobiography as an accompaniment to his request for admission to the examination for high school teachers. It is in the third person, somewhat stilted, and reveals his reflective turn of mind. Problems of health and money weighed heavily on the young man.

Mendel studied at the Philosophical Institute at Olmütz. Illness and lack of money interrupted his studies. Passionately devoted to learning and without financial support, he turned to the Church, which offered both. In 1843 he was admitted to the Königinkloster as a novice. As was common, students and scholars worked alongside the clerics. At the monastery was a small garden, attended by a distinguished botanist, Pater Aurelius Thaler. Thaler died and Mendel was given responsibility for the garden. Mendel attended Brünn Theological College and the University of Vienna in addition to the institue at Olmütz. He taught at Znaim High School and Brünn Modern School.

By 1856 Mendel was thirty-four years old, equipped with a patched-together education, secure in his livelihood, having custody of a garden 120 feet long and 20 feet wide. He was ready for serious research. He read botany, everything he could get his hands on. The reasons for pursuing this interest can only be surmised. Perhaps his love for growing things and the availability of the garden were decisive; on such mundane matters the course of scientific discovery may rest. What ideas were churning in his head we cannot know. He kept his thoughts to himself as befitted a monk in search of secular answers to questions long considered to be in the province of God. His subject was hybridization. For his experiments he chose the edible pea, an ideal species. It is naturally self-pollinated, can readily be cross-pollinated, and the hybrid is fertile. The different forms of the plant are easily distinguishable from one another. There are minimal problems with interassociations among the various forms of the plant. Pea plants grow readily and were of a size suited to his garden.

Mendel selected seven pairs of characters: (1) shape of the ripe seed (round or wrinkled); (2) color of the pea (yellow or green); (3) tint of the seed coat (white or colored); (4) shape of the ripe pods (simply curved or constricted); (5) tint of the unripe pods (green or yellow); (6) position of the flowers (axial or terminal); and (7) stature of the plant (tall or dwarf).

Mendel opened the flowers just before they were ready to open by themselves. He removed the male element (stamens) and dusted the female element (pistil) with pollen from a plant showing the opposite character. He made the cross both ways, known as reciprocal crossing. When he crossed two plants, each from a pure line and unlike one another with respect to the attribute in question, all the offspring (which we have learned to call the F_1 generation) almost invariably showed the attribute of one parent. This character Mendel called "dominant." The attribute of the other did not appear. Though present it was masked; Mendel called it "recessive." In the next generation, F_2, the plants being self-fertilized, the attributes in question appeared in a ratio of 3 to 1, 3 showing the dominant character and 1 the recessive.

Mendel continued his experiments for six or seven generations, with like results. One-fourth of the total number of individuals were dominant, one-fourth recessive, and two-fourths, though outwardly exhibiting the dominant character, did not breed true—thus, in appearance, the persistent 3:1 ratio. Mendel took pains to count all the offspring, in contrast to earlier studies of hybridization. Some, like Darwin, focused on the modal forms. Most observers and experimenters were preoccupied with the bizarre and the grotesque. Perhaps nothing reveals so well Mendel's scientific bent as this examination of all forms and quantification of his findings. R. A. Fisher, the famous English statistician, says of Mendel's results that they appear more like demonstrations than like experiments; his findings approach his hypothesis closer than is likely on the basis of chance.

Mendel's work was later summarized as having identified two "laws of heredity." One is the "law of segregation," which holds that when the reproductive cells are formed the alternative units of heredity separate from one another, as for example the characters for smooth or wrinkled peas. The second is the "law of independent recombination," which holds that in the newly formed individual the units of heredity for a particular character recombine themselves in random fashion.

Mendel's findings have been modified by later discoveries. For example, the discovery of linkage, crossing over, and mutations made necessary some alteration of Mendel's simple findings but did not invalidate his work. What had Mendel's experiments demonstrated? They showed that heredity belonged in the realm of science, not the occult, thus refuting the mythology that had long been dominant. They showed that genetic attributes were determined at the time of conception, thus invalidating the Lamarckian idea that acquired characters can be inherited. The experiments revealed that male and female parents contributed equally to the makeup of the offspring. We could forget male prepotency. The genetic contribution of a parent was shown to diminish by half with each generation. Thus the great-grandson of an outstanding elder received only one-eighth of his heredity therefrom. If an individual's ancestor came over with the Mayflower he or she probably received about three-thousands of 1 percent of his/her biological inheritance from that person. So much for the long honored bloodline. Mendel showed that nature, in its wisdom, keeps broadening the genetic base.

The work showed that life has continuous flow from one generation to another. The idea of spontaneous generation, empirically disproved by Spallanzani and Pasteur, was dealt an additional blow.

Vigor in the hybrid offspring, previously known to Darwin and characterized by him as "luxurisation," must have appeared in Mendel's plants but went unreported. When this principle became generally known with the work of Shull in 1908, the myth of the pure line would be dispelled. Hybrid corn and the crossing of purebred livestock lines would be the accepted techniques.

Did Mendel perceive these potential consequences? We cannot tell. His paper was scrupulously limited to his observed results; there was no visualization. In its spare, depersonalized style it became the model for subsequent scientific papers. Those who heard his report foresaw none of these profound consequences. The paper involved methods and concepts unknown to his listeners and therefore incomprehensible. His hearers were accustomed to abstract theory, not to arithmetic ratios. Einstein said, "It is the theory which decides what we can observe." Not comprehending a theory underlying Mendel's findings, his listeners observed nothing. Mendel's findings were not attacked, they simply went unnoticed.

Mendel ceased his experiments after this disappointing reception. His inner thoughts he kept to himself. He said, "My time will come," as indeed it did. After Mendel's work had slumbered for thirty-four years it was reaffirmed and published within a few months' time by three separate researchers. The new genetic theory caught on quickly. The world was more ready to learn of genetic experiments in 1900 than it had been in 1865.

Mendel learned how attributes are passed from one generation to another, giving continuity to a species. Darwin learned how natural selection occurs, providing for change. The twin principles apply to plants, animals, and people. Thus come both continuity and change, and for all creatures, plants, animals, human beings.

Rebuffed in what he had hoped would be received as a major scientific discovery, Mendel put aside interest in things scientific. He became prelate of his monastery in 1868, a crotchety man, doing battle with the government over tax matters. He served as prelate for sixteen years, growing more corpulent, smoking his cigars, tending his desk. He died of Bright's disease on January 6, 1884 when sixty-two years old and was buried at Brünn.

What kind of man was Mendel? The facts of his life are reasonably clear. But Mendel the man eludes all of us, including his biographer. Was he a simple peasant, educated beyond his capability, as his colleague Nägeli seemed to think? Was he a brilliant scientist, untimely born and so unappreciated in his day? Was he an opportunist, attaching himself to the Church for bed and board? Was he truly a reverent man, searching out the wonders of God's creation? His driving force seems to have been the one he expressed in his poem as a schoolboy, to "dispel the gloomy power of superstition which now oppresses the world."

REFERENCES

Bateson, W. 1913. *Mendel's Principles of Heredity.* Cambridge: Cambridge Univ. Press.
Iltis, H. 1932. *Life of Mendel.* Trans. E. and C. Paul. New York: Norton.
Magner, Lois N. 1979. *A History of the Life Sciences.* New York and Basel: Marcel Dekker.
Mendel, Gregor. 1865. "Experiments in Plant Hybridization." *Proceedings of the Brünn Society for the Study of Natural Science.* Reviewed in Iltis, *Life of Mendel.*
Nardone, R. N. 1968. *Mendel Centenary: Genetics, Development and Evolution.* Washington, D.C.: Catholic Univ. Press.
Olby, R. 1966. *Origins of Mendelism.* New York: Schocken.
Sootin, H. 1959. *Gregor Mendel: Father of the Science of Genetics.* New York: Vanguard.
Stern, Curt, and Eva R. Sherwood. 1966. *The Origin of Genetics. A Mendel Source Book.* San Francisco: Freeman.
Stubbe, Hans. 1972. *History of Genetics.* Cambridge, Mass.: MIT Press.
Sturtevant, A. H. 1965. *A History of Genetics.* New York: Harper and Row.

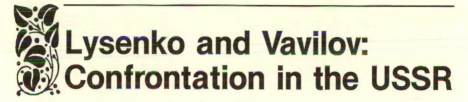

CHAPTER 8

Lysenko and Vavilov: Confrontation in the USSR

We shall go to the pyre
we shall burn but we shall
not renounce our convictions.
— N. I. VAVILOV, *March 1939*

THIS CHAPTER, like the preceding one, is on genetics. It has the ingredients of drama: hero and villain, confrontation and clash, defeat and victory. The battle was between ideas, between institutions, between methods, and between people. The stakes were survival or death. We begin by describing the opposing camps.

After Mendel, genetics proceeded on a two-track course, destined ultimately to clash. On one path were the followers of Mendel, committed to the discipline of science. They formulated hypotheses, tested them, and discarded those that did not survive. They specified the conditions surrounding their studies and quantified their results. They accepted only those findings which could be reproduced by other researchers. They welcomed new findings which superceded their own. In the post-Mendelian tradition were, among others, Weismann, Morgan, Muller, and Vavilov, the latter a Russian and the hero of this chapter.

The other track was in the tradition of Lamarck, the French biologist who was mentioned in the previous chapter. Lamarck's major theme was that acquired characters could be inherited. Lamarck said, "The production of a new organ in an animal results from a new need which continues to make itself felt." He and his followers believed that environment was more important than heredity. Change could be induced and could occur abruptly. Of central importance in the legacy of Lamarck is the Russian horticulturist Ivan Vladimirovich Michurin, born in 1855 of an impoverished noble family. Michurin grew seedlings and grafted them onto the varieties he wished them to resemble, a kind of Johnny Appleseed with a high school diploma. Culmination of the Lamarck line came with the Russian Trofim Denisovich Lysenko, who lived from 1898 to 1976. Lysenko was the leader of Lamarckist thought in the clash with orthodox genetics and is the other central figure in this chapter.

The setting which would bring these rival schools into confrontation was the Russian Revolution. Before 1917 Marxists showed only desultory interest in biology though there is a hint of Lamarckism in a fragment of Engels's work. Social theory and politics were the consuming passions. It is significant that Marx and Engels as well as their followers considered environmental factors to be enormously important in shaping human beings. This is the essence of dialectical materialism, central to communist thought. With exploitation overcome, conflict between human beings would cease and the classless society would emerge. People would produce in accordance with their ability and consume in keeping with their need. This they would do without coercion; the arm of the state would wither away. Needed to achieve this state of human perfection was a conducive environment. The evil in men was not genetically based; it was the product of evil institutions. The revolutionary task was to throw out the evil institutions that had corrupted men. That environmental conditions might be decisive for plants and animals as well as for human beings was readily believable.

The Revolution ended the intellectual autonomy of the scientists. The new duty of the scientists was to serve the country in ways specified by the political leaders. There was a felt need to develop a unique Marxist science, distinct from "bourgeois" science. Marxist thought was to be expressed both in the social sciences and in the life sciences. Some part of "bourgeois" social science was rooted in Malthus, a pastor, and some part of life science stemmed from Mendel, a priest. That followers of an atheistic ideology would be inclined to reject such origins is not surprising.

Above all there was a terrible urgency to get food produced. The Soviet Union has hunger and starvation as part of its history; it is a country with a short growing season, limited rainfall, erratic climate, and large areas of unproductive soil. Naum Jasny, the Russian farm expert, said long ago that agriculture was the Achilles' heel of the Soviet Union. The commissars were famine fighters. Faults they had, but lack of zeal was not one of them.

In such a setting the Lamarckian promise for sudden transformation of agriculture and a consequent spurt in food production carried enormous appeal. Attractiveness of a purposeful leap out of agricultural backwardness is caught by Bertolt Brecht's poem:

> Let us thus with ever newer arts
> Change this earth's form and operation,
> Gladly measure thousand-year-old wisdom

> By new wisdom one year old.
> Dreams! Golden If!
> Let the lovely flood of grain rise higher!
> Sower, what
> You will create tomorrow, call it yours today!

Chief architect of the brave new world for agriculture was T. D. Lysenko. He was born of farm parents in Karlovka, a village near Poltava, in the south of Russia. He entered the Horticultural Institute at Poltava in 1913 and a similar institute at Umansk, remaining until 1921. He joined the newly funded research station at Gandza in Azerbaidjan. *Pravda,* with unaccountable colorfulness, thus described him in 1927, when he was just short of thirty years old:

Skinny, with prominent cheekbones and close-cropped hair (later replaced by a lank forelock), . . . this Lysenko gives one the sensation of a toothache. God grant him health, he is a man of doleful appearance. Both stingy with a word and unremarkable in features, except that you remember his morose eye crawling along the earth with such a look as if he were at least getting ready to kill someone. He smiled only once, this barefoot scientist. . . .

At Azerbaidjan Lysenko developed what he called "vernalization," which brought him worldwide fame. The intent of vernalization was to avert the killing, during the winter, of wheat seeded in the fall. Lysenko moistened and chilled the seed of winter wheat and planted it in the spring. A small trial did well. The success was widely publicized by Lysenko, a master of propaganda. But the effort could not be generalized. The plant breeder Konstantinov carried out an extensive five-year experimental check and found no significant statistical difference between vernalized wheat and the standard practice. So vernalization expired. But Lysenko survived. Strangely, his advocacy of this failed practice propelled him to a position of prominence.

Lysenko had considerable official backing in political circles. He had the necessary qualifications: humble origin, aggressiveness, flashes of insight, a known name, loyalty to the Revolution, and willingness to challenge bourgeois science. For a sample of his style, here is a passage from his speech in 1935 at the Second All-Union Congress of Shock Collective Farmers, delivered in the presence of Stalin. Lysenko described the vernalization debate in these terms:

Tell me comrades, was there not a class struggle on the vernalization front? In the collective farms there were kulaks and their abettors who kept whispering (and they were not the only ones, every class enemy did) into the peasant's ears: "Don't soak the seeds. It will ruin them." This is the way it was, such were the whispers, such were the kulak and saboteur deceptions, when, instead of helping collective farmers, they did their destructive business, both in the scientific world and out of it; a class enemy is always an enemy whether he is a scientist or not.

At the end of this speech Stalin exclaimed, "Bravo! Comrade Lysenko, bravo!"

Lysenko's star rose. He entered political life and was for a time vice-president of the Supreme Soviet. He was twice awarded a Stalin Prize and received the Order of Lenin. In May 1945 he was made a Hero of the Soviet Union. In 1938 he was elected president of the Lenin All-Union Academy of Agricultural Sciences. For thirty years he was the virtual czar of "agrobiology" (his word) in the Soviet Union.

N. I. Vavilov, Lysenko's rival, was a very different man. He took his first steps in science at the Moscow Agricultural Institute under Pryanishnikov, who occupied the chair of plant breeding. Vavilov had worked in England under the great geneticist Bateson and he had published valuable research before the Revolution. While still a young man he was appointed head of the All-Union Institute of Plant Industry and a little later also became head of the Bureau of Genetics under the Academy of Sciences. His work came to the attention of Lenin who, when he set up the Lenin Academy of Agricultural Sciences, put Vavilov in charge. In 1926 he was awarded the Lenin Prize.

Vavilov's major interest was in a series of expeditions to regions where various crop plants were presumed to have originated. He collected an enormous amount of living plant material from which he hoped to develop new and more productive crops for Russia. Vavilov created centers of advanced research that won great respect in the international community of scientists. When the Revolution came Vavilov gave it his support, though he did not become a party member. He was then thirty years old and already a man of note.

In 1929 the party launched a five-year plan for agriculture, setting as a goal a 35 percent increase in average grain yields. The agricultural scientists were enlisted in support of the plan. Their cooperation was supplied with some misgivings; the goal seemed unattainable. But acceptance of the goal was the condition for continued support of scientific work.

The brief honeymoon was soon over. Hostility to the scientists was rising, especially so toward Vavilov. The assembly of foreign plant material of questionable value, repeated and often inconclusive tests, research on incomprehensible subjects, and the esoteric language of science all served to irritate the commissars. Agricultural science had to become useful by transforming itself from its bourgeois habits into the socialist mold. The pattern was Lysenko's model, with Michurin the rallying call,

Stalin the enforcer, and the ghost of Lamarck flitting about in the background. The issue was joined.

Numerous code words were developed by Lysenko. "Michurinism" connoted approval, "Mendelism" conveyed condemnation. It was no longer needful to describe a scientist's ideas; he was simply pigeonholed. To Lysenko and his supporters, a geneticist was either a "Michurinist" (one of "ours") or a "Mendelist" (one of "theirs," an enemy of the people).

Vavilov was charged with carrying out "reactionary botanical studies." In 1937 Lysenko's closest aid, Prezent, linked Vavilov to Bukharin, an apostate who had "sold out socialism." In 1938 a number of workers in Vavilov's Lenin All-Union Academy of Agricultural Sciences were arrested. The newspaper *Sotszemledelie* published an article proposing "To sanitize the Academy of Science. To root out mercilessly enemies and their yes-men from scientific establishments." Vavilov was named among the enemies of the people, charged with an attitude inimical to Lysenko's work. A Michurinist group formed within Vavilov's academy. Lysenko appointed a young specialist, Shundenko, as deputy to Vavilov. Shundenko, who was responsible only to Lysenko, tried to force Vavilov's resignation.

In March 1939, at a meeting in the All-Union Institute of Plant Breeding, there was an open clash between Vavilov and Lysenko. Lysenko spoke thus: "Nikolay Ivanovich [Vavilov], it is somewhat difficult for you to carry on your work. We talked of this many times and I was sincerely sorry for you. But, you see, you are being insubordinate to me. . . . I say now that some kind of measures must be taken. We cannot go on this way." Vavilov persisted, ignoring these attacks and continuing his scientific work. That same year he proposed, despite Lysenko's criticism, a move to hybrid corn. He was elected president of the International Congress of Genetics, which met in Edinburgh in 1939. But he was denied permission to go.

In August 1940 Vavilov was arrested. He was picked up by members of the secret police while on a plant-hunting expedition in the western Ukraine. On July 9, 1941, the military collegium of the Supreme Court, after a meeting lasting only a few minutes, passed sentence on him. He was found guilty of belonging to a rightest conspiracy, spying for England, leading the Labor Peasant party, sabotaging agriculture, consorting with white émigrés, and other offenses. The sentence was death. A first and second appeal were denied. But the sentence was not carried out immediately; apparently higher approval was necessary.

While Vavilov was in a prison in Saratov the death sentence was commuted to a ten-year imprisonment. He survived prison conditions until his death on January 26, 1943. Circumstances of his death and the place of burial are not known.

Vavilov was by no means the only scientist who was purged during the Stalinist Terror. The historian Joravsky lists by name 105 biologists, agricultural specialists, and other scientists who suffered repression.

Following Vavilov's arrest, Lysenko assumed Vavilov's post as director of the Institute of Genetics at the Academy of Sciences. Under Stalin's protection Lysenko's domination of agricultural science was complete.

There is no need to chronicle in detail the suppression of agricultural science that characterized the years of Lysenko's dominance. The mental state of those who capitulated to Stalin and Lysenko is illustrated by the writing of the biologist O. B. Lepeshinskaya. At the beginning of her book she wrote that Stalin had read it and approved. Later, after Stalin's death, she recounted in greater detail the secret of her success.

In these sorrowful days, I cannot help recollecting an incident in my life. It was in a difficult year when malicious metaphysicians, Old Testament idealists, bearers of the most reactionary ideas of Weismannism-Morganism took up arms against my work in biology. Once, when I felt especially wretched and miserable from the endless hostile attacks, the telephone rang in my room. I lifted the receiver and heard such a familiar, such a dear voice, that of Iosif Vissarianovich. . . . Encouraging me with friendly paternal word, Stalin gave me advice. And in his wise counsel there was such crystal clarity, such power of scientific prevision, that my heart stood still with pride. Pride that there is on this large planet a man intimate and dear, for whom all complex questions and problems are an open book, for whom, in all detail, the path of development of Soviet progressive science is clear.

It is time to move out of the theoretical dialogues, the public pronouncements, and the purges to see what was happening on the farms of the Soviet Union during the years of Lysenkoism.

As might be surmised, on-farm experience with the Lysenko initiatives often failed to conform to the plan. Vernalization, Lysenko's original proposal for transforming Soviet agriculture, died a natural death. In 1935 new wheat varieties were released. Three of these were rejected in the year of submission. One, number 1163, was susceptible to smut and made poor bread and so was soon forgotten.

Prerevolutionary Russia had a proud tradition of soil science, having in fact given that body of knowledge to the world. But there came a man named Vil'yams (a Russianized name; his father was an American engineer named Williams). Vil'yams contended, contrary to known science, that the soil's structure, not its chemistry, was the source of fertility. (One senses here the ghost of Jethro Tull. The USSR seems inclined to embrace ideas that have been rejected by the West: the labor theory of value, the errors of Jethro Tull, and Lamarckism.) With Lysenko's support Vil'yams prescribed crop rotation with emphasis on grass to improve soil structure. He frowned on the use of fertilizer. The result was a diminution in the production of much-needed grain and an increase in the growth of forage, which the farmers were not in position to use. The system was given a trial for twenty-four years and was finally abandoned in 1961.

Lysenko denied the efficacy of using plant and animal hormones, thus choking off a promising new field of agricultural science. He opposed the adoption of hybrid corn. This technique had been developed by the reactionary Mendelists-Morganists and so was resisted.

One of the strangest of Lysenko's campaigns had to do with the transformation of one species into another, an idea in accord with the worst examples of seventeenth-century natural philosophy. He wrote thus: "Under the action of external environment which is unsuitable or little suitable for a given species, particles of a different species for which the conditions are more suitable arise in the body of the plant. From these particles rudiments (buds or seeds) are formed which develop into individuals of the other species." This was part of Lysenko's idea that stress or "shattering" would modify the species. Lysenko's journal *Agribiologiya* carried on a contest. Who would detect the most transformations? From 1950 to 1955 numerous articles appeared reporting the transformation of wheat into rye and vice versa, barley into oats, peas into vetch, vetch into lentils, firs into pines, hazelnuts into hornbeams, alders into birches, and sunflowers into strangleweed.

M. F. Ivanov, a successful animal husbandman who had died the year Lysenko launched his attack on modern biology, had taken a favorable view of genetic science. But Ivanov was proclaimed a founder of Michurinism and so transferred posthumously into the Lysenko camp.

The Lysenko affair was for geneticists a controversy concerning theory and method. For the party officials it concerned ideology. For the peasants it was a question as to what new and strange edict would be passed down to them from on high. For the consumers it was a steady diet of hopes and promises, most of which went unfulfilled.

In 1964 Lysenkoism faded. It had been on the defensive for some time. Thirty years of this nonscience had left the Soviet Union with an agriculture incapable of meeting food needs; the country had been transformed from a grain exporter to a grain importer. Some unreconstructed geneticists had gone underground and had been chipping away at the edges of Lysenko's monolith. Khrushchev's fall in October 1964 left Lysenko without the protection of the one high official on whom he relied for power. Instrumental in the downfall of Lysenko was Zhores A. Medvedev, the distinguished biochemist and the chief resource for this chapter.

Lysenko, the agricultural Rasputin, lost his power. He lingered on, the sands running out, the nominal head of agencies that finessed his orders. He died in 1976.

Thirty years of Lysenkoism produced a generation of students trained in the art of forensic agriculture rather than in the rigor of scientific method. Worldwide, studies of genetics and heredity were advancing, but not in the Soviet Union. The fountain of scientific literature in the field was stopped up. It would take time to staff the research stations with people adequately trained to work in the life sciences.

Meanwhile in the physical sciences, where ideology was not a real constraint, the scientists and the engineers of the Soviet Union forged ahead. Witness the rapid industrialization, the dams, and the power plants. Lysenko's well-publicized errors had led the Western world into an unwarranted derogation of all Soviet science; the launching of *Sputnik* in 1957 brought a needed reappraisal.

By 1977, biological science had again become respectable in the Soviet Union. That country to its great credit turned its back on error and sought to make amends. Vavilov's rehabilitation was proclaimed by the Russian scientist K. N. Khuchua:

The multifaceted, splendid, and brilliant life of a great scientist, founder of new directions in biology, was cut short on January 26, 1943, when he was 55 years old. His untimely death was a very serious loss for all our Soviet science.

In marking the 90th anniversary of the birth of Nikolai Ivanovich Vavilov, we bow our heads with reverence and a feeling of great gratitude before him as an outstanding scientist and thinker of our time, who devoted all his energy and his knowledge to the development of biological science in our country.

N. I. Vavilov was one of the few humans on the earth, around whose name his successors built legends. The life and activity of N. I. Vavilov was a whole epoch in science. As Academician N. P. Dubinin so aptly phrased it, "Time has supplied a deathless memorial to N. I. Vavilov."

A concluding comment. The Lysenko affair showed, to the satisfaction of scientists, that it was not possible, by ordinary environmental influences, to make basic changes in the character of plants and animals, changes that would be transmitted to the next generation. Irradiation would do this in the short run and evolution would do it in the long run. But Lysenko's method would not do it.

Does the same conclusion follow for human beings? Marxist doctrine casts the human being as having no element of the spirit but being purely biological and so subject to environmental and biological principles. The Lysenko affair must cast doubt on the Marxist postulate that human perfectibility can be achieved by cultural conditioning.

REFERENCES

Hudson, P. S., and R. H. Richens. 1946. *The New Genetics in the Soviet Union.* Imperial Bureau of Plant Breeding and Genetics, School of Agriculture, Cambridge, England.

Huxley, Julian. 1949. *Heredity East and West.* New York: Henry Schuman.

Joravsky, David. 1970. *The Lysenko Affair.* Cambridge, Mass.: Harvard Univ. Press.

Khuchua, K. N. 1977. *Life and Activity of Academician N. I. Vavilov on the Ninetieth Anniversary of His Birth.* Washington, D.C.: National Agricultural Library.

Magner, Lois N. 1979. *A History of the Life Sciences.* New York and Basel: Marcel Dekker.

Medvedev, Zhores A. 1969. *The Rise and Fall of T. D. Lysenko.* Trans. I. Michael Lerner. New York: Columbia Univ. Press.

CHAPTER 9

The Land Grant Trio

BY THE MIDDLE OF THE NINETEENTH CENTURY agriculture was still in its historic pattern. Hand labor, the ox, and the horse were the sources of power. The rake, the flail, the hoe, and the cradle were familiar tools. An Old Testament prophet magically transported to a nineteenth-century American farm could have recognized almost everything he saw and named almost every tool. American farms were similar to farms in much of the Third World today.

But technical change was coming. Liebig and McCormick had already begun their transforming work. Pasteur and Mendel were on the horizon. But technologically American agriculture was premodern. At the outbreak of the Civil War 60 percent of all working people were still engaged in agricultural production.

Though farmers were strong in numbers they were otherwise weak. Typically, the man on the land was at a low level of education, poor in material possessions, and limited in his political power. Though we were purportedly a classless society, the farmer was in effect a second-class citizen. Education, wealth, social prestige, and governance were in the hands of the wellborn and the well-to-do.

Much of Southern agriculture was in large plantations worked by slaves. An owner-operated family farming system was the objective of the Free Soil Movement, progenitor of Lincoln's Republican party. So there was a clash of ideology. Lincoln became president and agrarian reform took place. Three institutional changes occurred:

On May 12, 1862, President Lincoln signed the Act to Establish a Department of Agriculture, giving farmers representation at the national level.

On May 20, 1862, he signed the Homestead Act, giving 160 acres of land to anyone who would settle on it, improve it, and live on it for five years.

On July 2, 1862, he signed the Land Grant College Act, providing federal assistance in the establishment of colleges to teach "Agricultural and the Mechanic Arts."

The history of these events is set forth with accuracy in a series of excellent monographs by Alfred Charles True.

The main driving force behind these institutional changes was the desire to improve agricultural efficiency and so increase the incomes of farmers. A reduction in the cost of food and the alleviation of hunger were secondary consequences, not professed goals, but they did occur.

Neither before nor since has the Congress enacted and the president signed laws of such sweeping importance to agriculture. Philosophically akin to them and flowing from them came other major institutional innovations: the transcontinental railway, improved roads, the reclamation service, rural free delivery, the Farm Credit Administration, rural electrification, vocational agricultural teaching in the high schools, and the soil conservation service. Together these federal actions would transform agriculture almost beyond recognition.

The purpose of this chapter is to examine the Land Grant College Act and what became its triple function (teaching, research, and extension); to focus on the men who were instrumental in shaping these initiatives; to trace the consequences of these reforms; and to speculate on the usefulness of this American model for the developing nations of the Third World.

Three men were instrumental in founding the land grant college system; we consider their separate contributions. One was Justin Smith Morrill, who helped initiate the teaching function. The second was Samuel Johnson, father of the experiment stations. The third was Seaman A. Knapp, who laid the foundation for the agricultural extension service.

Before 1860, higher education was largely limited to the well endowed and the well bred. Education was the privilege of those preparing for the clergy, the law, and medicine; governance and civic leadership came overwhelmingly from this elite class and from the landed gentry. Dirt farmers and artisans lacked the means for higher education and, had they had the means, almost nothing pertinent was offered. They were thus automatically kept in a low-income, low-prestige category and were largely excluded from leadership.

All this was abhorrent to a man named Justin Smith Morrill, one of five sons of a village blacksmith. Morrill was born April 14, 1810, in Strafford, Vermont. Too poor to receive formal higher education, he educated himself. Hard work and good fortune permitted Morrill to retire from business at thirty-eight years of age and enter the political world. He was elected to the U.S. House of Representatives as a Whig in 1854.

From his new base in Congress, Justin Morrill, ever mindful of his own lack of schooling, became an advocate of education for the farmer and the engineer, making this his special cause. He saw the vast areas of land then in the public domain and argued that certain of these lands could be granted to each of the states and sold by them to farmers. Funds thereby obtained should be used for setting up colleges to teach agriculture and the mechanic arts.

Representative Morrill introduced the first Land Grant College Bill on December 14, 1857, but it failed. In 1862 Morrill re-introduced his bill, which passed the Senate 32 to 7 and the House 90 to 25 and was signed by President Lincoln. The bill granted 30,000 acres of public land for each congressman. Public lands were then being sold for $1.25 an acre, so resources made available to the new schools were modest in amount.

Iowa was the first state to accept the provisions of the Morrill Land Grant Act, doing so on September 11, 1862. Vermont and Connecticut followed in that same year. By 1870 thirty-six states were committed. Some states disposed of their land quickly at depressed prices in an effort to obtain the funds for an early start of the new colleges. Other states, New York among them, held the lands while their value rose, providing an excellent endowment.

These schools started slowly. Ten years after passage of the act, the combined enrollment in agricultural and mechanical courses were New York, 151; Michigan, 143; Pennsylvania, 130; Maryland, 130; Maine, 103; New Jersey, 67; Rhode Island, 25; New Hampshire, 22; and Vermont, 21.

Difficulties were numerous. Many of the applicants, coming from substandard rural schools, were deficient in mathematical and communication skills, requiring special preparation before they could enroll. At first there was little to teach. Agricultural science was still in the gestation stage. Courses contained such limited biological knowledge as was available, plus the generally accepted practical arts. Folklore was a discernible ingredient. Bits of classical writings about agriculture, stemming from Varro, Cato, Pliny, and others, crept into the courses. The new institutions had to tolerate snide comments from the educated elite about "cow colleges." Gradually, as the body of scientific knowledge was built up, course content took on greater depth and strength.

In the early days the colleges were almost entirely for white students. In 1890 Mr. Morrill, by then a senator, introduced a bill to expand the Land Grant College Act to provide funds for colleges serving black students. This act was passed and resulted in schools for minority students in much of the South, schools now desegregated but still predominantly black.

Despite slow beginnings, the land grant colleges gradually caught on. Most of them, having begun teaching only agriculture and the mechanical arts, branched out into broader areas, becoming colleges within universities.

Almost all the agricultural colleges added graduate schools. Several of the original attributes, however, were in large measure kept: their predominantly tax-supported status and their preference for what is relevant over what is merely reputable.

By the time these land grant colleges (more accurately, state universities) reached the hundredth anniversary of the Morrill Act, they enrolled one-fifth of all the undergraduate students in the nation. Of the thirty-six then-living Nobel Prize winners in the United States, eighteen had earned land grant college degrees.

This profound development was the brain-child of a Vermonter who had been poor and denied education but realized its value. Rather than curse the darkness, Justin Morrill lit a candle.

We had the land grant colleges and instruction in agriculture. But the body of knowledge had not yet been built up and the educational offering was thin. Farm practice was still largely traditional; folklore was dominant. Conflicting claims and untested theorizing were emerging from the few centers of learning that addressed agricultural subjects. The case for experimental work to test new and old theories under field conditions is clear to those who view the situation in retrospect. It was also clear, at that time, to a limited number of farsighted people, chief of whom was a frail young man from New York State named Samuel W. Johnson, mentioned earlier in the chapter on Liebig. Samuel Johnson gets into this chapter by his work in establishing the first agricultural experiment station in the United States, an event which occurred in the State of Connecticut on July 2, 1875.

The case for tax-supported experiment stations is that new knowledge increases the efficiency of agricultural production, increased efficiency reduces cost, and the benefits of reduced production cost are shared by farmers in the form of larger net returns and by consumers in lower food costs. Most farms are not large enough to carry on their own research; tax-supported research is therefore needed if the desired efficiency gains are to be achieved. Experiment stations are in the public interest; it is therefore appropriate that they be tax supported.

Samuel Johnson was a scientist when agricultural science was still struggling to be born. He was the archetype of agricultural researchers – persistent in purpose, scrupulous in method, faithful to scientific findings, and impatient with claims based on personal authority. He was quiet, retiring, and thoughtful rather than effusive, but once he had fixed his purpose he had great tenacity.

Johnson was born July 3, 1830, at Kingsboro, Fulton County, New York, where his father was a prosperous merchant. A few years later the family moved to a large fertile farm north of Watertown, New York. Early in his career Johnson came through his reading under the influence of Liebig, who was then at the height of his fame. In May 1853 Johnson set off for Germany, where he acquired a good education in chemistry. At Möckern, in 1851, the world's first publicly supported agricultural experiment station had been founded, a farm of 120 acres. In 1854 Johnson visited this experiment station and was impressed. He became enthusiastic about the German experiment stations and was eager to bring them to America.

Johnson, the agricultural chemist, adopted early in his career a project of such potency that it took on a life of its own, carrying him with it, preempting time he would rather have devoted to other things. The circumstance was this: in the early days of enthusiasm for agricultural chemistry, various people had set themselves up as soil analysts. For five dollars they would tell a farmer precisely what kind of fertilizer he needed. Then other people (or sometimes the same person) would sell the farmer exactly the fertility supplement the soil reportedly required – lime, gypsum, marl, muck, phosphoric acid, bone dust, potash, charcoal, guano, or ammonia. The opportunity for fraud was obvious and was avidly exploited. The result, of course, was to discredit agricultural chemistry and with it all manifestations of agricultural science.

Johnson took on the cause of uncovering these frauds. The demand for this kind of service grew geometrically. The general perception arose that the sole or at least the major function of agricultural chemistry was to deal with soil analysis and fertilizer frauds. Johnson was almost overwhelmed.

But he saw a way of turning this event to his own purpose – the establishment of an experiment station. He believed that fertilizer analysis to expose the frauds inflicted on farmers was a service that could best be supplied by a publicly supported institution. This he saw as the opening wedge to get an experiment station started, to provide a beginning for his real purpose, which was research on important questions of agricultural science. Thus he recognized early an important principle of agricultural research administration – if you are doing work for a public institution, it is important to have a "pot boiler" with which to earn support for more important basic work.

Johnson, single minded as is many a scientist, pushed his experiment station idea with all vigor. He spoke, wrote, taught, cajoled, organized meetings, headed committees, and gathered converts. Finally, in 1875, after a twenty-year campaign, the legislators of the State of Connecticut took the necessary action. They set up an experiment station at Middletown and voted $2,800 a year for two years for its support. Two years later it was moved to New Haven. The station was set up on the German model. It was primarily tax supported but private contributions were also accepted. The legislature, confronted with ideological alternatives, a privately or publicly supported institution, provided a pragmatic answer, which is the genius of the American political system.

Other states soon followed the Connecticut lead, being kindred in form and purpose, making later collaboration relatively easy. By 1887, before federal financial help was given, twenty-eight states were doing experimental work in agriculture. Federal action of 1887, which integrated the system of experiment stations, was more an act of funding than of founding. The Hatch Act provided $15,000 in federal funds to every experiment station. Funding for the system began at $585,000 in 1888, the first year, and grew fairly rapidly thereafter. The federal legislation was named after Congressman William Henry Hatch, Democrat from Missouri, chairman of the House Committee on Agriculture. Participating in the campaign for the Hatch Act were all three agricultural men who are highlighted in this chapter. Besides Johnson there were Justin Morrill and Seaman Knapp, who would become the leading light for the extension service. Thus the founders of the triad that sprang from the agrarian reform showed early affinity and cooperation.

The states responded rapidly to the Hatch Act. During the year following its passage the legislatures of all thirty-eight states gave assent to its provisions.

There were problems. The number of available scientists trained in agriculture was limited and it was hard to staff the stations. Farmers were not conditioned to accept findings that came from laboratories. General administration, correspondence, printing, and distribution of publications took up much of the funds, leaving little for original scientific investigations.

Before long, however, new knowledge, both basic and applied, began to flow from the new institutions. Among the more dramatic developments were hybrid corn, streptomycin, the Babcock test for butterfat, and the discovery of vitamins A and B. Less dramatic than these breakthroughs but in sum very effective were discoveries regarding plant, animal, and human nutrition, tillage practices, improved crop varieties, better livestock sanitation, pest control, advances in agricultural engineering, and improved marketing. Responding to need, the institutions grew, slowly at first, then more rapidly. As intended, these scientific advances soon found their way into the teaching programs. The utility of joint appointments for research and teaching was quickly demonstrated.

The experiment stations, as an institutional invention, must rank in the forefront among the ways of organizing agricultural science for human improvement. Samuel Johnson's cause was a rare and fortunate commitment that has led to a better-fed world.

By the turn of the century we had agricultural education at the college level and tax-supported agricultural research. But only a few of the operating farmers had attended the land grant colleges. And new knowledge generated by the experiment stations was slow getting into use. Forty years after the land grant colleges had been established per acre yields showed little increase and agricultural efficiency was almost stagnant. Needed was some potent way of extending new agricultural knowledge to the rank and file of farmers. The human dynamo who would energize the system was Seaman Knapp, whose life spanned the years from 1833 to 1911. He was born at Schroon, in Essex County, New York. (How many of these pioneers for agricultural betterment came from the Northeast!)

Seaman Knapp was a solid middle-class fellow. For generations his family had been farmers, blacksmiths, country doctors, and craftsmen. Seaman was the first Knapp in eight generations to have higher education; he studied the only curriculum available to him – classical Latin and Greek – at Union College in Schenectady, New York, and was a member of Phi Beta Kappa.

Knapp had multiple careers: farmer, businessman, banker, preacher, land speculator, editor, author, salesman, superintendent of a state school for the deaf, professor, and briefly president of Iowa Agricultural College. Farming did not assume major importance in his life until he was thirty-three years old, when he was forced into it by an injury that required a life in the open. He went to Iowa and started to raise Merino sheep, about which he knew nothing. All his sheep died, perhaps a crucial event in American agriculture, because it drove home for Knapp the idea that practical affairs are governed by principles that must be discovered, taught, and used, and that there are penalties for violating these principles. This became the guiding tenet of his life.

Having failed at sheep he turned his attention to hogs and in ten years' time became one of the most successful swine producers in the state. He used his own farm for demonstrations; he had become convinced that seeing an improved farm practice was more effective than reading or hearing about it.

Suddenly Knapp pulled up stakes and went to the Cajun country of Louisiana, where a vast tract of undeveloped land had been acquired by speculators who wanted to divide it and sell it to farmers. Local farmers greeted the enterprise with laughter. Knapp's job, as manager for the investors, was to turn this situation around. Within twelve years he had done so. He saw the potential of this new area and did not overlook the opportunity to acquire some of the choice land for himself. Once a suitable farming system had been worked out Knapp set up demonstration farms, judiciously placed throughout the area.

In 1902 when Knapp was in his seventieth year, his old friend James Wilson, who had become secretary of agriculture, gave him responsibility for "improvement of agriculture throughout the South." As it turned out, this became an assignment for coping with the boll weevil, the destroyer of cotton that had crossed the border from Mexico in 1892 and was causing widespread havoc in Texas. The Bureau of Entomology of the U.S. Department of Agriculture had developed a way of combating the boll weevil involving changed cultural practices such as early planting, use of early-maturing seed, and different tillage methods. This was at best only partly successful, but it was all that could then be done.

Superintending a force of twenty-four special agents with funds provided by the U.S. Department of Agriculture, Knapp organized one thousand meetings. Seven thousand farmers agreed to use their land as demonstration farms. Knapp delivered his famous dictum, which became the key concept of the extension service: "What a man hears he may doubt. What he sees he may possibly doubt. But what he does himself he cannot doubt." The campaign against the boll weevil was the most visible single endeavor of Knapp's life. It became a classic example of what can be accomplished by cooperative action when vigorous leadership addresses a felt need with a credible program.

Knapp's strategy for combining the efforts of government agents and farmers became known as "cooperative demonstration work." In 1906 the General Education Board, with a substantial contribution from John D. Rockefeller, gave a boost to this work. In that year there were altogether 157 agents in eleven states, all of them in the South, of whom about half were paid by the federal government and half by the General Education Board. The first county agent, W. C. Stallings, was appointed in Smith County, Texas, November 12, 1906. In 1909 agricultural extension work was given a strong boost by the report of the American Country Life Commission, appointed by President Theodore Roosevelt and chaired by Liberty Hyde Bailey of New York State.

With growing support, the number of agents increased rapidly. The work expanded in scope as well as magnitude. Boys' Clubs began in 1907 and Girls' Clubs started in 1910. Club work became a potent vehicle for change. Many a father, dubious about some new method, would consent to its use in his son's club project. If successful (and many were), the new idea would be accepted. Thus began the famous 4-H Clubs. Home demonstration work for women, a natural associate of the girls' 4-H Clubs, was well under way by 1914.

Cooperative demonstration work, undertaken with such gusto for boll weevil control, was quickly adapted to other farm problems. By 1914, on the eve of passage of the Smith-Lever Act, there were 1,138 men and women agents in the Southern states, most of them graduates of the land grant colleges.

It was inevitable that this scattered work would become structured and funded in an organized way. This was recommended in 1908 by Kenyon L. Butterfield of the Rhode Island State College, president of the Association of American Agricultural Colleges and Experiment Stations. There was some skepticism, in the country and in the Congress, about nonfarmers telling farmers how to run their business at the expense of the federal government. "Book farming" was a term of derision until recent times. There was much argument about the division of responsibility between the local communities, the states, and the federal government. And there was apprehension about how the then privately financed agricultural advisors at the county level would fit into the new system. Knapp was not a party to these discussions; he had died in 1911. But his name was invoked, his experience was cited, and his indelible stamp was placed on the final product.

Democratic congressman Asbury F. Lever of South Carolina, chairman of the House Committee on Agriculture, and Senator Hoke Smith of Georgia, member of both the committees on agriculture and education, also a Democrat, gave their names to the bill which set up the Federal Extension Service. The Smith-Lever bill passed both houses and was signed by President Wilson on May 8, 1914. It provided for cooperation between the federal government and the states in both funding and supervision. It assured that each state would receive $10,000 of federal funds annually and additional amounts based on rural population, this from a fund that began at $600,000, increasing annually by $500,000 for seven years. The states were obligated to match the federal appropriations. In most cases this requirement was overscribed.

The triad was now complete: first came classroom teaching, then discovery of new knowledge, and finally dissemination of that knowledge directly to the farm people. Logic would suggest that the discovery of knowledge should precede the other two, but institutional evolution does not necessarily adhere to the Darwinian model.

Seaman Knapp had helped craft each of the three legs of this stool. He had been president of a land grant college, he had helped promote the experiment stations, and he had designed the format for the extension service. It is a pity that he did not live to see them brought together.

The triad grew and prospered. By 1962, one hundred years after the Land Grant College Act was signed, the combined effort in research, teaching, and extension was employing 28,000 agricultural scientists and teachers in a program costing nearly half a billion dollars.

It took time before the three parts of the land grant college system caught on, but when they did they developed a synergistic action that astounded even their strongest advocates. It was during World War II, three decades after adding the last limb of the triad, that production really took off. Witness the profound changes that have come about with the modernization of American agriculture, flowing in large part from the institutional initiatives described in this chapter:

1. The volume of agricultural production has increased. The United States now feeds three times as many people as at the turn of the century on essentially the same acreage, and feeds them better. In addition it exports one-fourth of its agricultural output.

2. With mechanization, the drudgery of farm work has been dramatically reduced.

3. The efficiency of agricultural production increases; output per unit of input now stands at two and a half times its 1930 level. This rising efficiency has resulted in a relative reduction in the price of food to the consumer, who buys groceries with a lower percentage of income than ever before or in any other country.

4. Food quality is improved, so dietary diseases, formerly widespread, have almost disappeared.

5. Per capita farm income has risen both absolutely and relatively, so the income disadvantage of farm people has been greatly reduced.

6. The educational disadvantage of farm people has been reduced.

7. The amenities of rural living – electricity, transport, schools, telephones, health service – have all improved and in many cases are now on a par with those in the cities.

Agriculture is losing its uniqueness. Formerly farm people were readily distinguishable from nonfarmers by speech, dress, and manner. This is no longer true. With modern agriculture it is becoming difficult to tell who is and who is not a farmer. Farmers are entering the mainstream of economic, social and political life.

The land grant college system itself is changing. Originally the colleges of agriculture enrolled white young men of farm background and taught them production agriculture with the expectation that they would be farmers. Now it recruits white and nonwhite young men and women from farm and nonfarm families, teaching them a wide variety of farm-related subjects, preparing them for farm and nonfarm careers. Years ago the experiment stations were almost the sole generators of new agricultural knowledge. Presently that role is deeper in substance and shared with agribusiness firms, a wide variety of nonfarm agencies, the international research network, and the biology departments of other colleges. The extension service was for a time the main conduit between the laboratory and the farm; now the clientele is broadened and farmers get new information from those who supply them with feed, fertilizer, chemicals, and machinery. The land grant college system is such an effective agent for change that it is transforming itself.

Is the American model useful to a country in the developing world, now at a stage comparable with that of the United States in 1860? The answer is, It depends. Ohio State University, working in cooperation with the Agency for International Development, successfully used a modification of the American model in helping India with wheat production. Cornell University similarly assisted the Philippines, and Purdue helped establish the teaching-research-extension triad in Minas Gerais, Brazil. But in Iran, development efforts based in part on the American model moved in a direction and at a speed unacceptable to the power elite and the effort failed.

The system cannot be *adopted* by other countries; it can be *adapted*. Different agricultural endowment, population densities, educational systems, religious heritage, social structures, and political climates all require modification of the American approach.

To be successful with the American model the developing country must have an economic system sufficiently open so that farmers can make their own decisions and so that aspirations of the common man will not be choked off. There must be patience. It was not until many years after initiation of the American system that strong agricultural development really began.

For how much of the world were Morrill, Johnson, and Knapp developing their agrarian reform? The United States only? Other countries as well? We look more deeply into this question in the next chapter.

REFERENCES

Berghorn, C. William. 1962. *After 100 Years*. A Report of the State of Vermont Morrill Land Grant Centennial Committee, Strafford, Vermont.

Cochrane, Willard W. 1979. *The Development of Agriculture: A Historical Analysis*. St. Paul: Univ. of Minnesota Press.

Marcus, Alan I. 1985. *Agricultural Science and the Quest for Legitimacy: Farmers, Agricultural Colleges and Experiment Stations, 1870–1890*. Ames: Iowa State Univ. Press (the Henry A. Wallace series on Agricultural History and Rural Studies).

Mawby, Russell G. 1983. *Seaman A. Knapp Memorial Lecture*. National Association of State Universities and Land Grant Colleges, Washington.

Rossiter, Margaret W. 1975. *The Emergence of Agricultural Science, Justus Liebig and the Americans, 1840–1880*. New Haven: Yale Univ. Press.

Sandburg, Carl. 1954. *Abraham Lincoln, the Prairie Years and the War Years*. New York: Harcourt Brace.

Schertz, Lyle P. 1979. *Another Revolution in U.S. Farming?* Washington, D.C.: USDA.

Scott, Roy Vernon. 1970. *The Reluctant Farmer: The Rise of Agricultural Extension to 1914*. Urbana: Univ. of Illinois Press.

True, A. C. 1912. *The United States Department of Agriculture, 1862–1912*. Washington, D.C.: USDA.

_____. 1928. *A History of Agricultural Extension Work in the United States, 1785–1923*. Washington, D.C.: USDA Misc. Pub. 15.

_____. 1929. *A History of Agricultural Education in the United States, 1785–1925*. Washington, D.C.: USDA Misc. Pub. 36.

_____. 1937. *A History of Agricultural Experimentation and Research in the United States, 1607–1925*. Washington, D.C.: USDA Misc. Pub. 251.

USDA. 1962a. *Century of Service, the First 100 Years of the United States Department of Agriculture*. Washington, D.C.

_____. 1962b. *After a Hundred Years*. USDA Yearbook. Washington, D.C.

CHAPTER 10

T. W. Schultz
and the Economizers

ECONOMISTS ARE SCIENTISTS OF A SORT, dealing with human beings rather than with molecules. They are intent on the efficient use of available means in achieving some given end. They wish to economize the use of scarce resources; hence the name of their discipline.

In the case before us, the objective is agricultural development, to provide food for people and a better livelihood for the farmers who produce it. The resources are land, labor, and capital. How can these resources best be combined to move toward a well-fed world? Agricultural development is not alone for the physical and biological sciences; it is also an economic problem. In medical equivalence, the agronomist, the engineer, the geneticist, and the chemist are specialists; the agricultural economist is a general practitioner.

In 1979 the Nobel Prize for Economics was given to a tall, lean emeritus professor of economics from the University of Chicago, Dr. T. W. Schultz, whose major professional effort had been focused on agricultural development in the countries of the Third World. What are Professor Schultz's ideas about agricultural development? How can the agriculture of the less developed countries be made more productive and rewarding?

Some say the principles of economics are culture bound, limited in their relevance to the industrial countries where these principles were first enunciated and so not useful to the countries of the Third World. Schultz says, "No, the principles are general," a position of major importance underlying the whole approach to agricultural development. The following paragraphs summarize many of his views.

On Traditional Agriculture. "There are comparatively few significant inefficiencies in the allocation of the factors of production in traditional agriculture." The rival view is that traditional agriculture is inefficient, largely because of ignorance, and that changing the existing combination of land, labor, and capital could result in large production increases.

On Technological Change. "In order to break this dependency (on a long established mix of land, labor and capital) farmers situated in traditional agriculture must somehow acquire, adopt, and learn to use effectively a profitable set of new factors." The opposed idea is that agricultural development need not await research and the discovery of new knowledge but can make substantial advance within the given resource endowment.

On Human Investment. "In general, estimates of the rate of return to schooling are much higher for elementary than for secondary schooling or higher education, although the rate for the latter two also exceeds the rate to conventional investments." Education as an investment is a relatively new concept, of which Schultz is a major exponent. The old idea was that education was in large part a consumption good and that measuring the rate of return therefrom was a crass thing.

On Research. "In India this investment in agricultural research has produced excellent results. An analysis by states within India shows that rate of return has been approximately 40 percent, which is indeed high compared with returns from most other investments to increase agricultural production." In attempting to measure the productivity of research, as well as in his effort to compute the return to education, Schultz is a pioneer.

On Politically Inspired Economic Development Models. "From the point of view of those who manage the political market, the lowly cultivator is viewed as indifferent to economic incentives because it is presumed that he is strongly committed to his traditional low level of productivity. Thus the stage is set for the doctrine that industrialization is the mainspring of economic growth, and economic policy is designed to give top priority to industry, and this includes keeping food grains cheap." This is a criticism of the Soviet Union's model of economic development, which has been emulated by a number of Third World countries, mostly with disappointing results.

On Poverty. "The community is poor because the factors on which the economy is dependent are not capable of producing more under existing circumstances." Schultz challenges the view that attributes poverty to laziness, ignorance, or exploitation.

On Food Aid. "The United States is providing Egypt with massive amounts of aid. . . . With agricultural products at concessional prices from abroad, Egypt maintains her cheap food for consumers and very low prices for farmers. What is sad is the raw deal the poor Egyptian farmers are dealt." But Schultz sees the usefulness of food aid in circumstances that are temporary and urgent: "When a sudden destruction of resources occurs, whether it is caused by the vicissitudes of nature or by war, foreign aid is, as it should be, a humanitarian response." Thus Schultz is somewhere between those who look on all food aid as unwise and those who would be open-handed under almost any circumstance.

On Development Assistance. "The international donor community has become a comfortable club that abides by a live-and-let-live policy. Critical statements about the performance of any member of this club are deemed to be in poor taste with one exception, namely, that the United States is allocating too small a share of her gross national product to foreign aid." Schultz has a lover's quarrel with the international donors. He loves them when they finance research and education and quarrels with them when they fund monumental and unpromising capital projects. He is at odds both with those who love foreign aid without quarreling over it and those who quarrel about it with no love in their hearts.

On Motivation. "Farmers the world over, in dealing with costs, returns, and risks, are calculating economic agents." Sociologists and anthropologists, who are fellow social scientists, generally dispute this view.

On the Market Economy. "No government which has abolished markets has been successful in modernizing agriculture." This is the issue which divides the world. Schultz comes down clearly on the side of competitive markets.

Schultz sounds like an exponent of the American development model described in the previous chapter, which he is. What evidence does he marshall in support of his views? With what authority does he speak? We examine the career and contributions of this extraordinary man.

Theodore William Schultz was born near Arlington, a small town in eastern South Dakota, on April 30, 1902. This rural background gave him an understanding of agriculture and a liking for farm people that would stay with him throughout his life. He obtained his undergraduate degree from South Dakota State College at Brookings in 1927. He received his Ph.D. degree from the University of Wisconsin in 1930. He sees his Wisconsin venture thus: "Reared in the protest culture of the Dakotas which was then nurtured by the Non-Partisan League and LaFollette, I sought intellectual comfort at the University of Wisconsin." One sees in Schultz's professional life the influence of such dissidents as Bob LaFollette and John R. Commons.

After obtaining his degree, Schultz went to Iowa State College, becoming head of the Department of Economics and Sociology. After thirteen years in Iowa Schultz became the focal point of an issue that changed his career. Up to that time the politically powerful leaders of agriculture had looked on land grant colleges such as Iowa more or less as their captive advocates. In 1943 one of Schultz's colleagues, working on food strategy in wartime, published a pamphlet asserting (correctly) that in nutritional value margarine "compared favorably with butter." The powerful dairy interests rose in protest. As department head, Schultz backed the author of the pamphlet. The ensuing political-academic fracas led to the scattering of the lively young Iowa faculty. Schultz resigned, thereby enhancing his reputation for scholarship and integrity. He moved to a much better position at the University of Chicago, which has been his academic home since leaving Ames. The encounter with the Iowa political powers no doubt contributed to Schultz's preference of the academic over the political world.

At the University of Chicago Schultz and his graduate students plunged immediately into farm policy issues, particularly the prospective postwar status of the big commodity programs to control the production and support the prices of wheat, corn, and cotton. He launched research of his own, he participated in round table discussions, and he read everything in sight. In 1945 he produced a landmark book, *Agriculture in an Unstable Economy,* the first of a long list of prestigious writings. The central thesis of the book is found in the preface: "the basic causes for the farm problem—the low earnings of most farm people and the great instability of income from farming—are not *within* agriculture but elsewhere in the economy."

Though correct, this appraisal was received with misgiving by the agricultural establishment and indeed by many agricultural economists who were then convinced that the well-being of American agriculture was directly dependent upon the government's price support and production control programs. Schultz testified before the agricultural committees of the Congress and was given a rough time. He concluded, correctly as it turned out, that the time was not then ripe for economic rationality regarding these farm programs. He turned his interest to other subjects: economic development in the Third World, welfare in rural areas, the economic value of education, investment in human capital, and the economics of the family.

In 1964 he produced his most noteworthy book, *Transforming Traditional Agriculture,* decisive in his winning of the Nobel Prize. This small book, 212 pages, is Schultz at his best as keen observer, logician, and polemicist.

Schultz's model for agricultural development. The assessment of traditional agriculture as presented in the book is that farmers in a long-established setting are wise in the use of their resources, having over many generations come to make the best use of the land, labor, and capital available to them. An advance can be made only by improving their resources and adding to their knowledge. Paths to improvement, therefore, are to produce new knowledge through agricultural research, to improve the level of understanding by education, to permit markets to function, and to limit the role of government in the development process. Given the opportunity to make decisions, farmers will use their new opportunities wisely. They will produce more food if the price rises and less if it falls, in accordance with economic principles.

Schultz's case has its preconditions. Education is useful only if a changed pattern of resources is available. Agricultural extension will fail unless there is something worthwhile to extend. Schultz's prescription for agricultural betterment can be aborted by politically influential landowners; the inference is that political and institutional change may be needful before agricultural advance can occur.

There is little in all this that will surprise an American farmer. But to people who deny the received economic principles, or to those who dislike the American system, or to impatient politicians who want quick results, or to activists who have strong faith in the power of government, Schultz's thesis was displeasing.

Rival theories are briefly outlined.

The Industrialization Model. A plan for economic development, based largely on the experience of the Soviet Union, is to hold down prices of farm products by government action, thereby extracting forced savings from farmers. These savings are used to build up the capital plant which in time will produce additional goods, to the advantage of farmers and nonfarmers alike. Holding prices down at the farm level will not inhibit agricultural production, according to the advocates of industrialization, because at low prices the farmers will be forced to produce additional amounts of food in order to maintain their incomes. Farm labor is assumed to be redundant in this assessment; it can be transferred to industry without loss to agricultural output. This prescription calls for strong government action.

The plan helped the Soviet Union to industrialize but at substantial cost in reduced food production and loss of human life. India emulated the Russian pattern in its early development strategy but met with adverse results and revised its policy.

Schultz rejects the industrialization strategy because it jeopardizes the food supply, is inequitable to farmers, aggrandizes government, and demeans the individual. He challenges the idea that farm labor is redundant and that reducing the price to farmers will induce them to increase output.

Balanced Growth. A compromise strategy is to advance agriculture and industry in synchronized fashion. This can be done with relatively free institutions, as in Taiwan, or it can be done by strong central direction, as in the People's Republic of China, where the plan is to "walk on two legs," with agriculture and industry advancing together.

The balanced growth strategy, if in a setting of relatively free institutions, gives Schultz no problems.

These are the three basic strategies. Within them are numerous variations: "big push" versus "incremental growth," and "capital intensive" versus "small is beautiful" versus "intermediate technology." The ultimate equivocation is "appropriate technology"; who can quarrel with what is appropriate? There are arguments as to whether the focus should be on "the poorest of the poor," a welfare concept, or on "change agents," who are inclined to be the larger and better-off farmers. Some wish to satisfy "basic needs"; others are willing to have the market system identify the beneficiaries. Wherever strategies are discussed, economists will debate these alternatives.

Some well-meaning people ignore these models and the assumptions that undergird them. They want to go ahead with agricultural development without assumptions regarding any particular strategy—"Just get busy and start doing good." But this is itself an assumption: that the development process is without any authentic principles, a highly implausible premise.

Farmer preference seems to be for Schultz's enterprise-oriented model. Change from it has generally been resisted and advocacy for it has usually been welcomed. Whether this preference arises from its efficiency or its individual freedom is not clear; it seems to possess both attributes.

There is the danger that those who work at agricultural development may, in their zeal, undertake to manipulate people and design their lives for them. Anthropologists are particularly worried about this. They see that agricultural development will transform existing cultures. Unwilling to set up criteria for judging, they generally consider one culture to be as good as another and so are wary of the development process. But there can hardly be grave misgivings about helping people achieve the goals to which they themselves aspire. And surely an adequate food supply is a universal and valid aspiration.

T. W. Schultz lifted the whole level of debate on agricultural development to a higher plane, better grounded in fact and theory. He helped bring the results of education and research into the realm of measured phenomena. He treated the farm household as an enterprise; previously economists had focused exclusively on crop and livestock enterprises. He helped improve the role of farm women. He placed his compassion, his intellect, and his reputation in support of studies of poverty. He took a courageous albeit lonely position on matters of domestic farm policy. He taught classes, wrote books, and supervised graduate students, thereby extending his influence into a new generation.

Honors came. Especially valued was the Frances A. Walker Award, conferred in 1972 by the American Economic Association "to the economist who has in the course of his life made a contribution of the highest distinction in economics." There were honorary doctorates. And there is the Nobel Prize.

The life and career of T. W. Schultz show that one can sometimes find green pastures when one leaves the herd. Leaving the herd is a hazardous thing; the wolves may pick you off. But that danger does not seem to deter Professor Schultz.

REFERENCES

Bowman, Mary Jean. 1980. "On Theodore W. Schultz's Contributions to Economics." *Scandinavian Journal of Economics* 82. Reprint.

Day, Richard H., ed. 1982. *Economic Analysis and Public Policy*. Ames: Iowa State Univ. Press.

Haney, L. H. 1949. *History of Economic Thought*. New York: Macmillan.

Marshall, Alfred. 1948. *Principles of Economics*. 8th ed. New York: Macmillan.

Martin, Lee R., ed. 1977. *A Survey of Agricultural Economics Literature*. Vol. 1, *Traditional Fields of Agricultural Economics, 1940s to 1970s*. St. Paul: Univ. of Minnesota Press, for the American Agricultural Economics Association.

Schultz, T. W. 1945. *Agriculture in an Unstable Economy*. New York: McGraw-Hill.

———. 1963. *The Economic Value of Education*. New York: Columbia Univ. Press.

———. 1964. *Transforming Traditional Agriculture*. New Haven: Yale Univ. Press. Paperback edition, Univ. of Chicago Press, 1983.

———. 1971. *Investment in Human Capital: The Role of Education and of Research*. New York: Free Press, Macmillan.

———. 1972. *Human Resources: Fiftieth Anniversary Colloquium 6*. New York: National Bureau of Economic Research.

———. 1975. *Economics of the Family: Marriage, Children, and Human Capital*. Chicago: Univ. of Chicago Press, for the National Bureau of Economic Research.

———. Dec. 1979. "The Economics of Being Poor." Nobel Memorial Lecture, Univ. of Chicago.

———. 1981. *Investing in People: The Economics of Population Quality*. Berkeley: Univ. of California Press.

———, ed. 1972. *Investment in Education: The Equity-Efficiency Quandary*. Chicago: Univ. of Chicago Press.

———, ed. 1978. *Distortions of Agricultural Incentives*. Bloomington: Indiana Univ. Press.

CHAPTER 11

Scurvy and the Hidden Hunger

STARVE TO DEATH with a full stomach? Famine in the midst of plenty? It seems incredible but it can happen and does today in some parts of the world. The focus of this chapter is nutritional deficiency, the hidden hunger that kills people or incapacitates them. Total food intake may be sufficient but there can be critical lack of some particular nutrient or nutrients.

Of all the diseases related to nutritional deficiency, scurvy is perhaps the most repulsive, the most debilitating, the easiest to cure, and the nearest to eradication. The present chapter will review the conquest of this horrible disease. The villain is the Admiralty of the British navy; the hero is Dr. James Lind, a Scottish physician.

Scurvy is caused by a deficiency of Vitamin C, the antiscorbutic vitamin found in many fruits and vegetables, especially citrus. When the body is denied this vital nutrient a weakness develops in the walls of the capillary vessels and the cells, which rupture, causing the escape of blood and other body fluids. Internal hemorrhaging is the striking manifestation of this disease. The parts of the body most affected are the gums and the legs. In severe cases the escaped blood and other body liquids cannot be handled by the overloaded urinary system. The accumulated fluids putrify, the legs swell, the body discolors, ulcers develop, the breath becomes offensive, the gums take on a sponginess, the teeth fall out, the victim becomes listless, the tendons contract, control of the body is lost, and the bones lose their strength. Vomiting, retching, irregular fevers, and fainting fits are characteristic of the disease. Unless the diet is remedied death occurs. Mercifully, few people of our generation are victimized by this disease.

79

In time past the disease struck mostly at sea, and it was not until the long sea voyages beginning in the fifteenth century that the problem became critical. Rations on British ships were fairly standard: 1 pound of biscuit daily, 2 pounds of salt beef twice weekly, 1 pound of salt pork twice weekly, 2 ounces of dried fish thrice weekly, 2 ounces of butter thrice weekly, 4 ounces of cheese thrice weekly, 8 ounces of dry peas every four days, 1 gallon of beer daily.

The total caloric value of this ration was adequate, as it supplied about four thousand calories daily. However, it was extremely deficient in vitamins, particularly in Vitamin C. Vitamin C is stored in the body, and the symptoms of scurvy do not appear until some time after the dietary deficiency has begun. The dental surgeon F. C. Cady says this may be as long as four to six months, while Louis H. Roddis, the American naval surgeon, says it may be two to eight weeks. In the early days British ships were engaged in short voyages—the coastal trade, shipping to the Continent, or naval warfare with the European powers. There was frequent shore leave during which the crews would unknowingly regenerate the bodily supply of this critical nutrient. Scurvy was not then a great problem. But with the great voyages of discovery, with the India trade, with the long predatory naval campaigns against the Spanish, and with the slave ships, British vessels would sometimes be at sea for long periods, with infrequent visits to port. Scurvy then struck with full force.

Scurvy seemed the special curse of the British. The other sea powers of the day—the Dutch, the Spanish, the Portuguese—had far less trouble. In retrospect it is not difficult to see why this was so. The Dutch provisioned their ships with sauerkraut, a good source of Vitamin C. The Spanish and the Portuguese came from a land where citrus fruit flourished; this was a part of the sea ration and served to ward off scurvy. Both sauerkraut and citrus were deemed inappropriate foods for British seamen, the sauerkraut because it was despised as the lowly food of a rival nation, and the citrus because it was grown in an enemy country and was expensive. To the British, meat and biscuits were proper fare for sailing men. They had served well throughout the centuries, and when the scurvy struck the inclination was to look for the cause elsewhere than in the ration.

Historically scurvy has been a problem where one or another or all of three conditions prevailed. It occurred when unwholesome diets were prescribed by people in authority, as was the case for armies, navies, prisons, and slave ships. It was found where foods bearing Vitamin C simply were not available, as in high latitudes, north and south, where winters were long and fruits and vegetables did not grow. It also existed where poverty was so great that the needed foods could not be purchased.

The evidence is that if the needed foods are available and if there is the money to buy them, the people will do a fairly good job of balancing their own rations and scurvy does not develop. In large measure the scurvy story is the tale of blind men in authority governed by tradition or by misguided motives of thrift who thought they knew more about what was good for their men than did the men themselves.

Many reports of British experience with scurvy on long sea voyages are available. Two will suffice. One originally told by a chronicler named Samuel Purchas concerns a Sir James Lancaster who left from Tor Bay, England, on April 18, 1601, bound for India. He commanded four ships: the *Dragon* with 202 men; the *Hector* with 108; the *Ascention* with 82; and the *Susan* with 88. There also was a victualler, the *Guest.* By the time this expedition approached the Cape of Good Hope, scurvy had set in: "very many of our men were fallen sicke of the Scurvey in all our ships, and unlesse it were in the Generals ship only, the other three were so weake of men, that they could hardly handle the sayles."

The chronicler comments thus regarding the crew of the *Dragon,* the ship of the commander, Sir James, referred to as the General:

And the reason why the Generals men stood better in health than the men of other ships was this: he brought to Sea with him certaine Bottles of the Juice of Limons, which hee gave to each one, as long as it would last, three spoonfuls every morning fasting. . . . By this means the Generall cured many of his men, and preserved the rest; so that his ship (having the double of men that was in the rest of the ships) he had not so many sicke, nor lost so many men as they did, which was the mercie of God to us all.

Before arriving at the Cape, the expedition lost 110 men, mostly from the 278 who had started on the three smaller ships.

The best experience was that of the great explorer Captain James Cook, who made three long voyages. The first, begun in 1768 and completed in 1771, took him to the South Pacific, New Zealand, and Batavia. The second, from 1772 to 1775, was an exploration of the Antarctic region. The third and last departed England in 1776, ranging from the South Pacific to the Bering Sea. Though Cook was killed in Hawaii, the expedition returned safely to England in 1780.

Cook was particular about the food for his crew. He never touched land without procuring fruit, vegetables, fresh meat, eggs, fowl, and similar foods. He fed sauerkraut to his men, and after overcoming their early aversion to this despised Dutch food his sailors ate it so greedily that it had to be rationed. The variety of foods provided by Cook made it difficult to determine which one or ones prevented scurvy. In any case, Cook's experience was unique. During the first voyage he lost 34 men from a crew of 94, but the deaths were from dysentery, not scurvy. On his second voyage he embarked with 193 men and lost none. On the third trip there were only two deaths, one from tuberculosis and the other being Cook himself, from a skirmish with the natives of Hawaii.

It is impossible to say how many British lives were lost from scurvy during the three hundred years between 1500, when the long ocean voyages began, and 1800, when adequate preventive measures against the disease were in general use. Roddis says it is certain that during this period scurvy killed as many seamen as the combined losses resulting from naval battles, shipwreck, other nautical hazards, and all other diseases affecting sailors. Four or five thousand deaths a year from scurvy for the British navy and one-fourth as many for the merchant marine is Roddis's estimate. This totals in excess of a million deaths for the three hundred–year period.

What was the cause of this dread disease? This was hard to answer. How, in an unscientific age, relate an event to a cause that had preceded it by weeks or months? How establish credibility for an explanation that ran counter to entrenched ideas?

The fallacious explanations were so many that they obscured the correct answer. Here is a partial list:

The Sea. People were healthy on land and sick at sea. There must be a mysterious something about the sea itself that caused scurvy.

Bad Climate, particularly the cold and damp encountered at sea.

Unwholesome Atmosphere. This was a favorite early explanation for many illnesses, including scurvy.

Contagion. It was alleged that whatever the original cause, the disease spread on contact.

Fornication. The disease was confused with syphilis. The symptoms had some similarity.

Unwholesome Water. On long sea voyages the water often became stale, and this seemed a logical cause.

Unwholesome Food. Meat, though salted, would sometimes become putrid, a credible cause for ailment.

Salt. Salty meat and the sometimes salty water ingested by seamen was put forth as an explanation. Strangely, salt was also put forward as a cure.

Divine Punishment. The inscrutable purposes of the Almighty were seen in the ravages of this dread disease.

Interspersed with these misleading appraisals and obscured by them were correct explanations pointing to dietary deficiencies. Pliny had listed this cause, among others, in the first century of the Christian era. Solomon Albert in 1593 pointed to dietary deficiency as the cause and mentioned orange juice as a cure. Eugalinus in 1604 pointed to diet as the cause of the problem and recommended, as antiscorbutic medicine, scurvy grass and brook lime, both unknown to our generation. Felix Plater in 1608 recommended oranges. In 1617 John Woodall, an Elizabethan surgeon, proposed the use of lemon juice as a cure for scurvy. In 1674 de la Böe, professor of medicine at Leyden, said oranges would cure scurvy. In 1696 Dr. William Cockburn pointed out the value of fresh fruits and vegetables. Up to the time of James Lind's work in 1753, more than eighty books and papers had been written on scurvy, and in many of them the use of acid fruits and their juices was recommended. The practical experience of Lancaster in 1601 and of Cook's three voyages from 1768 to 1780 should have been enough to drive the point home. But none of this appeared to have a decisive effect on the rations for seamen prescribed by the Admiralty. Evidence is excluded if it does not conform to the model.

The earliest efforts to overcome scurvy constitute a recitation of ridiculous bumblings. Various medicines were prescribed, among them ipecac, camphire, sage tea, camomile, whiskey, tobacco juice, myrrh, alumwater, and oak-bark decoction. Cinnamon and whey were used. Joshua Ward, a notorious quack who lived from 1685 to 1761, offered a violent diuretic composed of antimony, dragon's blood or balsam, and wine. Sweating was recommended. Laxatives were prescribed. Bloodletting was found not to be helpful, which was understandable as blood was already leaking into the body through the ruptured capillaries at an alarming rate. A unique curative effort arose from the perception that the severity of the disease was lessened when sailors reached land. Holes were dug and scurvy-stricken men were buried therein up to their chins and left for several hours in the hope that the mysterious healing power of the land would restore them to health.

The man who cut through this confusion was Dr. James Lind, a Scotsman. Lind was born in Edinburgh in 1716 of an upper-middle-class family. He was apprenticed to an Edinburgh physician, George Langlands, at age fifteen. He entered the Royal Navy in 1739 when twenty-three years old.

On May 25, 1747, Lind, then a surgeon on the seventy-four-gun-ship *Salisbury,* carried out an experiment with human subjects which demonstrated without question that citrus juice was the specific treatment for scurvy, that its use would cure that disease in near magical fashion, and that it had the power to prevent scurvy. He selected twelve patients, all with advanced cases of scurvy. He tried six different treatments, two patients for each. The respective daily prescriptions and the amounts for each man were as follows:

First two patients: a quart of cider
Second two patients: twenty-five drops of elixir vitriol
Third two patients: two spoonfuls of vinegar
Fourth two patients: seawater, unlimited amounts
Fifth two patients: two oranges and one lemon
Sixth two patients: an electary, "the bigness of a nutmeg," three
                        times a day, consisting of garlic, mustard seed,
                        horseradish, balsam of Peru, and gum myrrh

Lind's findings are best reported in his own words:

The consequence was, that the most sudden and visible good effects were perceived from the use of oranges and lemons; one of those who had taken them,
being at the end of six days fit for duty. The spots were not indeed at that time
quite off his body, nor his gums sound; but without any other medicine than a
gargle for his mouth he became quite healthy before we came into Plymouth
which was on the 16th of June. The other was the best recovered of any in his
condition; and being now pretty well, was appointed nurse to the rest of the sick.

In 1753 Lind published his *Treatise of the Scurvy,* a lengthy scholarly
document. Stewart and Guthrie, chroniclers of Lind's contribution, comment thus on Lind's treatise: "This work demonstrated beyond all doubt
that scurvy, a disease which both at sea and on land was costing thousands of lives every year, could readily be cured or—even more important—prevented."

Like many another great work, this epic received scant notice at the
time of its publication. Lind's proposal for adding citrus juice to the ration
long lay idle. In 1772, 19 years after publication of Lind's treatise, James
Cook, the prestigious captain who was given credit for the conquest of
scurvy because of the excellent health of his crew, recommended against
implementing Lind's proposal on the grounds of expense. A man of enormous influence, Cook's adverse counsel postponed the adoption of an
improved official ration for another twenty-three years.

Finally, in 1795 the Royal Navy reluctantly began to provide a regular
daily allowance of lemon juice. This was 194 years after Lancaster
showed the beneficial effect of citrus, 42 years after Lind's definitive
treatise, and 24 years after Cook's successful experience with a variety of
antiscorbutic foods.

When the order was fully in effect, success was dramatic. The number of scurvy patients in Haslar, the great naval hospital near Ports-
mouth, totaled 1,754 in the year 1760. By 1806 there was only one. But
the British merchant navy put off the use of antiscorbutics for 59 more
years, adopting them generally in 1854. The juices of all the citrus fruits

were called "lime juice" by the British. Hence the slang terms "Limeys" and "Lime Juicers" were applied to British ships and sailors.

Wading through this history, one is torn between celebrating the victory over scurvy and agonizing over its long delay. Herbert Spencer, who deplored officialdom, took the latter course. He commented: "Thus two centuries after the remedy was known, and forty years after a chief medical officer of the Government had given conclusive evidence of its worth, the Admiralty, forced thereto by an exacerbation of the evil, first moved in the matter."

All this occurred without knowing what it was in the fruits and vegetables that made the difference. Dr. Thomas Trotter, a disciple of Lind's, commented thus around the close of the eighteenth century: "Whatever, therefore, may be the theory of sea scurvy, we contend that recent vegetable matter imparts a *something* to the body, fortifies it against the disease." This *something* was Vitamin C, not to be identified until 1911 by Sir Gowland Hopkins.

Scurvy is but one of the hidden hungers. In addition there is rickets, a weakness of the bones in children caused by a lack of calcium in the diet and a lack of Vitamin D. And there is goiter, an enlargement of the thyroid gland which results from a lack of iodine. There is pellagra, manifested in a number of symptoms, including nervousness, lassitude, rough skin, paleness, indigestion, and other disorders, caused by a lack of niacine and Vitamin B complex. There is kwashiorkor, the protein-deficiency disease, sometimes fatal to the young. There is beri-beri, a Sinhalese word for "I cannot," the symptoms of which include stiffness of the legs, paralysis, pain, and anemia. Beri-beri results from eating polished rice; for aesthetic reasons the nutritious dark outer layer of the grain, which contains thiamine, is milled off and fed to the animals, who thrive wondrously. Human beings sacrifice health for psychic satisfaction. Fascinating stories could be written about each of these.

In the United States these nutrition-related diseases are in retreat. In 1975, when the American diet was under attack for its alleged shortcomings, I called the statistician at the then Department of Health, Education and Welfare to learn how many cases of these nutrition-related diseases we had. "We don't know," he replied. "There used to be a great many but they have become so few that we have stopped reporting them."

This cannot be said for all countries. The American people live in a favored land at a favored time. Hidden hunger, subtle starvation, and shadowed forms of famine continue to exist in much of the world. Physical impairment resulting from nutritional deficiency is just as crippling as debility resulting from an overall lack of food, and death is just as final. A difference is that, being hidden, the origin and remedies are harder to find, and cause and cure, once found, often lack credibility.

REFERENCES

Cady, F. C. 1937. "The Association of Scurvy and Oral Diseases." *Public Health Reports* 52, pt. 2 (Oct. 29):1526–30.

Lloyd, Christopher, ed. 1965. *The Health of Seamen.* Printed for the Navy Records Society. London: Spottiswoode, Ballantyne.

Mosteller, Frederick. 1981. "Innovation and Evaluation." *Science* 211, no. 4485 (Feb. 27):881–86.

Purchas, Samuel. 1965. *Hakluytus Posthumus, or Purchas His Pilgrimes.* Vol. 2. New York: AMS Press.

Roddis, Louis H. 1950. *James Lind, Founder of Nautical Medicine.* New York: Henry Schuman.

Stewart, C. P., and Douglas Guthrie, eds. 1953. *Lind's Treatise on Scurvy.* Edinburgh: At the University Press.

Whelan, Elizabeth M., and Frederick J. Stare. 1975. *Panic in the Pantry.* New York: Atheneum.

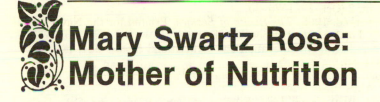Mary Swartz Rose: Mother of Nutrition

THE INVENTORS OF AGRICULTURE, by all competent accounts, were women. But the scientific advancements in agriculture since that time, if this book is to be believed, have been made overwhelmingly by men. This is so because for centuries and in many cultures women were considered soft, delicate, emotional, and noncompetitive. The stereotype for science is almost exactly the opposite: tough, rigorous, rational, impersonal, and unemotional; in a word, masculine. A woman scientist would therefore be a contradiction. Hardly anyone expected middle-class women to hold jobs outside the home, let alone take on scientific endeavors. Raising sons who would work and vote was their task. If women chafed at this assigned role they might be told, gently, that "the hand that rocked the cradle ruled the world."

Women finally rose in opposition to the ostracism from science imposed on them. These attempts took two forms. One was the confrontational strategy, demanding that society reject all stereotypes and accept the goal of full equality. The other approach was to accept the prevailing inequality and sexual stereotypes, using them for short-term gains such as staking out areas of "women's work." Mary Swartz Rose was such a one, a nonconfrontationist whose scientific work on food we describe in this chapter. She was a gifted and persistent teacher and scientist who became known as the Mother of Nutrition.

The field of nutrition was a prime candidate for study by female scientists; it had received limited attention. Wilbur O. Atwater of the U.S. Department of Agriculture published in 1896 an extensive table of food values, an important but relatively small beginning. Work in human nutrition, a logical extension of Liebig's work on plant and animal nutrition, was difficult to do. One could readily experiment with plants and animals but not with people. Efficient conversion of feed into flesh had a direct payoff for hogs and cattle, which in America are better fed than the people who are free to place aesthetics above nutrition. What dollar dividend would come from better-fed human beings? If there was an improvement in nutrition, what proprietary financial reward would flow from it? In promoting nutrition, profit seems more important than concern for human health.

So human nutrition, unenlightened by science, was an inseparable mixture of folk wisdom and myth. Animal fat was held in high esteem. During World War I the civilian population ate discredited whole-wheat bread so that the preferred white bread could be provided to the fighting men. Thus the field of nutrition was in need of study. But who would study it? Women! They prepared food in the home and it seemed a short step to studying it in the laboratory. Work on food was no direct threat to the male scientists. There was no hierarchy to challenge or displace.

It was into this kind of world that Mary Davies Swartz was born on October 31, 1874, in Newark, Ohio, the first of five children. She had a conventional upbringing in a midwestern home of refinement and achievement. She had an infectious smile, a nimble wit, and an energetic manner. She was graduated valedictorian of her high school class and received a degree of bachelor of letters from Denison University in 1901.

About this time something happened to her career objectives; she changed from liberal arts to applied work. She began taking courses in domestic science at Mechanics Institute, Rochester, New York, receiving a diploma in 1902. Then for three years she taught home economics in the high school at Fond du Lac, Wisconsin, after which she entered Teachers College, Columbia University, in New York City to work toward a bachelor of science degree in chemistry and a diploma in dietetics.

She took her combined degree in chemistry and dietetics in 1906. In 1907 she received a traveling fellowship to study physiological chemistry at Yale University. There she met Anton R. Rose, a fellow student. The two were married in 1910, when Mary was thirty-six years old. Indicative of her liberated but nonconfrontational style, she kept her maiden name, added her husband's name, and dispensed with the "Mrs." Professionally she became Mary Swartz Rose.

This budding woman scientist did well at Yale. She was accepted into the science honorary, the Society of Sigma Xi, a much-sought prize. She became a member of the American Association for the Advancement of Science and the Connecticut Academy of Arts and Sciences. She received the Ph.D. degree in physiological chemistry in 1909. She was not just collecting trophies; she was shaping tools for a dedicated career.

Ever the institutionalist, Mary Swartz Rose went back to Teachers

College at Columbia, becoming the first full-time person to develop a program in nutrition. In 1910 she became the first woman to have a professorial appointment in nutrition. The remainder of her life she spent at the college, teaching, doing research, and writing. Nutrition had emerged as her commitment and teaching had become her profession. Her concern was for the malnourished and the ill fed.

She was teaching a subject for which facts were scarce. Her research was undertaken to find the facts with which to do the teaching that would alleviate nutritional problems of the vulnerable groups in society. She did not have to delve deep for the mother lode; she picked up nuggets that lay everywhere in a field which few had prospected.

Mary Swartz Rose taught her students to carry on education in nutrition in the public schools. Over the years she had twenty-seven graduate students, all of them women; a total of eleven thousand undergraduate students took her classes. Her graduate students worked with groups of twelve or eighteen children in the eight- to ten-year-old age bracket, two assigned to each class. One would teach the class, using a standard lesson plan. The other would supervise home visitation. From all this came, in 1932, her book *Teaching Nutrition to Boys and Girls*.

She didn't stay in the classroom. Some of this work was with malnourished children at the Stuyvesant Neighborhood House on the Lower East Side of Manhattan Island. Early in her career she did basic metabolism studies of young people and later turned her attention to the food needs of the elderly. She carried on her own scientific studies and supervised the research of her graduate students so that she could base her teaching on facts, not myths. She studied the biological efficiency of protein, using white rats, then a new proxy for people. She looked into the mineral needs of the human body. She examined the effect of cooking, freezing, maturing, and sprouting on the Vitamin B content of peas and beans. In all this she insisted on the disciplined method she had learned at Yale. Her students, earning their degrees in teaching, acquired rigorous laboratory experience and a respect for facts.

From her own research and from her wide reading she advocated milk as the best food for children of all ages. Whole grain cereals, eggs, fruit, fresh vegetables, and liberal amounts of water were endorsed. Meat was not recommended for children under eight years of age if eggs and milk were provided. She worried about excessive use of sugar and about obesity long before these became general concerns. She identified the vulnerable groups in society: mothers, infants, children, the elderly, and the poor. She advocated school lunches long before the public developed an interest in them. Thus the subject of nutrition was introduced in the public schools. Her students, moving into teaching jobs, carried method and subject matter with them. They developed a growing network of ideas and personnel, pervading the educational system with nutritional knowledge. It was the classic process by which a new discipline becomes established. All of this fit into the growing new subject, home economics. The nutritional work of Mary Swartz Rose was eagerly adopted into the home economics agenda, which was rather sparse in the early years.

Mary Swartz Rose and her husband, Anton, made their home in Edgewater, New Jersey, and by all accounts it was a happy one. Richard Collin Rose, their only child, was born in 1915 when his mother was forty-one years old. She died, rich with honors, on February 2, 1941, at sixty-six years of age.

Mary Swartz Rose helped put nutrition on the public policy agenda, where it had not been before. By her efforts and those of others, nutrition-related diseases have gone into steady decline. The height of children has been exceeding the height of their parents now for several generations. Athletic records are steadily being broken. The average life span is lengthening. She helped identify the groups in society that are nutritionally vulnerable.

The subject of nutrition has continued to grow in importance. Domestically, there came publicly supported food aid initiatives such as the Direct Donation Program, the School Lunch Program, the Food Stamp Program, and the Program for Women, Infants, and Children. Internationally, the Food and Agriculture Organization of the United Nations was formed, with a strong emphasis on nutrition. In 1963 the FAO set up the multilateral World Food Program. Food aid to hungry people abroad is provided by scores of private religious and philanthropic organizations, as well as by government agencies such as Public Law 480, Food-For-Peace. What had begun as a modest effort in research and education had grown and been transformed into a series of direct action programs.

Mary Swartz Rose helped initiate a movement whose purpose is no less than the objective she had spelled out in 1936: "the collective obligation to provide mothers, infants, children and poor persons with an indispensible nutrition minimum; the creation in all countries of a definite nutrition policy; and the creation of organizations to give life to that policy."

The field that had been characterized by research and education became subject to controversy about food additives, adulterants, and contaminants. Subject matter, style, and program thrust all were changed. The banner of nutrition has been carried with every conceivable strategy and by a great number of people, especially women. One of them, Hazel K. Stiebeling, of the U.S. Department of Agriculture, worked in Rose's tradition, with persistent, low-key, fact-faithful method. Others, like Carol Tucker Foreman, chose the confrontational technique.

The other current of the stream in which Mary Swartz Rose worked was woman's rights, the aspect of it that opened professional and scientific endeavor to females. Here the gains were enormous. Women students enrolled in scientific studies and undertook scientific appointments. Their achievements were recognized. Barbara McClintock, Nobel laureate for her work in genetics of the corn plant, is a case in point.

These twin currents, nutrition and woman's rights, different though related, became mighty parallel streams. To what degree did Mary Swartz Rose help initiate these twin flows and to what degree was she borne along by the flood? It matters little. The tides were too strong for narrow attribution. Both currents are a part of today's and tomorrow's worlds; it is good to reflect on how one woman's life was related to their beginnings.

Mary Swartz Rose was above all else an educator. Her research was in support of her teaching. In that respect she was somewhat unique among the scientists in this book. There are others who taught: Liebig, Mendel, and Schultz, for example. But none of the others personally lifted the teaching role to so widespread and enduring a level in the fight against hunger as did this resolute woman.

REFERENCES

Eagles, Juanita Archibald, Florence Pye Orrea, and Clara Mae Taylor. 1979. *Mary Swartz Rose, 1874–1941, Pioneer in Nutrition.* New York: Teachers College, Columbia University.

Rose, Mary Swartz. 1932. *Teaching Nutrition to Boys and Girls.* New York: Macmillan.

Rossiter, Margaret W. 1982. *Women Scientists in America: Struggles and Strategies to 1940.* Baltimore: Johns Hopkins Univ. Press.

Stiebeling, Hazel K. 1959. "Food in Our Lives." In the 1959 *Yearbook of Agriculture,* pp. 1–6.

Todhunter, Elizabeth Neige. 1959. "The Story of Nutrition." In the 1959 *Yearbook of Agriculture,* pp. 7–22.

USDA Yearbook. 1959. *Food.* Washington, D.C.: Government Printing Office.

CHAPTER 13

Henry Wallace and Hybrid Corn

HENRY WALLACE was a bundle of contradictions. He was a great promoter of increased corn production and at the same time was the architect for a massive effort to curtail corn output. This was not the only paradox. He was variously (and sometimes simultaneously) scientist and mystic, entrepreneur and government planner, idealist and pragmatist, philosopher and activist, party loyalist and political maverick.

This book is about the conquest of hunger. Wallace's contributions as developer of hybrid corn, agricultural scientist, agribusinessman, and humanitarian are within the scope of the book and thus are treated. Other authors may attempt to untangle the many additional threads that constitute the fabric of this complex man.

Henry Agard Wallace, subject of our chapter, was the son of Henry C. Wallace, secretary of agriculture under Harding and Coolidge. Our Henry was the grandson of Henry (Uncle Henry) Wallace, founder of *Wallaces' Farmer* and a noteworthy agriculturalist in his own right. Henry A. was the father of yet another Henry Wallace, Henry B., a successful poultry breeder and businessman. In agricultural circles, when you say Henry Wallace you have to indicate which of the four you mean, for all are well known. In broader circles Henry Wallace means Henry A.

Corn, otherwise known as maize, was domesticated by the Indians probably in what is now Mexico some eight thousand years ago. The Indians have many legends about its origin. A blackbird brought it from the west, say some. A beautiful maiden shook it from her hair, say others. The Mayans believed that their god-hero Gucumatz, knowing that human beings needed corn, went through grievous perils to bring it to them.

Modern scientists know a little more about the origin of corn than do the Indians but not much more; corn is a crop with no agreed ancestor, its genetic history tangled with teosinte and tripsacum. Corn has become so reliant on human care that it cannot exist on its own. Primitive corn ears were about two inches long and as big around as a person's finger, but by the time Henry Wallace came on the scene selection and breeding had increased the length and circumference by about four times. Corn, which is a feed, a food, and an industrial crop, will produce more edible biomass per acre than any other plant species.

Corn held a fascination for young Henry Wallace. He was born in Iowa, our greatest corn state, the son and grandson of agricultural leaders who were steeped in the culture of corn. As a five-year-old child he tagged along after the legendary scientist George Washington Carver, professor of agriculture at Iowa State College. He studied agriculture at Iowa State College, disciplining his natural curiosity. Independent reading and reflective thought prepared him to see opportunities that were invisible to others.

The story of corn is told by Wallace himself in collaboration with William Brown in the excellent small book *Corn and Its Early Fathers*. Brown published, in 1983, the definitive article, "H. A. Wallace and the Development of Hybrid Corn." Edward and Frederick Schapsmeier published a scholarly book, *Henry A. Wallace of Iowa: The Agrarian Years 1910–1940*. The story that emerges from these writings is that of research on corn done chiefly by men at the agricultural experiment stations of the land grant college system, coupled with the practical application of this knowledge by Henry A. Wallace using agribusiness channels.

Corn bears its male and female organs on the same plant, the pollen in the tassel and the ovary on the ear, reached by the silk. The ovary is fertilized by wind-borne pollen from the same or other plants. Selection of desirable ears, the historic method of corn improvement, involved controlling the female but permitting indiscriminate male parentage. It was like trying to improve a beef herd by carefully selecting the heifers but giving no attention to the bulls. What the hybridizers did was to control the male as well as the female.

There were four great scientists who pried out the secrets of corn genetics and made hybrid corn possible: (1) William J. Beal of Michigan Agricultural College, who in 1877 made the first known controlled crosses between different varieties of corn for the purpose of increasing yields. This was before the discovery of Mendel's breakthrough genetic experiment. (2) George Harrison Shull who, beginning in 1904, working at Cold Spring Harbor on Long Island, showed by self-pollinating and crossing the corn plant that open-pollinated varieties of corn were a "mass of very complex hybrids" and that crossing different lines resulted in hybrid vigor, which he termed *heterosis*. (3) Edward Murray East, first at the University of Illinois and later at the Connecticut Experiment Station, who, working independently of Shull but at the same time, showed that inbreeding reduced vigor but crossing restored it. (4) Donald F. Jones of the Connecticut Experiment Station who, in 1917, invented the "double cross," using four inbred lines instead of two, making hybrid seed production practical. Other researchers working on corn genetics, gradually building up the fund of knowledge, were Hoffer of Indiana, Kiesselbach of Nebraska, and Richey of the U.S. Department of Agriculture. These early scientists did not learn the physiological or genetic reason for hybrid vigor, nor did anyone else. Scientists treat it as an unexplained but useful attribute.

The discoveries of these pioneers, the result of the search for pure knowledge, languished for a decade or so. There was no felt need for application. The extension service had not yet been set up to bridge the gap between laboratory and field. Before Wallace, no businessman seized the opportunity for profit in growing and selling hybrid seed.

Aesthetics took priority over economics. During the early decades of the twentieth century corn shows were in vogue. Farmers selected ten-ear displays of uniform cylindrical ears for exhibition at county, state, and national contests. These entries were ranked according to a standard agreed to by the reigning corn judges. Such was the mania for high-ranking corn that a grand champion ear sold for $150. The unexamined inference was that these blue-ribbon ears would produce beautiful high-yielding corn in the next generation.

Young Henry Wallace had his misgivings about blue ribbons for beautiful corn. In Iowa corn was a feed grain and Wallace asked the question, What's beauty to a hog? In 1904, when Wallace was a sixteen-year-old high school student, he set up a test plot and conducted his first experiment with corn. One of the most prominent judges had ranked forty ears of corn according to the standard then current. The young man took kernels from each of the ears and planted a row representative of each one. He tended the plot carefully and weighed the resulting yield. His experiment showed conclusively that the appearance of the corn had no correlation whatever with its yield. This finding supported Wallace's natural skepticism about conventional wisdom.

Experiments similar to Wallace's were subsequently repeated with like results. But such was the commitment to corn shows that they persisted for a time even after their economic irrelevance had been demonstrated. The same cycle of shows and prizes, followed by their demonstrated economic insignificance, occurred for poultry, cattle, and hogs.

Henry Wallace entered Iowa State College in 1906, already a serious-minded student. He pursued his special interests, going beyond the prescribed curriculum. He wrote articles for his father's paper and took a walking trip through Iowa, recording his observations in a feature story titled "On the Trail of Corn Belt Farming." He read scientific articles, including of course the work of Darwin and Mendel. He followed with avid interest the publications of Shull, East, and other researchers who worked on corn. He was interested in corn breeding not just as a matter of scientific inquiry but as a way of increasing yields and boosting income.

In 1913 Wallace began his own inbreeding of corn and in 1919 he started crossbreeding inbred strains. He shifted his operations to a 40-acre piece of land just outside of Des Moines. Small successes in 1921 and 1922 spurred him on and in 1923 he produced a single-cross hybrid, the parents of which were a Leaming inbred and a line out of a red variety named Bloody Butcher. The reddish color was expressed in the hybrid and Wallace named it "Copper Cross." Entered in the Iowa Corn Yield Test in 1924, it won a gold medal for high yield. In the early years hybrid corn outyielded open-pollinated varieties by about 25 percent. The margin of superiority increased with the years as breeding was improved.

Wallace, the entrepreneur, saw the success of his Copper Cross not as the occasion for an article in a scientific journal but as an opportunity to bring improved corn to midwestern farmers. He contracted with George Kurtzweil, a salesman for the Iowa Seed Company, to produce an acre of Copper Cross seed in 1923 and sell it for a dollar a pound. A new industry was born. The hybrid seed corn industry has a good thing going for it; if seed from the commercial crop is planted it produces a wild assortment of individuals with unsatisfactory yield. The corn farmer has to buy new seed each year.

In 1926 Wallace, with a few of his friends, founded the Hi-Bred Corn Company. Production and sales increased at a geometric rate. Agreements were made with other seed companies to produce and market Hi-Bred seed on a royalty basis. The Henry Field Seed Company was one such firm and Roswell Garst's operation at Coon Rapids, Iowa, was another. This was the Garst who gained fame in 1959 by hosting Nikita Khrushchev. By 1932 Hi-Bred Corn Company was producing hybrid seed on 220 acres. In 1935 the company's name was changed to the Pioneer Hi-Bred Corn Company. By 1986 the company had become Pioneer Hi-Bred International, Incorporated, with five thousand employees and net sales of $885 million. It was by far the largest seed corn company, with 38 percent of North America's seed corn sales, more than the next six companies combined. It had expanded into sorghum, wheat, soybeans, alfalfa, and sunflower seed. The company had moved into microbial cultures and retail computer systems. It had become truly international, with operations in Europe, Asia, South America, and Africa as well as North America. In this continent alone it had 124 research scientists working on plant breeding and genetics, plant pathology, entomology, and plant physiology, half of them working on corn. The Wallace family continued active in the company: John P., a nephew, and Robert B., a son of Henry A., were shareholders and members of the board of directors.

The adoption of hybrid corn was one of the most rapid innovations in all of agriculture. Within the ten years from 1936 to 1945, the planting of hybrid corn in the corn belt—the ten states including and surrounding Iowa in the American Midwest—increased from 5 percent to more than 90 percent. The reason for the rapid acceptance was the obvious superior yield and the fact that the hybrid required neither new tillage equipment nor reorganization of the farming system. All it required was more storage space to hold the larger crop.

The national average of corn yield per acre has increased more than four times since Wallace began his work. Perhaps half of that increase is attributable to genetics, expressed in large part through hybridization. This is a massive increase in the production of food and feed and a significant step in the conquest of hunger.

The advent of hybrid corn is testimony to the fruitful collaboration of three entities: research scientists working in the laboratory, farmers ready to adopt practices that pay off, and businessmen seeking a profit.

Hybrid corn was Wallace's absorbing concern, but he had other interests. He was competent in mathematics and worked on statistical methods, applying his techniques to prices and to the weather. He was instrumental in setting up the Statistical Laboratory at Iowa State College, enlisting the aid of Professor George Snedecor in this enterprise. As an early agricultural economist he worked on the elasticity of demand, a measurement of central importance in agricultural policy. In 1920 he published *Agricultural Prices,* a pioneering work in market analysis. In 1921 he took over from his father editorship of *Wallaces' Farmer.* His alma mater honored him in 1934 by conferring on him the honorary doctor of science degree.

Wallace had keen interest in economics and was largely self-taught in this subject. Because of his misgivings about mainstream thought he was attracted to the nonconformist economist Thorstein Veblen. Like his father and his grandfather, Wallace was interested in public policy particularly as it related to agriculture. He and his father were in the forefront of the agrarian struggles of the 1920s. In his role as editor of *Wallaces' Farmer* he gave unequivocal commitment to the agrarian cause.

With the coming of the New Deal Wallace went to Washington to be Franklin Roosevelt's secretary of agriculture, serving in a Democratic administration despite his family's Republican roots. The country was in the depths of the Great Depression and farmers were in desperate straits. The prevailing diagnosis of the problem was surplus production. Wallace set up the Agricultural Adjustment Administration, cutting the acreage of major crops, including corn, and paying farmers for nonproduction. This writer believes that the problem of the Great Depression was inept monetary policy rather than excess supply of farm products and that supply management was an inappropriate solution. The program had some merit as an emergency measure in an extreme situation but it has been continued for more than half a century, long past its time, with manifold abuses. This, of course, was no fault of Wallace's and he frequently spoke out against the continuation of these policies.

The Washington experience, which spanned 1933 to 1948, was a time of turmoil and controversy, radically different in both substance and style from the Iowa years. During this time Wallace served as secretary of agriculture (1933–40), vice-president (1941–45) and secretary of commerce (1945–46). In 1948 he was the unsuccessful presidential nominee of the Progressive party. Three incidents from these years reflect Wallace's humanitarian side.

In 1933, as secretary of agriculture, Wallace set up the Federal Surplus Relief Corporation, through which surplus food products were made available to hungry people who had been victimized by the Great Depression. In 1939, also while secretary of agriculture, Wallace put a food stamp plan into effect to make food available to low-income people on a partially subsidized basis. This program was closed out during World War II but was revived in 1961 and became the prototype for the present food stamp plan. In 1941, while Wallace was vice-president, he was called upon by Raymond B. Fosdick, president of Rockefeller Foundation. The foundation was planning to set up an agricultural development center in some foreign country and Fosdick, aware of Wallace's competence as an agriculturist, sought his advice. Wallace, who had spent a month traveling in Mexico and talking with government officials, advised Fosdick to choose Mexico, where the population was increasing rapidly and food production was lagging. The advice was followed and initiatives were taken that led to the International Center for the Improvement of Corn and Wheat, the base from which Norman Borlaug transformed wheat production. This center has produced a "hybrid" corn, open pollinated but selected and fixed from a series of crosses and inbreeding, for use by subsistence farmers of Latin America who cannot or in any case do not buy new hybrid seed each year. This is a second-best solution, sacrificing something in yield as compared with a regular hybrid but gaining greatly over the native varieties that the farmers would otherwise plant. This corn has good-quality protein and promises to improve the level of nutrition among the poor, for whom corn is the staple food. Thus do great events flow from seemingly small beginnings.

Following his political defeat in 1948, Wallace resumed his intense interest in genetics. He settled at South Salem, New York (he did not go back to Iowa) and worked with strawberries and gladioli as well as corn and chickens. He loved this type of activity and continued it until his death on November 18, 1965.

What can we say of Henry Wallace? Does he belong in the company of others in this book? Indeed he does. He helped improve world food production, actual and potential. He assisted in bridging the gap between the laboratory and the farmer's field. He helped lay the foundation for institutionalized food aid. He was a successful agricultural scientist, writer, statistician, economist, and businessman who in midlife entered the political world, thereby eclipsing his contribution as an agriculturist.

REFERENCES

Bender, Barbara. 1975. *Farming in Prehistory: From Food-gatherer to Food-producer.* London: John Baker.

Brown, William L. 1983. "H. A. Wallace and the Development of Hybrid Corn." *Annals of Iowa* 47 (Fall).

Lord, Russell. 1947. *The Wallaces of Iowa.* Boston: Houghton Mifflin.

MacDonald, Dwight. 1947. *Henry Wallace: The Man and the Myth.* New York: Vanguard Press.

Poppendieck, Janet. 1986. *Breadlines Knee-Deep in Wheat: Food Assistance in the Great Depression.* New Brunswick, N.J.: Rutgers Univ. Press.

Schapsmeier, Edward L. and Frederick H. 1968. *Henry A. Wallace of Iowa: The Agrarian Years, 1910–1940.* Ames: Iowa State Univ. Press.

Wallace, H. A. 1920. *Agricultural Prices.* Des Moines, Iowa: Wallace.

Wallace, Henry A., and William L. Brown. 1956. *Corn and Its Early Fathers.* Chicago: Michigan State Univ. Press. Reprint. Iowa State University Press, 1988.

CHAPTER 14

Norman Borlaug: Hunger Fighter

JEAN HENRI FABRE, the nineteenth-century French naturalist, once said, "History records the battlefields on which we lose our lives, but it disdains to tell us of the cultivated fields by which we live; it can tell us the names of the king's bastard offspring, but it cannot tell us the origin of wheat. Such is human folly."

Countering Fabre's generalization, we offer in this chapter the story of wheat, the story of cultivated fields, and the story of a hunger fighter named Norman Borlaug. The story begins in Mexico in October 1944, when Norman Borlaug went to that country for the Rockefeller Foundation to improve its agriculture. There followed a chain of events, partly planned and partly the result of chance, that transformed world agriculture. How did Borlaug orchestrate the role of the experimenter, the institution builder, the educator, and the public official? How did he, a Westerner, take a free gift of the East, reshape it, and return it immensely enriched? How did he help the New World discharge its debt to the Old?

Norman Borlaug was born in 1914 on a farm in northeast Iowa near the little town of Cresco. He is of medium size, erect and lean, of Norwegian stock. There is intensity in his manner and animation in his gestures. Borlaug's conversational comments reveal his thought processes. "Plant breeding is like poker," he comments. "If you have a bad hand, throw it in. If you've got a good one, don't be afraid to bet." "Small differences can be decisive," he says. And his intense focus leaves no doubt about his ability to discern these small differences. He thinks in terms of challenge. "A man has to be a torero, a bullfighter," he says. "He has to sidestep bureaucracy and red tape."

Borlaug is a product of the land grant college system. He did both his undergraduate and graduate work at the University of Minnesota, his advanced work in plant pathology under Dr. E. C. Stakman, an eminent scientist whose specialty was fungus diseases of plants. Borlaug's career carried him into genetics. To follow through his wheat improvement work, he had to develop a good understanding of ecology, soil science, plant nutrition, meteorology, hydrology, engineering, economics, demography, administration, and group dynamics. How does he describe his work? "I don't know what I am," he says with a trace of regret, typical for a scientist who has been pulled out of his original field. But it is perfectly clear what he is: he is an integrator of the scientific disciplines while differentiation has been the fashion. Therein lies the special uniqueness of Norman Borlaug and the reason that he has been able to make a greater contribution to the alleviation of world hunger than any other living man.

The Mexico to which Borlaug came in 1944 was primarily an agricultural country, with three-fourths of the people living on the land. Fields had been cultivated, some of them for thousands of years, with virtually no replenishing of soil nutrients. Plants and animals were ravaged by almost every known disease. Insect damage went unchecked. Corn and wheat yields were a fraction of those in the United States. Beyond all this the numbers of people were increasing at a rate that would more than double the population in the next twenty-five years. As a consequence of the population explosion the food supply was in jeopardy. Imports were rising, asserting a troublesome demand for limited foreign exchange. The foreseeable result, if these trends were to continue, was stark disaster.

How should Borlaug proceed? Self-appointed counsellors would have had him operate in the same fashion as other development planners. Some, the "necessary prior condition" advocates, discounted the possibility of doing anything until certain conditions had been met: a comprehensive agricultural development plan must be prepared, or a number of basic scientific questions must be answered, or the educational institutions must be made over on the model of the American system, or land reform must be completed, or we must work on family planning, or the political situation must be stabilized. These counsels of perfection—most of them are in fact aplogies for inaction—were all rejected. Instead, Borlaug set up a program with these unique features:

First, priorities were established and adhered to. The number one priority was to improve wheat yields in order to feed hungry people. Second, no distinction was made between basic and applied science; emphasis was on whatever was needed to advance toward the program objectives. Finally, career scientists were placed in charge and given long-term assignments. Native young people were trained through internships and outstanding men were given advanced study with the purpose of preparing them to take over the program.

Borlaug did not begin as an interdisciplinary scientist; that came later, after he had exploited his skills within his own field, pathology. He began with a particular crop, wheat, and with a particular problem of that crop, the fungus disease known as rust, which cut deeply into yields. One acre of badly rusted wheat can carry as many as 50 trillion tiny spores, which suck out the plant's moisture. They rise in clouds at harvest time, settling on man and machine in a fashion repulsive to eye and spirit. The grain from a rust-infected field is shriveled and shrunken. A severe case of rust can cut the yield in half or reduce it to zero.

It was clear that until the rust problem was brought under control no real progress would be possible. So began the program to breed wheat for rust resistance. Borlaug started by gathering as many of the Mexican wheat varieties as possible, from various altitudes and latitudes, some 8,500 samples altogether. Then he tested them. Only two of Borlaug's selections showed resistance to rust.

Wheat breeding involves crossing, a delicate operation performed with tweezers and magnifying glass. Over a period of twenty years, Borlaug and his associates made more than thirty thousand of these wheat crosses. The two Mexican lines that had shown resistance to rust were crossed with the more promising of the other lines. In addition, there were crosses with rust-resistant wheat introduced from the United States, Kenya, Australia, and Morocco. Some of these crosses produced wheat that had a fairly high degree of rust resistance.

Borlaug came to the conclusion that his improved wheat should not be highly specific in its environmental adaptation, so he set about to develop a limited number of wheat varieties with general rather than specific adaptation. It was this approach, whether instinctive, fortuitous, or reasoned, that permitted the rapid spread of his wheat not only within Mexico but outside the country, from Morocco to India. Borlaug bred photoperiod sensitivity out of his wheats; that is, he bred wheats that utilize about the same number of days to maturity regardless of whether the hours of daylight are lengthening or shortening. This was an enormous gain. Wheat thus bred can be adapted within a range, north and south, of perhaps five thousand miles instead of the customary five hundred.

Closely built into Borlaug's wheat research was a trainee program resembling an apprenticeship arrangement. Over the years, young scientists from scores of nations participated in his program, learning his methods and absorbing some of his enthusiasm. They slogged through the mud, choked on the dust, withstood heat and cold, mastered delicate skills, absorbed the meaning of scientific integrity, and, perhaps most important, learned the dignity of manual labor. They returned to their countries, often carrying the new wheat varieties with them. These were the "wheat apostles" who laid the groundwork for the later rapid expansion of the Mexican wheats.

The wheat-breeding techniques used in Mexico were not designed by Borlaug. What was unique was the execution of the plan, the adherence to the goal, the depth of his commitment, the reliability of funding, and the continuity of personnel. Add to this the serendipity that somehow seems to attend the bold and venturesome.

Throughout these years, Norman Borlaug's commitment became completely clear to his associates. The science had to be good, but that was not enough; it had to contribute toward his objective: "To help put bread in the bellies of hungry Mexicans." Of all the scientists whose careers are reported in this book Borlaug is unique in the degree of his dedication to fighting hunger. All other objectives were subordinate.

In a single season Borlaug's crew made from two thousand to six thousand individual crosses. Each year they studied the performance of forty thousand varieties and lines in various stages of development, most of which were planted in several locations. "Some of these kernels may be gold nuggets," said Borlaug. "Find them!" Finding them was a case of meticulous selection and relentless rejection. In twenty years of work with their forty thousand lines, they created and distributed some seventy-five new varieties, of which four subsequently comprised the bulk of the wheat grown in Mexico.

By 1951 it began to look as if the battle against wheat rust had been won. The disease seemed checked by the resistant varieties. Then suddenly Race 15B appeared, a type of rust previously of little importance. It spread throughout Mexico, the United States, and Canada with explosive force, ruining fields that promised 40 bushels an acre. Race 15B was deadly to two of Borlaug's four varieties, but the other two came through well. Reliance was shifted to these varieties and the threat passed.

In 1953 another variant of rust, Race 139, arose to strike down the remaining two of his established varieties. A series of new crosses, using lines carried in the wheat nursery, produced the resistant Chapingo 52, Chapingo 53, Bajio, and Mexe. These withstood the new rust and provided the basis for Borlaug's successful updated varieties.

By 1957, thirteen years after his work began, Borlaug was able to say that he had the rust problem under control. A number of new lines had been released; 70 percent of the Mexican area cultivated to wheat was seeded to these new varieties. The national average yield had been increased from 11.5 to 20 bushels per acre as the depredations of the rust had been checked. This was success, unprecedented and unquestionable.

Had Borlaug been only a pathologist he might have congratulated himself on a job well done and tapered off his labors. He would have kept some work going to stay ahead of such new races of rust as might develop. He could have had a sinecure for the remaining years of his professional life and congratulated himself on staying within his profession.

But not Norman Borlaug. For him this gain meant only that the enemy, hunger, was vulnerable and that he should press the attack. Yields were still low. Soil fertility was limited and the capacity of his wheat varieties to take up soil nutrients was likewise limited. Soil fertility could be increased with fertilizer, but Borlaug's wheats responded by growing tall and lodging, falling flat with rain and wind rather than producing more grain. A small application of fertilizer helped some. But beyond that point the more fertilizer, the lower the yield.

What was needed was germ plasm that would permit the wheat to assimilate a large amount of soil nutrients and convert these nutrients to grain, standing stiff and erect in doing so. These attributes had to be capable of being incorporated into his adapted rust-resistant Mexican wheats. He had no such germ plasm. Where could he find it?

From Japan came this last major component of Borlaug's miracle wheat. S. C. Salmon, a scientist from the U.S. Department of Agriculture, was in Japan with General MacArthur immediately after the war, helping get that country back on its feet. He saw, at the Morioka Branch Experiment Station in northern Honshu, a number of remarkably stiff, short-stemmed wheat varieties, heavily fertilized and producing high yields. The short-stemmed wheats have as many leaves and hence as big a manufacturing surface per stem as other wheats. They have shorter intervals between the leaves and so waste less effort in erecting an unproductive stem. And they have many more stems per plant. Furthermore, and extremely important, they have the capacity to take up large amounts of soil nutrients and convert them to grain.

News of the short-strawed wheat reached Norman Borlaug in Mexico. As always, he had his antennae up for anything new or promising. In 1953 he obtained some of the early crosses and breeding lines from Orville Vogel of Washington State, who had received them from Salmon. Working with his now well-developed techniques, Borlaug crossed Vogel's wheats with his Mexican varieties, obtaining the desired adaptation, disease resistance, and dwarf character. He found, and words cannot express his jubilation, that the increased yield potential of the new dwarf wheat was due not only to its nonlodging characteristic but also to its greater number of stems, the greater number of grains per head, and its better grain-filling qualities. Growing two crops a year, Borlaug had two varieties, Pictic 62 and Penjamo 62, ready for release by 1961, eight years after he first received the parent stock.

The new dwarf wheats had such voracious appetites for soil nutrients that they pushed far beyond the known range of fertilizer application. So new research had to be done. Optimum nitrogen application for the old wheats had been about 40 pounds per acre; the new wheats made efficient use of 120 pounds. Increased amounts of phosphorous and potash were also needed, as were some of the minor elements. Balancing the nutrition for these new wheats required research in soil fertility and plant response, which Borlaug and his colleagues incorporated into the work of the Rockefeller project along with pathology and genetics.

The new wheats were so prolific that all kinds of undertakings, previously unprofitable, became paying practices. Herbicides, for example. And use of insecticides. And additional irrigation. Borlaug moved into these areas with his research, recruiting necessary personnel, readily stepping from one scientific discipline to another, invading fields thought to be the special reserve of this or that subdivision of science, disregarding "keep off the grass" signs erected by scientific protocol. He was more concerned with how much hay he put up than with how much grass he kept off of.

Once he got the practices orchestrated, yields of these wheats were phenomenal. Better farmers, using improved methods, were able to get yields as high as 105 bushels per acre, two and a half times the top yields of Borlaug's earlier varieties. The advantages of these varieties were so great that in four years they took over 95 percent of the area cultivated to wheat in Mexico. The wheat was so attractive to farmers that virtually all of the first crop and much of the second were used for seed. National average wheat yields per acre, which had almost doubled from 1943 to 1957, increased another 10 bushels by 1963. Borlaug shifted to the new dwarf wheats and put aside the varieties on which he had labored so hard for twenty years.

With this success the old Rockefeller project was renamed and expanded. The new institution was called the International Center for Improvement of Corn and Wheat. In Spanish it was El Centro Internacional por Mejoramiento de Maíz y Trigo, or CIMMYT. It has been CIMMYT ever since.

Everything Borlaug had done seemingly worked together for good. Broadly based disease resistance, varieties insensitive to day length, the readily evident superiority of his wheat, the speed with which it could be multiplied, the readiness with which it could be adopted, the trained apprentices who spread the word, together with an immense resource of good will earned by his years of devoted labor — all of this catapulted his wheat into rapid adoption.

This was a breakthrough, a quantum leap, an event unusual in agriculture, where advances typically are gradual. And the breakthrough in genetics touched off revolutionary changes elsewhere. As it became clear that the new wheat would make fertilizer pay fabulous returns, fertilizer use trebled in a single year. The use of insecticides and herbicides was stepped up. Irrigation increased. Storage and transportation expanded. Businessmen stepped forward to service the new needs. Researchers on other crops caught a new vision now that wheat had experienced this great success. Extension men, working on adult education with Mexican farmers, now had something meaningful to push. Consumers bought increased amounts of the now-abundant wheat and upgraded their diets by substituting wheat for corn in their tortillas. The Mexican government felt satisfaction in the improved food situation and took pride in its part of the program. Agricultural development people throughout the world noted the Mexican success. The International Research Network came into being modeled on the Mexican wheat experience.

There were several things about this breakthrough that make it special and gave it particular significance. It came in a hungry part of the world, not in those countries already surfeited with agricultural output. It came in the tropics, which had long been in agricultural torpor, not in the temperate climates, where change was already occurring at a pace more rapid than could readily be assimilated. It produced new knowledge and technology that could be used by farmers on small tracts of land, rather than being, like many technological changes, useful only on large farms. It was a breakthrough that came voluntarily, up from the grass roots, rather than being imposed arbitrarily from above.

And what of Norman Borlaug amidst all this success? The banquet circuit, honors and awards, and well-earned applause from his peers? He had little time for these things. He was already looking to Asia, Africa, and other countries of Latin America where he hoped to establish his new wheat.

And the need for his new wheat in the Third World was prodigious. The balance between humans and their food supply was being threatened. With the decline in the death rate and the resulting world population explosion, the danger of hunger, never distant in much of the world, took on a new and harsh immediacy.

In India and in Pakistan, agricultural practices had changed but little for centuries. It was much as it had been in Mexico. The two Asian countries were experiencing more than their share of the population explosion and less than their share of agricultural development.

In this setting Borlaug's new high-yielding Mexican wheats began to appear. Dr. M. S. Swaminathan of the Indian Agricultural Experiment Station had requested and received a few kernels of Borlaug's wheat, which had performed remarkably well. Swaminathan arranged an invitation to Borlaug to visit India which was accepted. The timing could not have been more propitious. Thus began the Green Revolution in South Asia, of which we read in the next chapter. As before, Borlaug's work seemed to the product of benevolent destiny, though on close analysis it appears that destiny undertakes few ventures on its own; it awaits the actions of the bold and courageous.

On Octber 20, 1970, Norman Borlaug was in his wheat field in Mexico, working with a group of trainees. On one side of him were two young Romanians; on the other a Brazilian. A car approached. In it was his wife, Margaret, obviously agitated. "What's wrong, Margaret?" he asked. "Nothing is wrong, Norman, nothing. You've just won the Nobel Peace Prize."

Borlaug couldn't believe it. He stayed on in the wheat field, working with his trainees. His privacy lasted forty minutes. Then an American television crew arrived. To Borlaug's dismay one of the cameramen trampled the wheat in order to get his picture. Such privacy as Borlaug had hitherto enjoyed was deeply eroded, beginning on that October morning.

"The peace prize?" asked many. "One of the science prizes, well enough. But how come the peace prize?"

The Nobel committee had the right prize for him. Throughout this story runs a hopeful and transcendent theme—the triumph of peaceful efforts at human betterment over the destruction of war. It was during World War II that the Mexican wheat project was launched. It was from the wreckage of postwar Japan that the needed germ plasm came. The antecedents for Borlaug's new wheat came from both sides of the Iron Curtain. Trainees at the Mexican wheat improvement center worked together amicably, Pakistanis and Indians, blacks and whites. There is about agriculture some strange and unifying principle. Science is oblivious to skin color, ancient animosities, and ideological confrontation. It may become the bridge of understanding.

To be a hunger fighter is to work in a cause conducive to peace. The victory over hunger may yet be won and the winning of it may heal the heart as well as nourish the body. This thought helps sustain those who work to provide our daily bread.

REFERENCES

Baum, Warren C. 1986. *Partners against Hunger: Consultative Group on International Agricultural Research.* Washington, D.C.: World Bank.

Bickel, Lennard. 1974. *Facing Starvation: Norman Borlaug and the Fight against Hunger.* New York: Readers Digest Press, E. P. Dutton.

Borlaug, Norman. Dec. 1968. Personal interview with the author, Mexico City.
_____. Sept. 22, 1986. "Accomplishments in Maize and Wheat Productivity." CIMMYT's Twentieth Anniversary Celebration, El Bataan, Mexico (mimeographed).
Hanson, Haldore. 1986. *Fifty Years around the Third World*. Burlington, Vt.: Fraser.
Paarlberg, Don. 1970. *Norman Borlaug—Hunger Fighter*. Washington, D.C.: U.S. Government Printing Office.
Stakman, E. S., Richard Bradfield, and Paul C. Mangelsdorf. 1967. *Campaigns against Hunger*. Cambridge, Mass.: Belknap Press of Harvard Univ. Press.

CHAPTER 15

M. S. Swaminathan and the Green Revolution

THE GREEN REVOLUTION was and is primarily a phenomenon of high-yielding wheat and rice. While it began in Mexico and spread throughout much of the world, it had its greatest impact in South Asia.

More than any other person, M. S. Swaminathan promotes the revolution, bridges the two principal crops, and symbolizes the area. A native of India, he first worked with Borlaug to introduce high-yielding wheat into his own country and then headed the International Rice Research Institute (IRRI) at Los Baños in the Philippines.

Swaminathan is a pleasant, open man, soft-spoken and congenial. A competent scientist and a devout Hindu, he is respectful of his Indian heritage and at home in the Western world. He is an ideal person through whom to understand the Asian transition from a traditional to a modernizing agriculture.

Momkombu Sambasivan Swaminathan was born in 1925 in Kumbakonam, a small town in Tamil Nadu in the south of India, the son of a land-owning surgeon father and a well-born mother. He began studying agriculture to prepare himself for managing the family plantation but soon became deeply interested in science, particularly genetics. He received a bachelor's degree in agriculture from Coimbatore Agricultural College in Madras and went on to the Indian Agricultural Research Institute at New Delhi, concentrating on genetics and plant breeding, completing his study there in 1949. Then followed study abroad, at Waginengen, Netherlands, with the help of a UNESCO fellowship, and at Cambridge, England, where, in 1952, he received his doctoral degree. He did not at once return to India but took a position as research associate in genetics at the University of Wisconsin for two years. He then went back to India and had his first close look at rice as assistant botanist at the prestigious

Central Rice Research Institute at Cuttack in Orissa. After a short stay he accepted a post as cytogeneticist at the Indian Agricultural Research Institute in New Delhi, where he had studied six years earlier. A well-trained geneticist, thirty-eight years old, already established and influential, full of good motives and common sense, he was there in 1963 when Norman Borlaug met him.

Borlaug's wheat had found its way into test plots throughout the world. Swaminathan had observed some of these short-strawed high-yielding varieties in the New Delhi plots. These wheats, which looked so strange alongside the tall Indian lines, resisted rust and responded vigorously to fertilizer and irrigation. They outyielded the native Indian wheats by 2 or 3 to 1. Observant and decisive as he was, Swaminathan moved quickly. With his urging India ordered 10 bushels of seed from Mexico which Swaminathan planted at his Indian Agricultural Research Institute in the fall of 1963. Yield was sensational, so India ordered 250 metric tons seeded on 7000 acres, which produced a very good crop.

On this limited but highly successful experience Swaminathan and Borlaug proposed rapid adoption of the Mexican wheats. A strategy was developed. Swaminathan the scientist became Swaminathan the promoter, the same transformation Borlaug had experienced.

This was the plan: Half the wheat produced on the 7000 acres would go for commercial increase to make more seed available the following year. The other half would go for demonstrations, planted in small plots by hundreds of farmers. Meanwhile, breeding work would go forward to modify the Mexican wheats in accordance with India's special conditions, and there would be a step-up in the training of young scientists. The extension service would pitch in.

A great debate arose. The Mexican wheats had looked good, very good, but should a full commitment be made to the plan outlined by Swaminathan and Borlaug? Counsel was divided. The farmers wanted the wheat, but many of the scientists were dubious about staking so much on a wheat so new, subjected to such limited testing. Suppose there should be an outbreak of some plant disease to which the new wheats proved susceptible and the whole crop were lost? The food supply of the people and the credibility of the officials were at stake. The cultural practices recommended for the Mexican wheat were far beyond the experience of the Asian scientists. Where would the necessary fertilizer come from? Could farmers be taught to fertilize and irrigate properly? The doubters contended, incorrectly, that the Mexican wheats produced less straw— how would the bullocks be fed? The color of the wheat was red, while the Indians preferred amber. Baking qualities were not the preferred ones. With abundant supplies, the price would be driven down. And so on and on.

In all this Swaminathan showed great strength. He lobbied success-fully for the new wheats, his own career at stake, and the results of the demonstration-experiment were almost unbelievably successful. Farmers were enthusiastic, doubters were subdued, and India was off to its agri-cultural transformation.

Efforts to modify the Mexican wheats to meet India's needs were successful. At the Indian Agricultural Research Institute and under Swaminathan's direction, the reddish color was changed to the desired amber by induced mutation, using gamma rays and ultraviolet light. The high-yielding rust-resistant short-strawed characters of the Mexican wheats were retained. This was a scientific achievement of a high order. Crosses were made of native Indian lines with the Mexican wheats, re-sulting in a number of new varieties superior to both parents. Sharbati Sonora and Pusa Lerma were released. Thus was established an impor-tant principle: that the international research centers alone are not enough; they can be most effective when their work is associated with strong national research efforts.

There is one very precious thing about the wheat experience in Asia. The newly introduced wheats were called "the Mexican wheats," not "the Rockefeller wheats" or "the American wheats," though the Rockefeller Foundation had supplied the money for the Mexican initiative and Bor-laug had done his original study in America. The Rockefeller people had the grace and wit to buoy up the Mexicans and the Indians rather than claim credit for themselves. By so doing they increased the acceptability of the new wheats abroad and elevated the morale of the Mexicans.

Indian wheat production, which had stood at 12 million tons in 1964–65, more than trebled in eighteen years, reaching 42 million tons by 1982–83 in a country that supposedly was tradition bound. It was this amazing increase that, more than anything else, averted the mass starva-tion that had been widely predicted for India.

The high-yielding wheats spread to other countries. By the mid-1980s, more than half the wheat area in the Third World was sown to the high-yielding varieties. Swaminathan and Borlaug, one from the East and the other from the West, teamed up to transform wheat production. There is symbolism here as well as agricultural history.

India produces twice as many tons of rice as it does wheat. World-wide, the two leading staple foods are wheat and rice, the two staffs of life, and it is questionable whether we lean on one more than on the other.

Major trends were under way in the mid–twentieth century and new perceptions emerged. There was growing concern about world hunger. In South Asia, most of the tillable land was already in use. Agricultural science was spreading throughout the rice-growing area but rice yields had changed very little. An able cadre of Asian agricultural scientists had been formed but rice production had been little affected.

The idea of international agricultural research took hold. The principles of heredity know no national boundaries. Promising genetic material is not likely to be confined to any one country. The basic agricultural disciplines—physics, chemistry, biology—are not location specific. Epidemic plant diseases are a concern to all nations that grow the affected crop.

Recognition of these facts and action thereon came together in 1962 when the IRRI was dedicated in the Philippines with the collaboration of the two American founding agencies, the Rockefeller Foundation and the Ford Foundation, assisted by the facilities generously provided by the government of the Philippines. The objective was to improve rice. The multidisciplinary, mission-oriented, international approach used successfully in Mexico for wheat would be used in Asia for rice.

By the time IRRI was founded, rice scientists knew that there was a short-strawed variety of rice in Taiwan named Dee-geo-woo-gen. An immediate and credible hypothesis was that the short-strawed rice from Taiwan might have a yield-enhancing capability. Acting on this hypothesis, crosses were made and were successful. A new variety of rice was bred having double the yield potential of the traditional rice plant. The first variety, IR8, was released in November 1966, only four years after IRRI was established. It proved equal to its promise and became the "miracle rice" known throughout the world. It had a prodigious appetite for nutrients, stood erect despite heavy applications of fertilizer, and yielded amazingly well.

Subsequent varieties had better grain quality, greater resistance to insects and diseases, more variation in length of growing season, and improved adaptation to specific locations. In India, rice production had stood at 46 million tons in 1966 and rose to 80 million tons in 1980. By the mid-1980s more than half the Third World's rice area was planted to the high-yielding varieties.

The IRRI scientists, many of whom are Asians, worked at developing equipment and technology to accommodate the requirements of the high-yielding rice with minimal disturbance to established ways of doing things. Threshing machines have been developed that are small and portable, picked up and carried by two men. Dusters are of the knapsack type, suited to small fields. Tillage equipment is small-scale, as are grain driers.

Rice culture probably provides the greatest contrast in methods of any crop. In the United States rice fields are leveled with the help of laser beams, seeded from airplanes, and harvested with self-propelled combines. In Asia the typical tools are the mattock (tillage), the human hand (planting), and the sickle (harvest). Yet the production costs of the two systems, taking account of alternative opportunities, are similar. Asian rice competes effectively with American rice.

While all these changes were beginning for rice, Swaminathan was working away at the wheat revolution in India. Rice and wheat, both self-pollinating crops, call for similar plant-breeding procedures, so he had potential skills for rice.

In 1982, when Robert Chandler retired as director general of IRRI, the institute turned to Swaminathan, then fifty-seven years old. The wheat revolution was then well under way and Swaminathan the scientist-promoter was ready for a new challenge. He joined a going organization, adding his own prestige to it.

The Green Revolution has evoked both applause and criticism. Approval has come from those concerned with producing food and overcoming hunger. Disapproval comes from those whose prime purpose is to reduce inequalities in income among rural people. The high-yielding varieties generate deep-seated change, which conservatives mistrust and venturesome people accept. The Green Revolution has profound influence on established institutions. The terms for the division of the crop between landlord and tenant become outdated and need changing. With double-cropping the seasonal rhythm of rural activity is transformed. Some farmers are demoted from tenants to laborers as the landlords themselves undertake the now profitable farm operation. Some laborers are unemployed as a result of mechanization. Heavier production means lower prices. Problems of shortage may be replaced by problems of surplus which, though the more tractable of the two, are problems nonetheless. The disadvantaged and the dispossessed form the nuclei of dissident groups.

But these aspects of the Green Revolution, if dwelt upon, can immobilize the will, deify the existing state of affairs, negate every proposed change, and predispose a country to famine. Anyone who has visited the less-developed parts of the world and has seen hunger at close range will hesitate not a moment in trying to increase the availability of food. If this effort brings with it some associated problems, they are next in line for treatment.

The countries of the Third World look on IRRI as a major resource in the battle to overcome hunger. In April 1983 Dr. Swaminathan went to Beijing, China to receive the prize given by the Third World to IRRI for "its scientific contribution to improving the productivity of rice and rice-based cropping systems." The citation stated, in part, "IRRI's quiet, persistent, highly professional and wholly dedicated work touched the lives of millions in the Third World, improving the human condition in truly practical and lasting ways."

IRRI is an institutional invention of the first magnitude. The successes of IRRI in the Philippines and CIMMYT in Mexico have led to establishment of eleven additional institutes. The total list:

CIAT: Centro Internacional de Agricultura Tropical, Colombia
CIMMYT: Centro Internacional de Mejoramiento de Maíz y Trigo, Mexico
CIP: Centro Internacional de la Papa, Peru
IBPGR: International Board for Plant Genetic Resources, Italy
ICARDA: International Center for Agricultural Research in the Dry Areas, Lebanon
ICRISAT: International Crops Research Institute for the Semi-Arid Tropics, India
IFPRI: International Food Policy Research Institute, United States
IITA: International Institute of Tropical Agriculture, Nigeria
ILCA: International Livestock Center for Africa, Ethiopia
ILRAD: International Laboratory for Research on Animal Diseases, Kenya
IRRI: International Rice Research Institute, Philippines
ISNAR: International Service for National Agricultural Research, Netherlands
WARDA: West Africa Rice Development Association, Liberia

The thirteen centers are supported through the Consultative Group on International Agricultural Research (CGIAR), an international consortium of thirty-three governments and private agencies dedicated to the support and improvement of agricultural research in the Third World. By the mid-1980s there were about seven thousand persons employed within this network, including more than six hundred senior scientists from forty nations, having an annual budget of more than $200 million.

The major institutional inventions (the Experiment Station Systems of various countries and the International Research Centers of the Third World) provide quantum improvement in the world's food system. Using these agencies Dr. Swaminathan, Indian scientist, fights hunger and appears to be winning.

There has been no major famine in India since the high-yielding varieties of wheat and rice were introduced. There is no known previous period of equal length in India's history of which this can be said. During the later years of that period India outgrew, one hopes permanently, its need for food assistance from abroad. All of this happened despite phenomenal population growth. Credit for so significant an achievement must be shared by many—farmers, educators, government administrators, agribusiness firms, providers of food assistance, and, perhaps most significantly, agricultural scientists. Among these latter Swaminathan merits special recognition.

On June 18, 1987, Swaminathan was named winner of the first annual General Foods World Food Prize, an honor that carried with it an award of $200,000. The prize is intended "to recognize and reward those men and women who have made outstanding contributions to expanding and improving the quality, quantity, and availability of food throughout the world."

As this is written Swaminathan is again in India, assisting his native country in meeting the food problems that result from the 1987 drought.

REFERENCES

Bickel, Lennard. 1974. *Facing Starvation*. New York: Reader's Digest Press.
Chandler, Robert F., Jr. 1979. *Rice in the Tropics: A Guide to the Development of National Programs*. Boulder: Westview Press.
International Agricultural Research Institute. 1980. *Science and Agriculture: M. S. Swaminathan and the Movement for Self Reliance*. New Delhi: Indian Society of Genetics and Plant Breeding.
International Rice Research Institute. 1972. *Rice Science and Man*. Los Baños: Papers presented at the Tenth Anniversary Celebration of the International Rice Research Institute. IRRI.
Swaminathan, M. S. 1982. *Rice Research in the 1980s: Summary Reports from the 1982 International Rice Research Conference*. Los Baños: International Rice Research Institute.
_____. Nov. 1983. Personal interview with the author, Rome.
_____. 1983. "Biotechnological Research and Third World Agriculture." *Science* 218(Dec. 3):967–72.
_____.; Sept. 23, 1986. "The Green Revolution." CIMMYT's Twentieth Anniversary Celebration, El Bataan, Mexico (mimeographed).

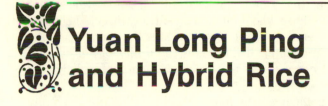

CHAPTER 16

Yuan Long Ping and Hybrid Rice

HUNGER HAS BEEN A MAJOR PROBLEM in China for most of known history. China already has almost one-fourth of the world's people and, despite a stern family planning program, population is growing at a rate of 1.3 percent per year. There is only a quarter of an acre of tillable land for each inhabitant; the United States has eight times as much. Any study that traces the hoped-for movement toward a well-fed world must take China into account.

During the Great Proletarian Cultural Revolution of the 1960s China was kept in turmoil. Education was interrupted. Scientists were torn from their laboratories and sent to the rural areas to work in the paddy fields in order to strip them of their alleged pretensions. Young activists, called Red Guards, disrupted town and country.

This period of chaos had tapered off by 1969. During the early 1970s, after much internal disorder and after long years of animosity toward the West, China opened itself to the United States. In 1980 the Ford Foundation received an invitation from the Chinese Academy of Social Science to send a team to China to study the country's rural economy. Five able people were named, competent in the full range of rural concerns. To their astonishment team members found that the Chinese had learned to produce hybrid rice. This was a scientific achievement that had eluded the prestigious International Rice Research Institute of the Philippines, the Central Rice Research Institute of India, the Agricultural Research Institute of Taiwan, and every free world researcher who had involved him- or herself in the effort. Hybrid rice outproduces, by about 20 percent, the varieties customarily planted in China. This was a breakthrough of great potential for meeting the food needs of China's millions.

115

How did it happen? Especially how did it happen during the time of insulation from the West, that supposed fountainhead of agricultural science? It is a story of the triumph of peaceful pursuits over violent uprisings and a lesson to those who think that a centrally directed country necessarily stifles the creative urge. It demonstrates the rising scientific competence of an Asian country. It illustrates the utility of agricultural science, the caprice of chance, and the accomplishment of a dedicated man.

Hybridizing a self-pollinated crop like rice is very difficult. Each tiny rice floret, progenitor of the rice grain, contains both the male members (stamens) and the female organ (pistil), so that the male ordinarily fertilizes the female of the same plant. To add to the problem, the stigma of the pistil is receptive to pollen for only a short time. The pollen is also viable for only a brief period. The stamens must be removed before they shed pollen and the pollen from the chosen male parent applied during the brief time the pistil is receptive. With such difficulties it is possible to make, individually, the limited numbers of crosses needed for experimental work but not the many needed for a commercial field.

In 1964, during the turmoil of the Cultural Revolution, China launched a research program on hybrid rice located at the Academy of Agriculture at Changsha, Mao Zedong's hometown in Hunan Province, South China. The purpose was to produce a hybrid for commercial production using large-scale methods, not a hybrid of fixed genetic composition that results from hand crossing and selection over a number of generations, as Borlaug had done for wheat and the International Rice Research Institute had done for rice. In other words, the intent was to hybridize rice, a self-pollinated crop, after the pattern of corn, a cross-pollinated crop. The effort met with no success. Six years later, in 1970, after the Cultural Revolution had subsided, the job of leading the hybrid rice project was given to Yuan Long Ping, then a forty-year-old plant breeder who had taught agriculture for seventeen years at An Jiang Agricultural School in Hunan Province. Yuan had been born in Beijing and had been educated at the Nanking Senior Middle School and the Southwest Agricultural College. He read and wrote English readily and had a fair command of Russian. These language skills gave him access to scientific work done outside his country. Some of this literature had found its way into China in the marvelous fashion by which learning penetrates political boundaries.

Yuan knew well enough from his studies the general course he must follow if he were to succeed. The lesson came from recent American success in producing hybrid corn without the need of detasseling. Yuan needed to discover and develop a male-sterile line that would be incapable of self-fertilization and would be receptive to the pollen of another parent. He must thwart nature. He would use the classic style of plant breeding: the discovery of some coveted bit of germ plasm and the transfer thereof to a desired line. The task was most difficult for Yuan; his subject, rice, had been designed by nature for incest rather than for the exogamy he had to impose. The conventional wisdom was that it could not be done. The prevailing judgment was this piece of dogma: "Since paddy rice is a self-pollinating crop, its flowering period short, its stigmata small and the percentage of fruiting by cross pollination is low, the hurdle of seed propagation will never be surmounted. No matter how strong heterosis of paddy rice is, it will not be applicable in reproduction."

But the conventional wisdom did not prevail. In the autumn of 1970, almost coincidentally with Yuan's arrival, came a breakthrough. Mr. Li Bi-hu, Yuan's assistant, while in search of the desired new germ plasm, discovered on Hainan Island off the coast of South China exactly the plant needed. It was a common wild rice plant, lying prone on the ground like its fellows, differing in that it had abortive pollen – it was male-sterile. Its later performance showed it to be a natural hybrid. This wild abortive plant, quickly dubbed WA, was crossed by hand with a normal line and was found capable of producing offspring which retained the male-sterile attributes through the successive back crossings with a normal parent. A back cross is a mating of father to daughter. By back crossing and selecting, Yuan found he could retain the male-sterile character while purging the line of its prostrate growth habit and its other undesirable characters: easy shattering, narrow leaves, and slim stems. When its desired attributes had been thus fixed, the male sterile line was crossed experimentally with various possible "restorer lines." Of the many potential lines tried, only 3 percent were found to possess strong restoring power; that is, the capability of re-establishing the attribute of self-fertilization to the offspring. From these was selected the male parent for the final hybridization.

It was now 1974, four years after the wild abortive male-sterile plant had been found. The carefully crafted hybrid was grown in a small demonstration field "with promising results." Improvements were achieved. Yields per acre were brought up to about one-fifth above ordinary rice. Distribution was made. The hybrid caught on rapidly, being readily accepted by both planning agencies and farmers. Planting increased from zero in 1974 to 17 million acres by 1983, 20 percent of China's total rice acreage.

What were the chances that this marvelous chain of events would occur? The probability of an outcome is the product of the probabilities of the separate events that bring it about. The likelihood of an outcross in rice such as produced the wild abortive plant is quite low. The chance that the offspring from such a cross would be male-sterile is more rare still. The probability that Mr. Li, on Hainan Island, would see this specimen and perceive its signifcance is even smaller. The likelihood that this wild abortive plant would be capable, when crossed, of transmitting its viable pistils and its sterile stamens to its offspring is indeterminately small. And the probability that the resulting male sterile line would respond to a restorer gene is likewise small. The probability of all these events happening together must be, in the statistical phrase, not significantly greater than zero. But it did happen.

One must be impressed, in reading the history of science related to agriculture, with the strong role played by chance events. Anton van Leeuwenhoek discovered microbes by idly peering through his microscope at a drop of stagnant water. Edward Jenner originated vaccination after noting that milkmaids escaped smallpox. Louis Pasteur advanced the germ theory by casually examining, for another purpose, two contrasting vats of beet pulp. Alexander Fleming discovered penicillin when a speck of soot from the smoky London sky landed in his petri dish. Selman Waksman found streptomycin in a clod of earth removed from the throat of a sick chicken. Ed Mertz and Oliver Nelson discovered high-lysine corn while running routine tests on their inbred lines. S. C. Salmon chanced upon a building block for Borlaug's high-yielding wheat at an experiment station in Japan. The list could go on and on.

There is one common feature to these diverse happenings: the investigator not only saw the event with his eye; he perceived it with his inner consciousness. This is the essence of scientific work. Chance favors the prepared mind.

In September 1982 my wife and I visited Dali Commune, a huge farm just outside Canton, in South China, which grows 9,000 acres of rice, twenty-five hundred of it hybrid. We met Ye Ping Wen, deputy chairman of the management committee. The commune was growing 500 acres of early season hybrid and 2,000 acres of late season hybrid. This was the third year of hybrid rice on the farm. Mr. Ye told us the hybrid seed cost eight to ten times as much per pound as ordinary rice seed, but the hybrid is vigorous and puts out so many shoots, said Mr. Ye, that it takes only 20 to 40 percent as much seed to plant an acre. The cost of hybrid seed amounts to about 10 percent of the value of the crop, so if it produces 20 percent better there is a clear advantage. As with all true hybrids, new seed must be bought each year. Mr. Ye, who had only five years' formal schooling, described with accuracy the system by which hybrid rice is produced.

We went out to see the rice. It was just beginning to head, waist-high, luxuriant, and vivid green. Blades were erect, stabbing the air like so many pineapple leaves. It would obviously make a good crop.

Yuan Long Ping has bought China valuable time with which to bring down the rate of population growth. As agricultural science advances, the threat of famine retreats. Yuan leads toward a well-fed world. He has also taught a valuable lesson for those remaining few who need it—that scientific achievement in agriculture has moved beyond the Wetern nations that first produced it.

With Yuan's achievement, the world's three great cereal crops, corn, wheat, and rice, have all been genetically transformed. This was done by the classic plant-breeding method: discovery of useful germ plasm and the transfer thereof to another line so as to produce a superior plant.

With apologies to the thousands of scientists who have contributed importantly but have been overlooked by the media, and with further apologies to those whose work has been reported but missed or underappraised by the author, and with full awareness of the dangers of interpersonal comparisons, here is a brief summary of the people and the institutions that have contributed to major improvement of the great crops:

Corn: William J. Beal of Michigan Agricultural College
E. M. East of the University of Illinois
D. F. Jones of the Connecticut Experiment Station
George H. Shull of the Carnegie Institute

Wheat: Norman Borglaug of CIMMYT, Mexico
M. S. Swaminathan of the Indian Agricultural Research Institute
Orville A. Vogel of the U.S. Department of Agriculture

Rice: The staff of the International Rice Research Institute, Philippines
Yuan Long Ping of the Hunan Academy of Agricultural Sciences, Changsha, People's Republic of China

The classic breeding technique, discovery and transfer of germ plasm, is giving way to the creation thereof by what is called gene splicing and genetic engineering. This amazing new development, full of questions and contention, is the subject of the next chapter.

However these things may be, no new techniques and no new names can erase the accomplishments of the great men listed above who achieved mightily in overcoming world hunger.

REFERENCES

Association of Japanese Agricultural Scientific Societies. 1975. *Rice in Asia*. To-kyo, Japan: Univ. of Tokyo Press.

Ford Foundation. October 1980. "Report on a Ford Foundation Rural Economy Team's Visit to China." Information paper for internal use.

Huaxue Tong Bao (Chemistry) January 1978. "National Production of Hybrid Rice Seeds by Chemically Induced Sterility." JPRS:072939, Article by Guandong Provincial Crop Heterosis Coordination and Cooperation Group No. 1, 21 (English).

Levin, Donald A. 1979. "Hybridization, an Evolutionary Perspective." *Benchmark Papers in Genetics* 11. Stroudsburg, Penn.: Dowden, Hutchinson, and Ross.

Lin, Shih-Cheng, and Yuan Long Ping. 1982. *Hybrid Rice Breeding in China, an Innovative Approach to Rice Breeding*. Los Baños, Laguna, Philippines: International Rice Research Institute, pp. 35–51.

Yuan Long Ping, January 1977, National General Information, "Key Techniques for High Production, Propagation of Hybrid Rice Outlined" (Genetics and Breeding) no. 1, 4–5 Beijing (English).

Yuan Long Ping. March 3, 1984. Correspondence with the author.

CHAPTER 17

Watson, Crick, and the Gene Splicers

BIOLOGY HAS UNDERGONE A TRANSFORMATION, indeed, a revolution. Its ascendancy came when physics, chemistry, and mathematics moved in to undergird the discipline. It came when team research and interdisciplinary work began to replace the single biologist working at his bench who stayed within his specialty. Change came when the electron microscope and X-ray crystallography made it possible to photograph the interior of the cell. It came when young men like James Watson, co-discoverer of the life substance DNA, appraised adversely the prospective results from yet more studies in traditional genetics. As a graduate student, Watson wearied of studying genetics based on laboratory work with the fruit fly. He judged that "Drosophila's better days were over and many of the best younger geneticists, among them Sonneborn and Luria, worked with micro-organisms." Plant breeders had focused on the manipulation of genetic material. To this now has been added the creation of desired germ plasm.

The work of James Watson and Francis Crick, which we describe in this chapter, was pure science, inspired by the desire to learn biology's best-kept secrets. What was the stuff that transmitted the attributes of life from the parent cell to the daughter? What was its structure and what was its chemical composition? The goal was to learn the structure of deoxyribonucleic acid, the life substance.

What was the status of the search for the life substance in 1951, when Watson and Crick first met? Science was on the trail. There were pieces of evidence: chemical, physical, genetic, and photographic. Numerous hypotheses were in existence, many of them in conflict with one another. Three research centers were leading the competition to learn the secret:

Cal Tech at Pasedena, California, with Linus Pauling as leader; Kings College in London, where Maurice Wilkins was preeminent; and Cambridge, England, with Watson and Crick, who were to win the race.

James Dewey Watson, probably the most brilliant of the scientists reported in this book, was born in Chicago on April 6, 1928, precocious from an early age. He was "discovered" by Louis Cowan, producer of the "Chicago Quiz Kids Show." He enrolled in the University of Chicago for a bachelor's degree in science at age fifteen. Paul Weiss, who taught him embryology and invertebrate zoology, commented thus: "He was (or appeared to be) completely indifferent to anything that went on in the class; he never took any notes and yet at the end of the course he came top of the class." Early on Watson read Schrödinger's book *What Is Life?* and, in his own words, "became polarized toward finding out the secret of the gene." He enrolled for the Ph.D. in genetics and experimental embryology at Indiana University. He did not have a fund of small talk; he would seek out the older men—Professors Muller, Sonneborn, or Luria—and talk with them. He would carry a book to a meeting and would read it if the speaker proved dull or unintelligent. Watson gravitated to Professor Salvador Luria, an Italian-trained microbiologist and a refugee from war-torn Europe. Luria's special field was viruses, those tiny entities that sometimes seem active and sometimes inert. Watson received his Ph.D. in 1950 at age twenty-two.

In 1951 Watson, with the support of a Merck fellowship, visited Cambridge, England and was invited to come there for his studies, an opportunity that appealed to him. The Merck people urged him to go instead to Caspersson's Institute of Cytochemistry in Stockholm, in which case his grant could run a full second year. His mother telephoned Paul Weiss, chairman of the board of Merck, imploring him, "Please stand your ground, for that boy for once needs to learn a lesson." But Watson overrode the counsel of his mother and the urging of his sponsor. He accepted the Cambridge offer. The son, judged by his mother to be in great need of guidance regarding his career, was less than two years away from the scientific discovery that would earn him the Nobel Prize.

So here was James D. Watson, Ph.D., twenty-three years old, freshly arrived at Cambridge. He was different in manner and brief in conversation. His curiosity was limited to scientific subjects. He was escaping from cytochemistry, microbial metabolism, and radiation biology. He appeared to be driven by the quest for knowledge and the honor that might come if he were successful.

Watson shared an office with Francis Crick, a confident, extroverted, ebullient, articulate thirty-five-year-old middle-class English experimental cytologist with a loud laugh and an insatiable curiosity. Together, despite lack of specific preparation, they would solve, within two years, the riddle of inheritance.

Francis H. C. Crick was born in Northampton, England on June 8, 1916. He studied at Mill Hill School and University College, London, where he received a second-class degree in physics in 1937. He opted for biology after reading, as Watson did, Schrödinger's book *What Is Life?*.

Crick, an avowed atheist, was moved by a desire "to try to show that areas apparently too mysterious to be explained by physics and chemistry could in fact be so explained." He sought to wipe out the old idea that living material possesses a vital force. At the Cavendish Laboratory in Cambridge Crick was introduced to biology and the biophysical techniques he would need in the field he had chosen: "the division between the living and the non-living, as typified by, say, proteins, viruses, bacteria, and the structure of chromosomes." He arrived at Cambridge in 1949 and made his career there.

It was inevitable that Watson and Crick would work together. Though opposites in lifestyle, they were complementary in their primary qualifications, Crick in crystallography and Watson in genetics. Watson had previously avoided work in physics, which seemed to him boring. His personal career as a chemist had been interrupted when he used a Bunsen burner to warm up some benzene. Watson provided the wings of the Watson-Crick bird, propelling it forward. Crick was the tail, keeping it on course. There was little delay in choosing a field; they set out to learn the structure of DNA. Their approach was to go beyond present knowledge in guessing its composition and then to check against known facts to see if their guess could be correct. But how make a good guess about something so small it can be seen only with the electron microscope and with X-ray crystallography, and even then without any details? The entities with which they worked are almost unbelievably small. If we were to take the DNA of one cell from each person alive today it could all be contained in a volume the size of a rather large drop of water. How could one conceive a model that would integrate the relevant and authentic contributions of biology, chemistry, and physics regarding this tiny bit of matter? How could one sort out and avoid the fallacious hypotheses generated by speculative microbiologists?

The two checked often with rivals at other institutions who were on the same quest, particularly with Maurice Wilkins and Rosalind Franklin at Kings College in London and with Linus Pauling, Max Delbrück, and R. B. Corey at Cal Tech in Pasadena. These people, at once friends and rivals, were all on the threshold of discovery. Papers were sometimes shared, sometimes filched, and sometimes sequestered. It was a race for knowledge and fame. Professional ethics were honored in the breach as well as in the observance.

When the work was well advanced Watson thought he had found the key, an elegant concept. He laid his solution before Jerry Donahue, an American crystallographer. Donahue told Watson he was using the wrong structural formula for three of the four DNA bases. Watson's "pretty model" was rejected.

The next day Watson got out his cardboard replicas and tried once more to fit the forms in compatible fashion. Suddenly his mind was flooded with a new perception. He saw that one pair of bases could be held together by two hydrogen bonds. If the other pair of bases was juxtaposed in a similar way, they too could be held together by at least two hydrogen bonds. However, any other pairing of the four bases would not give stable hydrogen-bonded structures. His new formulation satisfied Donahue's objection and was in accord with the accepted ratios. Crick, usually skeptical, quickly confirmed the validity of the solution.

It was now lunchtime, February 28, 1953. Watson recalls that Crick "winged into the Eagle [a pub] to tell everyone within hearing distance that we have found the secret of life." Watson was not quite twenty-five years old, on a fellowship, not yet a full-fledged professional. Crick was thirty-six, still without a Ph.D.

The two men quickly built a model which though crude in form was correct in all major respects. The model displayed the DNA molecule in the famed double helix form, corkscrewlike, the two spiraling backbones joined by the hydrogen bond cross-links. It was intricate, novel, consistent with recognized fact, and aesthetically pleasing.

Watson and Crick alerted their rivals of the discovery and specified its details. With professional aplomb but no doubt with disappointment, these competitors quickly confirmed the discovery's validity and offered congratulations. The findings were published by Watson and Crick in *Nature,* the renowned British scientific journal, the issue of April 1953. The discovery was quickly accepted by the scientific community.

Crick thought he had fulfilled his wish — to show that life could be explained totally by physics and chemistry. But other people viewed the matter differently. The artist Salvador Dalí said, "And now the announcement of Watson and Crick about DNA. This is for me the real proof of the existence of God."

Crick, Watson, and Wilkins received the Nobel Prize for their work on nucleic acids in 1962, the awarding officials having waited nine years to be sure the honor was warranted.

With DNA's physical form established and its chemical composition known, microbiologists moved in to advance knowledge farther. Some thirty years after the breakthrough the known facts were these:

The DNA molecule is a double helix; that is, a double thread, coiled like a spring and held together by the hydrogen bond cross-links. It looks like a spiral staircase or, more appropriately, a twisted rope ladder. All DNA molecules have this shape, whether of a cactus, a turtle, or a human being.

The DNA ladder consists of six pieces. The long threads that make up the sides of the ladder contain alternating units of phosphate and a sugar called deoxyribose. The rungs of the ladder are made of the four compounds called bases, abbreviated as A, C, G, and T. They are attached to the sugar units of the ladder's sidepieces. Each rung consists of two bases: A-T, T-A, C-G, or G-C. No other combination is possible because these pairs are chemically attracted to one another by their ability to form the stable hydrogen bonds.

Before the cell divides, the DNA duplicates. The ladder splits lengthwise, separating the bases of each strand. The separated strands are copied as the splitting occurs by synthesizing two new chains having the proper bases for pairing with the opposing bases in the original chains. When the cell divides, each new daughter cell thus receives DNA molecules identical with those of its parent.

RNA (ribonucleic acid), DNA's chemical cousin, is the "master copy," a substance that carries out DNA's instructions for protein production. It is somewhat different in chemical construction and acts as messenger, template, or mold to line up the amino acids in the exact order called for by the DNA of the genes. Occasionally, maybe once in 100,000 times, something goes wrong in this reproductive process; there occurs a mutation. Many of these are lethal and a few are inconsequential, but a very few are advantageous, giving the organism and its descendants greater prospect for survival. Thus evolution comes about.

Knowing now the chemistry, structure, and functioning of the hereditary substance, scientists were in a position to make applications. The stage was set for modifying the germ plasm by techniques variously known as recombinant DNA, gene splicing, and genetic engineering. Scientists went at this with the diligence comparable with that of Watson and Crick in their original discovery. During the 1970s scientists developed techniques for taking genes from a higher organism and splicing them into a piece of bacterial DNA. The resulting new piece of DNA, called recombinant DNA, can then be inserted into a bacterium. In 1980 scientists successfully inserted a new gene into a living animal.

The first applications were in medicine. By the late 1970s researchers had used recombinant DNA techniques to engineer bacteria that produced small amounts of insulin for treating severe diabetes, and interferon, a protein that fights viral infection. By the 1980s human growth hormones were being produced to treat individuals who would not otherwise reach normal height.

Mankind is heir to some three thousand genetically borne diseases. They encompass physical defects, retardation, blood disorders, and crippling diseases that go by such names as Down's syndrome, hemophilia, sickle-cell anemia, Tay-Sachs disease, Lesch-Nyhan syndrome, PNP deficiency, and cystic fibrosis. The potential posed by recombinant DNA for overcoming these human ailments is unpredictable but promising.

The agricultural people are not far behind the medical researchers. They have already developed genetically altered bacteria that can inhibit frost damage to farm crops. The following is a list of research undertakings, all uncertain as to their outcome, but all supportive of hope:

Development of bacteria that would degrade persistent pesticides. This would permit use of chemicals that would otherwise be a threat to the ecology.

Development of biological agents for regulating pests. There is the possibility that a plant virus might kill off unwanted vegetation and leave other life unharmed.

Synthesis of hormones that inhibit insect growth. Spraying these hormones during a critical stage in the life cycle could preclude maturation.

Development of bacteria capable of efficiently converting cellulosic waste to methane gas. This could reduce reliance on petroleum.

Modification of otherwise vulnerable farm crops so that they would tolerate herbicides and insecticides.

Building resistance to various fungal, bacterial, and viral diseases.

Development of plants with resistance to salt and water stress.

Parallel with recombinant DNA and related to it are other products of the new biology that are important to agriculture: embryo transplants, cloning, tissue culture, and growth hormones. Together these developments could raise food production to new heights and provide potent weapons against hunger.

Watson and Crick not only discovered the double helix, they also triggered the transformation of agricultural research witnessed by our generation. When these men began their studies the research paradigm was one man working at his desk or laboratory within a single discipline in the tradition of Liebig, Pasteur, and Mendel. Watson and Crick taught themselves related disciplines. They then associated themselves together as a team. After the breakthrough large multidisciplinary research institutions developed, combining basic with applied work and receiving support from both public and private sources. Henceforward individual contributions increasingly will merge into a team effort and it will be difficult to write a personalized book like this one.

There is widespread apprehension about recombinant DNA, some of it bordering on the hysterical. Horrible creatures are visualized creeping out from under laboratory doors. Already mice of twice normal size have been produced. Imaginary Frankenstein monsters emerge from test tubes. Visions of Hitler are invoked, with his rallying call "we will build a perfect race." There are fears that a hurtful form of bacterium might escape from the test tube to jeopardize the world. Gene splicing may be used by the military for the production of deadly new organisms, allegedly for defense. Who can tell how, when, or if such weapons of biological warfare might be turned loose?

There has long been, deep in the human psyche, a feeling that some knowledge is reserved for God, forbidden to man. In the Greek myth Prometheus was punished for stealing fire from the gods. The Book of Genesis has Adam and Eve banished from the Garden for eating the forbidden fruit of the tree of knowledge of good and evil. The danger of nuclear holocaust is alleged to be punishment for our having stolen the secret of the atom. To some the new biology seemed to usurp from God the power of creation itself. Was this to be condoned?

Counterposed against these misgivings and at the opposite end of the spectrum is the scientist's claim that the pursuit of knowledge of any kind is a proper activity for humanity, that nothing is forbidden. It is argued that constituted authority or public opinion are improper restrictions on scientific investigation. Cases in point: Socrates was condemned to drink hemlock because he asked questions in such a manner as to "make the worse seem the better cause." Galileo was required to recant his proposition that the earth went around the sun. And Vavilov, the Russian biologist, was jailed for opposing Lysenko, the officially supported quack plant breeder. These attacks on free inquiry were obviously contrary to the public interest and are used as a warning that arbitrary and uninformed interference with science is a dangerous thing.

Is genetic engineering in the public interest? Should gene splicing be curbed? Beginning about 1971 the issue was joined. The scientists themselves took the lead in public examination; the subject was considered in a series of seminars, controversies, and proposals. Out of all this came an agreed set of guidelines: experiments funded by the U.S. government must be approved for laboratory safety and scientific soundness by the National Institutes of Health and the Food and Drug Administration. Demands by activist groups for national legislation to govern genetic engineering were defeated. A more moderate approach was adopted — guidelines based on professional counsel.

But opposition to gene splicing continued, led by Jeremy Rifkin, an activist who heads the Foundation on Economic Trends. Rifkin brought suit to prevent scientists from testing their antifrost bacteria and won his case. President Carter set up a Presidential Commission for the Study of Ethical Problems in Medicine and Biomedical and Behavioral Research; the commission was continued under President Reagan. Its recommendation: proceed with caution. In its 1982 report on genetic engineering titled *Splicing Life,* the commission stated: "Human beings have not merely the right but the duty to employ their God-given powers to harness nature for human benefit. To turn away from gene splicing, which may provide a means of curing hereditary diseases, would itself raise serious ethical problems."

But a principle has been established, that the right of scientific activity is not absolute. Social considerations are relevant. Accountability is appropriate. For scientists, the age of innocence is over. Great powers imply great responsibility.

Some ancient issues were illuminated by the Watson-Crick discovery. The continuity of life was affirmed. The life material is split with each generation from the beginning to the present and forward as long as our offspring continue to reproduce. To a reflective person, this gives what Wordsworth called "intimations of immortality."

The theory that acquired characters can be inherited was further discredited. The idea of spontaneous generation was finally interred (except that Crick maintained it had occurred once, 3 or 4 billion years ago).

What of vitalism? Vitalism is the view that there is something additional in the biological realm which cannot be included under the heading of physics or chemistry. Crick thought the idea of vitalism had been disproved but that its ghost would remain, embraced by the lunatic fringe. But other scientists were less dogmatic, recognizing the difficulty of proving the nonexistence of any force or attribute. Can physics and chemistry explain conscience and reverence, those familiar attributes of humanity? People of religious faith found Crick's interpretation unconvincing.

To the scientist, the discovery of Watson and Crick was a sterling piece of research. To the medical doctor and the agriculturist, it was a breakthrough that promised to better the human condition. To those who were apprehensive, it set loose a new evil in the world. And to the person of faith, nothing had really been changed.

REFERENCES

Bareikis, Robert P., ed. 1978. *Science and the Public Interest: Recombinant DNA Research.* Bloomington, Ind.: Poynter Center.

Crick, Francis. 1966. *Of Molecules and Men.* Seattle: Univ. of Washington Press.

"Industrial Microbiology." *Scientific American* (Sept. 1981).

Olby, Robert. 1974. *The Path of the Double Helix.* Seattle: Univ. of Washington Press.

Schrödinger, Erwin. 1946. *What Is Life?* New York: Macmillan.

Stent, Gunther S., ed. 1980. *James D. Watson, the Double Helix, Text, Commentary, Reviews, Original Papers.* New York: W. W. Norton.

U.S. Office of Technology Assessment, U.S. Congress. 1981. *Genetic Technology: A New Frontier.* Boulder, Colo.: Westview Press, F. A. Praeger.

Watson, James D. 1980. *The Double Helix, a Personal Account of the Discovery of the Structure of DNA.* New York: W.W. Norton.

Watson, J. D., and F. H. C. Crick. 1953. "A Structure for Deoxyribonucleic Acid." *Nature,* April 25.

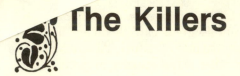

The Killers

PEOPLE OF ROMANTIC BENT like to think of nature as benign, supportive of humanity's noblest needs. Others, struggling with weeds and insects, think of nature as adversary. Actually it is neither; it has no inherent preference for any one kind of creature over another. Left undisturbed, it balances the various species of plants and animals with but one objective: the maximization of life.

People attempt to influence nature's balance in their own interest, killing weeds, insects, and diseases. But despite our best efforts these enemies cut food availability worldwide by about 30 percent. Without modern pesticides food production would be dramatically reduced. Not only would food production plummet, the rate of human survival would fall as well. Lice, flies, rats, mice, fleas, and mosquitoes would spring forth in an unnumbered host, carrying typhus, plague, cholera, yellow fever, and malaria. People, lacking both food and biomedical protection, would perish in unimaginable numbers. The "return to nature" sought by some environmental advocates would shrink both the supply side and the demand side of the food equation.

In this chapter we examine relatively recent scientific advances as they affect both the human population and food production. We look at the relevant fields, the people, and the killing agents. These are:

Antibiotics: Alexander Fleming discovered penicillin in 1928; Selman Waksman found streptomycin in 1944.

Insecticides: Paul Herman Müeller established the potency of DDT in 1939.

Herbicides: E. J. Kraus demonstrated the effectiveness of 2,4-D in 1944.

Biological Controls: Edward Knipling, a pioneer in a unique type of biological control, developed the sterile-male method of controlling screwworms in 1954.

All the pesticides are poisons, killers of insects, bacteria, fungi, weeds, predators, nematodes, and, unless great care is taken, human beings and their friends. All disturb the balance of nature. All are helpful to people in certain ways and are in other ways actually or potentially hurtful to them. So all are controversial.

The use of these killing agents surged during the years after World War II. Their early successes were so great that visionary people hoped for the total abolition of disease. The new wonder drugs were thought of as the "magic bullets" sought by the great German biologist Paul Ehrlich in the early twentieth century. Later and more sober judgments dulled the luster of those early hopes. But on balance and after much experience, these scientific advances represent an enormous net improvement in the human condition.

The first of the four categories, antibiotics, began as an effort to improve human health and spilled over to increase food production. The second, the insecticide DDT, was the product of commercial research and was launched simultaneously into the medical and agricultural fields. The third category, the herbicide 2,4-D, was a result of military research intended to deprive people of food and moved into the agricultural areas, increasing the food supply. The fourth, biological controls, originated in the agricultural area and stayed there.

The first category to be considered is antibiotics and microbial warfare. The number of microorganisms hosted by the average person is so great as to be almost incomprehensible. There are from 100,000 to 1 million microorganisms on a square centimeter of human skin. The alimentary canal contains from 10 to 100 million bacteria for each gram of tissue. The final census of living organisms which cohabit with the average person comes to approximately 100 trillion. Together they make up about a solid pound of living organisms. Under favorable conditions they are capable of doubling their numbers every twenty minutes. These tiny beings exist in proportionate numbers and in similar kinds in animals such as hogs, cattle, sheep, and poultry.

Some of these germs live in warfare with their hosts. Some live in combat with one another. Some are symbiotic, either with their host or their fellow microbes. The effects and side effects of these relationships on the human being may be good or bad as we see it; in any case they are incidental to the microbial purpose, which is to survive and multiply. In a healthy person these organisms exist in a sort of standoff. In an ill person a harmful species probably has gained the upper hand.

Alexander Fleming and Penicillin. Alexander Fleming was a cautious, taciturn, modest Scottish biologist, working at St. Mary's Hospital in London. In September 1928 he was studying a new antiseptic, mercuric chloride, which killed hurtful germs, though at a degree of concentration which the human body could not tolerate. In order to examine the colonies he had cultivated on agar in petri dishes, he had to lift the lids and leave the contents for some time exposed under the microscope, which meant running a risk of contamination.

As was his custom, he set the dishes aside after examination. It was not his habit to tidy up his bench after each operation; he sometimes saved his cultures for a second look, leaving the lids off. On this occasion he reexamined one of his dishes in the presence of his colleague, Merlin Pryce. On it were growing germs of the culture he had established, staphylococci, the cause of pimples, boils, and carbuncles. But there was more. A spore from the dull smoky skies of London had landed in the petri dish. Fleming was surprised to find that the invading organism was killing his culture. In Fleming's words, "This was an extraordinary and unexpected appearance and seemed to demand investigation."

Fleming followed up. Careful experiment established the killing power of the invading mold. He published his findings, giving his mold the name "penicillin" after the killing fungus, penicillium.

The scientific community need not have been surprised at this discovery. Three thousand years ago Chinese physicians used molds and soy flour poultices to cure boils, carbuncles, and infected wounds. Hippocrates, considered the father of medicine, recommended the use of toasted molds to treat disease. Often a country person of former days would apply a poultice of wet mouldy bread to a carbuncle or an infection to "draw the poison out."

But this was all traditional practice, unsupported by any established theory. Fleming supplied the scientific verification and the valid concept that moved a useful practice from the realm of folklore into the world of science. Nothing seems more obvious than a mystery after it is solved, and nothing appears more baffling than the solution to a problem before the answer is postulated.

Fleming's great contribution was to identify and help propagate an organism that has, in the overwhelming proportion of the cases, a benign effect on its human host. Penicillin has the special ability to attack and kill those organisms that cause strep throat, pneumonia, tonsillitis, scarlet fever, childbed fever, erysipelas, wound infections, gonorrhea, syphilis, anthrax, and gangrene.

The method by which penicillin kills is that of keeping the enemy organism from making a cell wall, so that the adversary simply disintegrates. Human cells have walls that are more resistant and so able to withstand attack. The early workers, including Fleming, did their experimental work in the absence of a clear notion regarding the intricacies of interbiotic warfare. That came later.

Fleming's discovery languished for twelve years. The active agent in penicillin could neither be isolated nor concentrated. Finally this problem was solved by Dr. Howard Florey of Australia and Dr. E. B. Chain, who had been born in Berlin. Together these two, working at Oxford, succeeded in freeze-drying the culture liquid, obtaining a brown powder. The antibiotic was used in a test on mice on May 25, 1940 with total success. Later, nine patients were treated with this antibiotic. In all cases the physicians reported, with typical British understatement, that "favorable therapeutic response was obtained."

Penicillin had its advent at the outset of World War II. The need was for an effective agent to treat wounds; penicillin was the ideal answer. It seemed that every report brought new acclaim to "the miracle drug." Preparation and use of the drug skyrocketed. As methods of production improved, costs dropped. In the early days penicillin was more precious than gold. During the war 300,000 units (the daily amount for treating pneumonia) were worth sixty dollars; by 1960 an equal amount sold for one cent. Honors were showered on Fleming; he accepted them with a combination of amazement, embarrassment, and pleasure. In July 1944 he was knighted. On October 25, 1945, along with Florey and Chain, he was awarded the Nobel Prize for Medicine.

Penicillin was receiving worldwide acclaim. But clouds were appearing on the horizon. The enemy organisms which the penicillin attacked were developing resistance, a form of immunity. Stronger doses were tried, but the development of new antibiotics proved a better approach. By 1974 there were at least three thousand different antibiotics and at least thirty thousand derivatives, of which some forty were in general use. Not more than one of every thousand antibiotics found its way into clinical practice. After its introduction a new antibiotic has, on the average, a life of ten years until resistance develops and it must be replaced.

The wide range of the new antibiotics, their low cost, their quick action, and the ease with which they could be administered made it possible to use them in general fashion for large groups of people. Antibiotics have had the clear effect of helping to bring down the human death rate in much of the world, thereby posing a greater challenge to food producers.

Selman Waksman and Streptomycin. Selman Waksman, a Russian-born microbiologist at the New Jersey Agricultural Experiment Station, believed that fungi should be useful for treating animals as well as human beings. He was fascinated by the microorganisms in the soil. He was impressed with the fact that something in the soil destroys harmful microbes. Everything goes back to the earth, all sorts of garbage, wastes, and corpses. Yet the earth counteracts all this, permitting trees and plants to grow and bloom. Fungus growth is the type of life that follows death.

Waksman examined thousands of soil samples, discovering innumerable molds, which are responsible for the characteristic odor of the earth. He described, tested, and classified them. Year after year he labored.

In September 1944 he and his colleagues discovered, in a clod of earth extracted from the throat of a sick chicken, a wonderful therapeutic substance produced by a mold. He called it streptomycin. It proved as effective as penicillin, attacking some of the same organisms and a number of others as well. It is particularly potent against tuberculosis, both in human beings and farm animals. One manifestation of its effectiveness is the closing of tuberculosis sanatoriums throughout the country and the conversion of many of them to retirement homes. Besides tuberculosis streptomycin also attacks pneumonia, infections of the urinary passages, typhoid fever, dysentery, undulant fever, and wound infections. In 1952 Waksman won the Nobel Prize for Medicine, as had Fleming before him.

The agricultural experiment stations, impressed with the work of one of their own, increased their investigations in microbiology, testing known antibiotics and making applications to plants and animals. They found that farm animals responded as readily to antibiotics as did people. The general applicability, the fast action, the low cost, and the minimum of allergic reactions contributed to therapeutic use. Mastitis, an important infectious disease of milk cattle that had long resisted treatment, was suppressed. Bovine tuberculosis, formerly widespread, was nearly eradicated.

Surprisingly, farm animals to which antibiotics were administered for therapeutic purposes not only threw off the disease but grew faster as well. So, instead of limiting the antibiotics to therapeutic use they were added to the feed for all the animals in the herd, well or ill. Various kinds of antibiotics increased the growth rate of chicks by 7 to 16 percent. Pigs showed a 15 percent faster growth rate. Growth rate of calves increased and the incidence of digestive disorders was diminished. These great gains in the rate of growth came at trifling cost; antibiotics were plentiful and cheap. The economic incentive for their use was powerful indeed.

This general use of antibiotics for entire herds and flocks had different results, depending on circumstances. The drug was more effective for young animals than for old, proportionately better for animals on poor than on good rations, more helpful to animals carrying some evidence of disease than to healthy herds, better for animals born as runts than for normal offspring, more advantageous for animals under stress than for those in adjustment, and more rewarding for animals under poor than good management. Animals raised in aseptic conditions show no response to antibiotics. The inference was that most farm animals carried some degree of subclinical infection and therefore were helped by antibiotics.

Antibiotics, which counteracted the bad effect of stress and unsanitary conditions, permitted farmers to manage their animals in huge flocks and herds rather than in the small groupings that had earlier been necessary. The size of poultry, swine, dairy, and cattle feeding establishments increased dramatically. Protests arose. Some people resented the transformation of agriculture permitted (caused?) by antibiotics. There was indignation at the inferior types of husbandry made tolerable by antibiotics. An indiscriminate aversion to chemistry and food additives had arisen for a variety of reasons and was directed at antibiotics. Perhaps most important, concern arose that general feeding of antibiotics would cause resistance to develop in the enemy organisms. These newly resistant microbes, it was feared, might escape to the human population where they would be immune to the standard antibiotics. The concern was that general treatment of animals might deprive the people of this wondrous new means of preventing human disease.

Evidence regarding this issue is in dispute. In April 1980, the National Research Council maintained that existing studies neither proved nor disproved a link between antibiotic use, resistant bacteria, and human disease. Restrictions on the use of antibiotics are in abeyance in the United States. For livestock production antibiotics mean a great gain but their use posed a potential danger for human health.

In the Third World antibiotics produced greater gains in population numbers than in food production. Were it not for other achievements, antibiotics would, on the average, have worsened the human condition in the developing countries. What is the gain in saving lives with medicine and then losing them by starvation?

The second category concerns insecticides, the high-tech assassins. Even after all our dusting and spraying, insects chew up or otherwise destroy approximately 10 percent of the crops and livestock in the United States. In countries where protection of plants and animals is less sophisticated the proportionate damage is far greater.

The loss to the human population through mortality and morbidity from insect-borne diseases (malaria, typhus, yellow fever, dysentery, plague, sleeping sickness) is beyond measure. Malaria is the number one killer of mankind. It affects one-sixth of the human race.

Until recent years methods of coping with insects were almost as hazardous to the applicator as to the insects. Lead arsenate was sprayed on apple trees to control the codling moth. Paris green was used to kill potato bugs, and hydrogen cyanide was applied as a fumigant. These chemicals, lethal to human beings, were often applied by people who knew little about their use so that death and injury to the applicators were at high rates.

In 1935, Paul Henry Müeller, a chemist employed by the Swiss firm J. R. Geigy, began to study insecticides. Müeller, a native Swiss, became convinced that a "contact" or "touch" insecticide would possess much better prospects than the oral poisons such as the arsenates then in use. Like Waksman, he ran hundreds of trials, spraying his chemicals into large glass chambers containing houseflies or other insects. A certain class of chemicals (chlorinated hydrocarbons) consistently seemed more effective than others. He dropped the less promising agents and focused more closely on those that were most effective.

Finally, in 1939, Müeller tried dichloro-diphenyl-trichloro-ethane, its name now mercifully shortened to DDT. This was a grayish-white powder whose preparation had been in the literature since 1873, described in the doctoral dissertation of an Austrian student named Othmar Zeidler. It had been considered of academic interest only and never as an insecticide. Müeller found DDT to be amazingly effective: "My fly cage was so toxic after a period that even after a very thorough cleaning of the cage, untreated flies, on touching the walls, fell to the floor."

Müeller perceived DDT to be relatively safe. It works through its effect on the nervous system and is a persistent, long-lived chemical, resisting biodegradation. Its effective life varies with its surroundings, being longer in field and stream than in the living body. The half-life of a pesticide is the amount of time required for half the original amount to be broken down or otherwise to disappear. According to clinical toxicologist Richard T. Rappolt, Sr., "The half-life of DDT in fat tissue is approximately three to six months." This is long by comparison with most other agents. The persistence of DDT was first thought to be a great advantage, reducing the need for frequent applications. Later, as we shall see, it was considered a major fault.

In past wars insect-borne diseases took far greater toll than did bullets, bombs, and bayonets. Not so in World War II. The Allies learned of DDT and quickly put it into use. The United States War Production Board conferred on DDT the same priority as on penicillin. It was used in the jungles of Burma, on the beachhead of Morotai, in European refugee camps, and on dozens of Pacific islands. Soldiers and sailors by the millions carried small cans of DDT powder to protect themselves from lice, bedbugs, and mosquitoes. DDT was one of the wonders of the age. In 1948, Paul Müeller was awarded the Nobel Prize for his discovery.

When the war was over the military men returned to their farms and their homes, intending to use this insecticide for the protection of their families and their crops. It was released for widespread civilian medical and agricultural use and production exploded. U.S. output increased from 10 million pounds in 1944 to over 100 million pounds by 1951. Production peaked at 188 million pounds in 1962-63. By 1976 William Lowrance would write that, worldwide, 4.4 billion pounds of DDT had been released into the biosphere. This is equal to a mass whose base is a city block and whose height is equal to that of a twenty story building.

With what consequences were these enormous amounts of poison released into the environment?

First, the effect on human health: This from a 1945 statement of Brig. Gen. James Stevens Simmons, chief of the U.S. Army's Preventive Medicine Service: "Armed with DDT, the Army has conquered the fear of typhus. For the first time in history, this ruthless companion of disaster, famine and poverty has lost all right to its murderous title of champion of the ancient plagues of war." And here is a passage from a 1973 technical report of the World Health Organization of the United Nations: "More than 100 million people are now living in areas that have been freed from the endemic form of the disease (malaria). . . . The withdrawal of this compound (DDT) from public health use at this time would give rise to immense problems and expose large populations to outbreaks of endemic and epidemic malaria." Lowrance wrote in 1976: "Massive occupational exposures, or accidental ingestions, even by children, have not been known to cause a single death anywhere in the world in the 35 years of DDT history."

Second, the effect on agricultural production: Farmers, seeing the effect of DDT and its related chemicals, quickly expanded its use. From 1939 to 1954 manufacturers' shipments of pesticides increased from $9.2 million to $174.6 million. During the period since World War II (the span that coincides with the availability of DDT and other insecticides), the per acre yield of crops in the United States doubled. It is impossible to measure the separate effects of insecticides, fertilizer, herbicides, better varieties, weather variations, and improved tillage. But the farmers' behavior makes clear their favorable assessment of DDT and its companions.

Third, the effects on insects: As DDT was poured on, insects began to develop immunity to it. They have been thus coping with and overcoming challenges throughout the ages. No insect species is known to have disappeared from the earth because of human activities. The rapid insect reproduction rates expedited the development of resistant insect strains. A pair of houseflies reproducing at maximum rate could multiply to an unbelievable 190 quintillion in just four months' time. Flies began to develop immunity, as did mosquitoes and field insects. Altogether some 150 species of insects and mites have developed resistance to major pesticides.

The pesticide companies brought out new chemicals, more effective and less persistent than DDT but sometimes more costly and more dangerous to the applicator. Soon the market abounded with insecticides, varied in their toxicity, specificity, cost, and persistence. Including herbicides, insecticides, and other poisons there are some two thousand pesticides used in the United States. To these new chemicals the insects began their adaptations. It was like warfare; the offense gains the initiative and the defense counters. Then a new offensive initiative and a new defensive move. And so on, endlessly. Ultimate and total victory for either protagonist seems unlikely.

Fourth, the effect on the biosphere: DDT, a persistent chemical, began to permeate the environment. Dairy cattle, housed in barns sprayed to control flies, picked up the chemical and transmitted it to their milk, to be ingested by children. Runoff from treated fields got into the streams. Birds ate insects killed by DDT, concentrated the chemical in their bodies, and died. Some wildlife species were reduced in numbers because of DDT. Human beings picked up the chemical through their food and lodged it within themselves. DDT was found in mothers' milk. It was found in the Arctic snows and in tropical streams. Everyone knew it was a poison; that was the reason for its existence. The demonstrated ability of DDT to cause cancer in test animals when fed in very large quantities led to the fear that its pervasiveness was causing an increase in human cancer. This whole matter came to a head in 1962 with the publication of Rachel Carson's influential book *Silent Spring*. The doleful title expressed the prospect that DDT and its companion chemicals would kill the wildlife and there would be no birds left to sing. So DDT was banned (except for limited special uses) effective December 31, 1972.

What happened to food production in the United States after DDT was banned? Crop yields did not decline; in fact, they continued to increase. Alternative methods of insect suppression arose, new chemicals, natural controls, better cultural practices, and integrated pest management.

And there is no real evidence that human health in the United States was affected one way or another. Some countries cut back on the use of DDT as they reduced their antimalarial campaigns, either because of concern for the environment or belief that the antimalarial campaign had been won. In recent years the incidence of malaria has increased. According to the World Health Organization, Sri Lanka, which had just 17 cases of malaria in 1963, had 149,000 in 1984.

What happended to the environment after DDT and some of its cohorts were banned? Some esteemed wildlife species increased (fish, eagles, songbirds). Some disfavored species also increased (mosquitoes, gypsy moths, fireants). Whether an observer considered the banning a success or a failure depended on whether he or she liked or disliked this combination of events.

Worldwide, DDT and its cohort of insecticides very likely increased the rate of human survival more than they increased the output of food. They increased the demand for food more than they increased the supply and so laid an additional challenge on food producers.

The third category, herbicides, involves "induced suicide." Weeds are as old as agriculture. According to the Book of Genesis, Adam, the first man, was punished for his sin by having to contend with thorns and thistles. By definition a weed is an unwanted plant. There are about eighteen thousand weed species in the world that are sufficiently important to cause serious economic damage. Weeds compete with crops for moisture, sunlight, plant food, and space. In 1965, losses from weeds in the United States equalled the combined losses from insects and diseases and were second only to those caused by erosion. In the Third World more labor is spent controlling weeds than on any other farm task.

There is a tendency to infer foreign origin for some of our most troublesome weeds. The Russian thistle, a weed of the Great Plains, is an example. The Jerusalem artichoke, a bad weed, is neither an artichoke nor is it from Jerusalem; it is native to North America. (The habit of blaming foreigners is not confined to weeds. There is the English sparrow, the European corn borer, the Dutch elm disease, and the Mexican bean beetle. No domestic bug is named the American beetle.)

For the first ten thousand years of agriculture, farmers tried to cope with weeds by pulling, hoeing, and plowing. Ten thousand years of fighting for their lives have made weeds tough. They propagate at prodigious rates. A single pigweed can produce 100,000 seeds. The seeds of curly dock have been known to lie in the soil, dormant but viable, for seventy years, awaiting the propitious time to sprout.

In the years since World War II there has been more progress in weed control than in all the previous years since agriculture began. This came with the development of herbicides, literally "plant killers." Herbicides are in the process of transforming agriculture.

The first major herbicide and the most widely used is 2,4-D, a soluble white crystalline solid, bearing the awesome technical name, 2,4-dichlorophenoxyacetic acid. 2,4-D was first intended as a weapon of war to destroy the growing crops of the enemy. It then became an instrument of peace, a killer of weeds. During the Vietnam War it reverted to the military arsenal. As this is written it is again a farm chemical.

Normally a plant grows through the influence and direction of hormones operating within the plant, telling it where, when, and how to grow. 2,4-D is a synthesized deranged growth hormone. It scrambles the normal messages so that the plant grows in strange and disorderly ways. The leaves twist, the stem is contorted, tumors are formed, photosynthesis is inhibited, and the vascular system becomes plugged. Death occurs in a matter of days or weeks. The plant literally grows itself to death; it is induced to commit suicide.

Most important of the scientists who worked on growth regulators was E. J. Kraus, head of the botany department of the University of Chicago. By 1942 he, with his students, had begun to understand the functioning of growth hormones and had acquired some ideas about how they could be manipulated. When World War II broke out the U.S. Army contracted with the University of Chicago for continuation of Kraus's experiments. The work was entirely war related, strictly secret, and intent on the destruction of crops. During 1944 and 1945 Kraus directed the synthesis and testing of nearly 1,100 substances, first in the laboratory and then in greenhouses. He was repeating the methods used by Fleming, Waksman, and Müeller in the discovery of penicillin, streptomycin, and DDT. From all this testing 2,4-D was singled out as the most promising.

In March 1944 experiments were made on the sensitivity of various plants to 2,4-D. Among these were common weeds, particularly bindweed. Broadleaf weeds, targeted with even very small amounts of a dilute spray, quickly became twisted and misshapen, dying in a few days. The grasses, including the cereals, appeared to tolerate the chemical.

2,4-D was not used in World War II. With the end of the war in the summer of 1945, the veil of secrecy was lifted. Workers in the state agricultural experiment stations began extensive field testing. Various crops and weeds were classified as to whether they were killed by the chemical or whether they were able to survive it.

The U.S. Department of Agriculture quickly sought to learn whether the chemical was toxic to human beings or animals; all tests proved negative. To clinch the point, Kraus announced that he personally ingested one-half gram of 2,4-D per day for three weeks with absolutely no effect. The U.S. Department of Agriculture concluded that the chemical was safe.

2,4-D was found to be biodegradable and nontoxic to soil organisms at normal field rates of application. Its half-life in the soil was found to be about two weeks. Appropriate practices were developed by the experiment stations. Timing, effectiveness, and methods of application were determined. Application was by hand-carried knapsack, tractor-drawn sprayer, and airplane. There was preplanting, preemergence, and postemergence application. Both dusts and sprays were used. The chemical was not only judged safe; it was easy to use, and it quickly became cheap. It cost $12.50 per pound in 1944; by 1950 a pound sold for $0.50. Use of the chemical skyrocketed. In 1945, total production came to 917,000 pounds; by 1950 production had increased twenty times.

Whole new families of herbicides were developed. Soon the market was plentifully supplied with an assortment of herbicides, increasingly specific for the more troublesome weeds, sparing the growing crop. Some eighty crops are protected by 2,4-D. There are thirty different herbicides used to protect corn alone. In 1984 herbicides were used on 93 percent of the corn acreage in the United States.

The development of herbicides constituted one of the most noteworthy scientific advances in agriculture. One of the great contributions of herbicides is that with proper use they permit limited tillage; that is, the growing of crops with minimal disturbance to the soil. On hilly ground this can reduce the amount of erosion by as much as 80 percent. In the long run this may turn out to be more important than their effect in killing weeds or contributing to the military effort. We shall read more of this in the next chapter.

The herbicides work to increase the food side of the equation that balances food with people. Working exclusively on plants, they do not increase the human population. Thus they increase per capita food supplies and better the human condition.

Not all is euphoric about the herbicides, though some early assessments gave the impression that it was. Air currents can carry the spray to adjoining fields, wiping out vulnerable crops. Weeds can develop resistance, and at least five major species have done so. Sometimes the killing of one weed species leads not to the flourishing of the crop but to the sudden appearance of a new weed species, tolerant to the herbicide. Excessive applications of particular herbicides can leave residue problems for next year's crop.

Though herbicides were not used during World War II or during the Korean War, the U.S. air force developed an operational capability. It began to look as if the herbicides had made a transition from their war-related origin to peacetime agricultural use. But this was not to be.

Associated with 2,4-D is its more lethal cousin 2,4,5-trichlorophenoxy acetic acid, known as 2,4,5-T. These two, mixed half and half, form Agent Orange, which was used to defoliate forests during the fighting in Southeast Asia. Dioxin, a contaminant sometimes found in 2,4,5-T, is one of the most dangerous of all poisons. Its fearsome chemical name is 2,3,7,8-tetrachlorodibenzo-P-dioxin and its shorthand name is TCDD. It was sometimes present, for the greater part unknown and its dangers unsuspected, in Agent Orange.

By 1969, 4 million acres in Southeast Asia had been sprayed. Rates of application were about 27 pounds per acre, up to ten times the usual recommended domestic rate. The results were considered militarily helpful; defoliation reduced the usefulness of the enemy's jungle hideouts and made ambushes more difficult. But associated effects were judged by most observers to be adverse. In December 1969 Dr. Arthur W. Galston, a Yale professor of biology, reported these effects to a subcommittee on national security policy:

1. *Ecological damage.* Mangrove forests along the river estuaries were killed. As a result, banks were eroded. Wildlife habitat was destroyed and therewith the wildlife itself.

2. *Inadvertent agricultural damage.* Useful plants were killed by the heavy rates of application. Truck crops and rubber trees perished. Deprived of their food supplies, refugees flowed into the cities.

3. *Effect on people.* The contaminant dioxin, which was often found in 2,4,5-T at the time the agent was used in Vietnam, is known from laboratory tests to be teratogenic; that is, it can modify the development of the fetus during gestation, producing abnormal offspring. It probably produces mutations. It is a tumor initiator, a carcinogen, a cancer producer. Dioxin is persistent. Its half-life in the soil varies from 200 to 340 days.

Great controversy arose. Apart from tests on laboratory animals, what were the actual effects on people? There was a conflict of testimony. The evidence from laboratory experiments with test animals is insufficient either clearly to condemn the suspected agent or to exonerate it. Dr. Samuel Epstein of the Cancer Research Foundation and the Harvard Medical School addressed this question. (Here the discussion broadens to include other chemicals, not just the herbicides.) Dr. Epstein pointed out that if a suspected agent produces cancer or birth abnormalities in one of ten thousand human beings, the chances of detecting this in a test group of fewer than fifty rats is very low. Hence, to increase the likelihood of detection the trials involve dosages far above normal levels, but this reduces the relevance of the findings. Furthermore, test animals may be either more or less sensitive to the suspected agent than are human beings. The drug Meclizine produces abnormal offspring in the rat but apparently not in a restricted number of human beings studied. With thalidomide apparently the reverse is true; human beings appear to be sixty times more sensitive than mice. Says Dr. Epstein, "Attempts to determine a safe level of thalidomide, based on animal teratogenicity data would clearly expose humans to significant teratogenic hazards." The inference is that the same is true of 2,4,5-T and its sometime contaminant, dioxin.

People argued that these chemicals affected the sperm and egg cells, that they were capable of producing monsters, and that because of genetic continuity it would not be possible to declare them safe until the offspring of exposed individuals were shown to be normal and to produce normal children for several generations. This of course made the case for total banning.

Throughout, there persisted the public perception—which scientists know to be an illusion—that absolute safety is a possible thing and that risk can be reduced to zero. To a people who had learned about the disastrous European experience with thalidomide, who had read Rachel Carson, who had come to think that science was running wild, and who were basically opposed to the Vietnam War, indictments such as Dr. Galston's were totally persuasive. Mightily reinforcing the antitechnology mood were the PBB, DBCP, Kepone, and Bhopal disasters.

When the Vietnam War came to an end the Agent Orange inventory, 8.7 million liters, was incinerated. Dioxin is the object of all-out opposition. 2,4,5-T has been banned except for limited use. 2,4-D and most of its companion herbicides continue in use as before, though under suspicion. As this is written the controversy still rages. Agriculture's chemical killers, whether antibiotics, insecticides, or herbicides, have drawn widespread public disapproval. In some respects it is an antichemical age. Whether the chemical danger is as great as is popularly believed is unclear, based on the evidence. But in public affairs the perception borders on the reality and becomes the guide to action.

Thus there has developed a search for biological controls so that the foes of food production, whether diseases, insects, or weeds, would be restrained by natural enemies rather than by man directly. To this field of science we now turn.

The fourth category, biological controls, or the "hired guns" is the final classification discussed. In the Old West when a man had an enemy he would like to see killed but considered it inappropriate to do the job himself he might engage a "hired gun." In a way that is how we now use biological controls to kill insects, diseases, vermin, and weeds. As in the Old West, it is important that the hired killers confine themselves to the enemy and don't shoot up the town.

The technical definition of biological contol is "the action of parasites, predators, pathogens, host resistance, autosterilization and genetic manipulation in maintaining another organism at a lower average than would occur in their absence." Organisms have their natural adversaries; the purpose of biological control is to tilt the scales against the undesired species. Biological controls have a long history. In the 1880s the U.S. Department of Agriculture imported vedalia beetles from Australia to control the cottony-cushion scale which threatened California's citrus crop. Another California pest, the grape leaf skeletonizer, was controlled by a virus disease brought in from Arizona.

The use of biological controls throughout the world peaked during the 1930s, when fifty different natural enemies of unwanted species had become established at various places. Despite some successes most attempts at biological control either have met with failure or have been only partially successful.

After World War II, when the chemical pesticides came in, biological controls were phased out. As seen by the enthusiasts for chemicals, the new killing agents replaced biological controls. It was thought that the chemicals could do the job without help. This began to change when pests developed resistance to the new chemicals and when some desired species were inadvertently killed. Public protest arose and certain of the chemicals were banned.

Biological controls have been used in an attempt to control the gypsy moth. They were used in Australia to suppress the rabbit population. They have been employed to kill weeds. The example we examine involves the use of a contraceptive technique in the insect world.

E. Knipling and the Screwworm. The screwworm is native to the tropical Western Hemisphere and is found in the Gulf Coast states. The adult is a large fly. The female lays two to four hundred eggs near the wound of a warm-blooded animal; cattle and sheep cut by barbed wire, castration, or dehorning are ready hosts. The eggs hatch within twelve hours and the maggots begin to feed on the damaged tissues. They burrow into the flesh and, if undeterred, can kill a full-grown steer in ten days.

Edward J. Knipling took on this formidable enemy. Knipling was born of German stock in 1909 in Port Lavaca, Texas, the ninth of ten children. He grew up on a small cotton and livestock farm along the Texas Gulf Coast, contending with two of the South's worst insect pests, screwworm and boll weevil, his interest in insect control being thus understandable. The only boy of his family to pursue a higher education, he received his bachelor's degree in entomology from Texas A & M in 1930 and his doctoral degree from Iowa State University in 1947.

Knipling had only one employer during his entire career—the U.S. Department of Agriculture. He worked with the new insecticide DDT when it was released but found it not well adapted to control of the screwworm.

In the back of Knipling's mind was an idea that had developed through conversation with his co-worker, Raymond C. Bushland, while working in the screwworm laboratory in Texas before the war. Here he learned the life cycle and the sex life of this insect. Knipling's notion was that if screwworm flies could be raised in large numbers in the laboratory, sterilized, and released, they would mate with native females, which would then be incapable of producing fertile eggs. Screwworm populations would therefore drop and the insect would no longer be a pest.

To succeed, Knipling had to (1) raise very large numbers of screwworm flies; (2) sterilize the adult males without reducing their competitive reproductive vigor; (3) estimate the numbers of the target population so as to know how many sterile males to release; (4) ascertain and assess the potential harm that might come from release; and (5) find a way to distribute the flies.

All of these things Knipling did. He raised his males, 2.75 billion of them, from maggots that fed on hamburger. He sterilized them with gamma rays from Cobalt 60. He released his flies from an airplane at precisely the right time.

The first trial was at Sanibel, an island off the coast of Florida. The result was indecisive. The sterilized males mated with the native females and reproduction was averted, as hoped. But the island was too close to the coast and new flies quickly came in. The next trial, in 1954, was on the island of Curaçao in the Caribbean, out of insect flight range from the mainland. This trail was completely successful.

Knipling's technique was used successfully in the southeastern United States in 1958. Suppression was achieved over the grazing lands of Texas starting in 1962. Mexico and the United States engaged in an effort to control the insect in all of Mexico north of the Isthmus of Tehuantepec. As this is written the screwworm has been virtually eliminated in the United States and most of Mexico except for sporadic outbreaks that are soon supressed. As the screwworm was overcome production of beef, lamb, and wool increased.

For his achievement Knipling received the Rockefeller Public Service Award and the prestigious Hoblitzelle Award. In 1966 he was elected a member of the National Academy of Sciences. His achievement must rank with the most innovative, newsworthy, and successful among the endeavors of agricultural science. The development of resistance, which had plagued those who relied on pesticides, was no worry to Knipling. Denied the normal process of procreation, screwworms have not been able to find an alternative.

How promising are biological controls? Can we expect that they will replace the antibiotics, the insecticides, and the herbicides? Not likely. There are thousands of weed species that cause economic damage. No one has done a census of the number of insects we would like to do without. And the species of disease-causing microorganisms are numerous beyond reckoning. The chances of coping with this horde of enemies by biological controls alone are quite remote.

In fact, no one technique is capable by itself of suppressing adequately the multitude of threats to plant and animal health — not chemicals alone, nor antibiotics, nor biological controls, nor cultural practices, nor breeding for resistance. These must be used together, in balanced fashion, as the U.S. Department of Agriculture is attempting to do with the gypsy moth. Much remains to be learned; we should not expect that in a single generation we would make optimum use of the tradition-shattering discoveries that have poured out of our experimental laboratories.

Antibiotics and insecticides were the key to bringing down the human death rate. Nothing like it had happened before. Table 18.1 shows that in the most populous parts of the world the death rate has been reduced by half in thirty years. This has permitted a doubling of the population. The amazing fact is that farmers and agricultural scientists have been able to feed these increased numbers of people. If agriculture is to continue this performance it will need all the tools an intelligent society can provide, including the enlightened use of chemicals. As with gene splicing, accountability is the key.

Table 18.1 Deaths per Thousand of Population, 1950 and 1980

	1950	1980	Percent Decline
Sub-Sahara Africa	29.3	17.7	40
Middle East and North Africa	24.0	12.6	47
South Asia	28.8	14.5	50
East Asia	27.1	10.5	61
China	27.3	7.9	71
Latin America and the Caribbean	16.6	8.5	49
Industrialized countries	10.5	9.1	13

Source: World Bank, 1984, *World Development Report,* 64.

REFERENCES

Antibiotics

Fleming, Sir Alexander. 1946. *Penicillin, Its Practical Application.* Philadelphia: Blakiston.

Goldberg, Herbert S. 1959. *Antibiotics, Their Chemistry and Non-Medical Uses.* Princeton, N.J.: D. Van Nostrand.

Lappé, Marc. 1982. *Germs That Won't Die.* Garden City, N.Y.: Anchor Press.

Maurois, Andre. 1959. *The Life of Sir Alexander Fleming.* New York: E. P. Dutton.

Stodola, Frank H. 1968. *Penicillin: Breakthrough to the Era of Antibiotics.* In *Science for Better Living,* USDA Yearbook.

Welch, Henry, and Felix Marti-Ibañez. 1960. *The Antibiotic Saga.* New York: Medical Encyclopedia.

Insecticides

Carson, Rachel. 1962. *Silent Spring.* Boston: Houghton Mifflin.

Ireland, C. H. de, and R. Truan. 1954. *15 Years of Geigy Pest Control.* Basle: Geigy.

Lowrance, William W. 1976. *Of Acceptable Risk.* Los Altos, Calif.: William Kaufmann.

Perkins, John H. 1982. *Insects, Experts, and the Insecticide Crisis.* New York: Plenum Press.

Ridgeway, R. L., J. C. Tinney, J. T. MacGregor, and N. H. Starler. 1978. "Pesticide Use in Agriculture." For publication in *Environmental Health Perspectives* (Jan.), proceedings of a workshop on Higher Plant Systems as Monitors of Environmental Mutagens, sponsored by the National Institute of Environmental Health Service, Marineland, Fla.

USDA Yearbook. 1952. *Insects.* Washington, D.C.: U.S. Government Printing Office.

————. 1968. *Science for Better Living.* Washington, D.C.: U.S. Government Printing Office.

————. 1975. *That We May Eat.* Washington, D.C.: U.S. Government Printing Office.

World Health Organization. 1973. *Safe Use of Pesticides.* WHO Technical Report 513, Geneva.

Herbicides

Bovey, Rodney W., and Alvin L. Young. 1980. *The Science of 2,4,5-T and Associated Phenoxy Herbicides.* New York: Wiley Interscience.

Klingman, Glenn C., Floyd M. Ashton, and Lyman J. Noordhoff. 1975. *Weed Science: Principles and Practices.* New York: Wiley Interscience.

Perkins, John H. 1982. *Insects, Experts, and the Insecticide Crisis.* New York: Plenum Press.

Peterson, Gale E. 1967. "The Discovery and Development of 2,4-D." *Agricultural History* 41, no. 3 (July):243–54.

Warren, G. F. 1980. "Integrated Crop Protection: State of the Art for Weeds and Their Control." Personal paper, West Lafayette, Ind.

Whiteside, Thomas. 1971. *The Withering Rain: America's Herbicidal Folly.* New York: E. P. Dutton.

Biological Controls

Charudattan, R., and H. L. Walker. 1982. *Biological Control of Weeds with Pathogens*. New York: Wiley Interscience.
Perkins, John H. 1982. *Insects, Experts, and the Insecticide Crisis*. New York: Plenum Press.
USDA Beltsville Agricultural Research Center (George C. Papavizas, ed.). 1981. *Biological Control in Crop Production*. Allanheld Osmun, N.J.: Beltsville.
USDA Yearbook. 1953. *Plant Diseases*. Washington, D.C.
_____. 1968. *Science for Better Living*. Washington, D.C.
_____. 1975. *That We May Eat*. Washington, D.C.
Van den Bosch, Robert, P. S. Messenger, and A. P. Gutierrez. 1982. *An Introduction to Biological Control*. New York: Plenum Press.

CHAPTER 19

Hugh Bennett and the Fight for Soil Conservation

We didn't inherit the land from our fathers,
we are borrowing it from our children.

—Old Amish saying

A THIN LAYER OF TOP SOIL is all that lies between us and disaster. No one has made that case more persuasively than Hugh Hammond Bennett, the father of soil conservation. Hear him on the subject: "So direct, in fact, is the relationship between soil erosion, the productivity of the land, and the prosperity of a people, that the history of mankind, to a considerable degree at least, may be interpreted in terms of the soil and what has happened to it as the result of human use."

In the Middle East, once a land of milk and honey, erosion has denuded the hills, exposing their rocky ribs. In China, the rolling lands of the interior have been eroded, the resulting silt raising the Yellow River above its floodplain to the peril of those who live in the lower valley. In the Himalayas, the Andes, Central America, and the mountains of Africa, population pressure has pushed cultivation farther and farther up the slopes, stripping away the protective forest, laying the soil bare to the pounding rain. Even in that new country the United States, opened for farming only during the last few centuries, wind and water erosion have already taken their toll. Throughout much of the world the rivers overflow, tawny with silt, after each heavy rain.

With the soil surface unprotected and with sloping land, this is what happens: raindrops strike the surface at a speed of about fifteen miles an hour, shattering the crumbly soil structure. If the land is saturated the detached particles are floated off, down the slope, in suspension. This is called sheet erosion. If the rain continues the moving water gathers and forms rivulets, cutting little ditches into the topsoil, a form of damage known as rill erosion. If the rainfall is heavy and the slope steep the runoff funnels to the natural waterway, gouging, widening, and deepening the trough, making an ugly scar. Such is gully erosion. American farming practice, following the teaching of the eighteenth-century eccentric Jethro Tull, aggravated erosion by deep plowing, frequent cultivation, tillage up and down the slope, and leaving the soil surface bare. An American Indian may have been right when he said, the first time he saw a ploughed field, "Wrong side up."

Wind erosion occurs when land surface is flat, rainfall is limited, fields are large, vegetation is sparse, and winds are strong. Then the topsoil is torn loose. Sharp, coarse particles, too heavy to be airborne, are hurled along the surface, cutting off tender young growth, piling up in dunes around fences and buildings. The lighter dust particles are lifted thousands of feet in the air and can be carried across the continent.

In 1938 Hugh Bennett estimated that 50 million acres of United States cropland, one-eighth of the total, were "ruined," and another 50 million were "severly damaged" by wind and water erosion. According to Bennett it takes from two hundred to one thousand years for nature to build an inch of topsoil. With clean tillage on slopes of from 8 to 10 degrees, an inch of topsoil could be eroded in from two to seven years. A covering of dense vegetation, says Bennett, is three hundred times more effective in retaining soil and six times more effective in retaining water than clean-tilled crops on the same kind of land.

Hugh H. Bennett was born, one of nine children, on April 15, 1881, on a 1,200-acre plantation in Anson County, in the Piedmont country of south-central North Carolina. The farm, hilly, erosive, and worn-out by continuous cropping of corn and cotton, imparted its difficulties to the family.

Young Bennett worked hard, saved money, and entered the University of North Carolina at Chapel Hill. For his studies he chose geology and chemistry, a reflection of his strong interest in the soil. He was exposed briefly to the principles of economics as found in the works of Adam Smith and John Stuart Mill, but this inoculation did not take.

Bennett, the young college graduate, was six feet one inch tall, broad of shoulder, outgoing and friendly, with an easy southern drawl. "Big Hugh" they called him. He had a way with language, written and spoken, and he had a way with people. He was full of enthusiasm, a worker, a showman, and a gifted promoter.

On graduation Bennett took a job with the U.S. Department of Agriculture as a soil surveyor in Davidson County, Tennessee. A soil surveyor tramps the land with his auger, classifying soil and topography. The purpose is to map the soils according to categories set up on the basis of parent material, chemical composition, internal drainage, and slope. The belief is that this will be helpful to anyone intent on using the land: farmers, foresters, roadbuilders, miners, and urban developers. Bennett invested a quarter of a century in thus acquiring direct knowledge of the land. He got into every state of the Union and many of the counties, assembling what was perhaps a greater practical knowledge of the soil than any other man before or since. After his reputation was established, Bennett did soil survey work in the Canal Zone, Alaska, Honduras, and Cuba. He became an internationally known soil expert.

Much of what he saw grieved him. In Stewart County, Georgia, was a "master gully" named Providence Cave, so called because it caved in the land near Providence Church. The gully, nearly 200 feet deep had swallowed up some of the best farmland in southwestern Georgia. It toppled a barn, a schoolhouse, a tenant house, and most of the churchyard with fifty graves.

In the United States, with its seemingly inexhaustible prairies and fertile valleys, the ethic of man's relation to the land was predominantly one of exploitation. That soil resources were finite and could be dissipated was not part of the general perception. In 1909, the Bureau of Soils, U.S. Department of Agriculture, released Bulletin 55, *Soils of the United States,* written by Bennett's chief. It contains this passage: "The soil is the one indestructible, immutable asset that the Nation possesses. It is the one resource that cannot be exhausted; it cannot be used up." This view had academic endorsement. David Ricardo, the foremost economic theorizer regarding land, whom many of the professionals in the U.S. Department of Agriculture had studied, wrote in the early nineteenth century of "the original and indestructible powers of the soil." Bennett took on the task of teaching people to love the land. This matchmaker promoted a romance that was variously ardent, contentious, and fickle. But after his intervention the relationship would never again be of indifference.

In 1927 Congress appropriated $160,000 for "investigation of the causes of soil erosion." Bennett was put in charge. He quickly initiated work in Oklahoma, Texas, Kansas, Wisconsin, Washington, Iowa, Missouri, Ohio, and North Carolina. The appropriation averaged less than $20,000 per project, a small amount even in that day. Obviously the investigations could not be deep. The objective was to get visibility as well as facts. In 1928, after a quarter-century in the field, Bennett wrote U.S. Department of Agriculture Circular 33, *Soil Erosion, a National Menace.* The fact that the department would publish it was evidence that interest was finally stirring.

Nature and politics combined to lay the basis for the conservation movement of the 1930s. Severe drought scorched the vegetation of the Great Plains, exposing the fragile soil. Fierce winds ripped up the dirt, piling it in drifts ten feet high and lifting it twenty thousand feet in the air, carrying it to the East Coast and hundreds of more miles out to sea. By 1933 Roosevelt's New Deal had taken over and change was afoot. Protecting our soul resources was an attractive initiative. The Soil Erosion Service was set up in the Interior Department. Bennett was put in charge.

President Roosevelt supported the new effort strongly and his cabinet quickly got the message. Three months after the agency was formed Bennett received $5 million from the Interior Department to support his program. Shortly thereafter came another $5 million. Then came yet another $5 million, which Bennett turned down because he couldn't gear up his program that fast. But the Interior Department insisted that he take it with instructions to turn it back to the Treasury only if he couldn't use it. Propelled by zeal and supplied with money, Bennett's Soil Erosion Service grew with amazing speed. In his first full year of operation he trebled the number of his employees to 6,622. He had demonstration projects going in thirty-one states, covering 4 million acres.

Bennett's home agency was the Department of Agriculture. He was instrumental in making the soil conservation initiative a permanent agency and transferring it from the Interior Department to the Department of Agriculture, where its name became the Soil Conservation Service. It grew at a prodigious rate. By 1937 Bennett had thirteen thousand technical, administrative, and clerical employees. His people were building terraces, constructing grass waterways, laying out contoured hillside fields, putting up dams, and digging ponds. They pushed the planting of kudzu, a Japanese ornamental vine that had extraordinary ability to grow on gullied land.

Able writers had in the past addressed themselves to the conservation issue. Among them were Gifford Pinchot, who wrote *The Fight for Conservation* in 1911; John Muir, author of *The Yosemite* in 1912; and Liberty Hyde Bailey, who published *The Holy Earth* in 1915. During the 1930s came a new outpouring as many excellent writers took up the cause. To what degree Bennett's initiative stimulated this flood is uncertain. In any case these writers broadened the base and deepened the commitment for the conservation movement. Here is a sample:

1932, Louis Bromfield, *The Farm*
1934, William Vogt, *The Agriculture of the Maya*
1935, Paul Sears, *Deserts on the March*
1935, Gove Hambidge, *Enchanted Acre*
1936, Stuart Chase, *Rich Land Poor Land*
1938, Aldo Leopold, *Conservation Ethic*
1938, Russell Lord, *Behold Our Land*
1939, Walter Lowdermilk, *The Eleventh Commandment*

The tone of these writings is portrayed by the Lowdermilk book. If

Moses had foreseen what would happen to the Promised Land after three thousand years, observed Lowdermilk, he would have added another commandment to the original ten, stated thus: "XI. Thou shalt inherit the holy earth as a faithful steward, conserving its resources and productivity from generation to generation."

Bennett and his colleagues sought and obtained support from teachers, bankers, club women, chambers of commerce, big industry, labor unions, religious leaders, bar associations, railroad officials, luncheon clubs, nature lovers, and public utility executives. The nonprofit educational organization Friends of the Land emerged from this enthusiasm with its influential quarterly journal *The Land*. The Sierra Club was a strong supporter. Conservation became a good word and a carrier for other liberal causes.

In 1939 Bennett launched a plan, endorsed by President Roosevelt, for soil conservation districts to be organized under state and federal law on a local watershed basis. In effect these were to be local units of government, voted into place by the farmers themselves, having democratically elected officials charged with the disposition of federal monies for conservation purposes. These funds would be used for putting conservation practices into use on private farm land. Drainage, terracing, pond building, tree planting, and establishing grass cover were among the practices. These soil conservation districts took off like a rocket. There soon were twenty-five hundred districts, almost one per county, virtually covering the country. Eighty percent of the nation's farms and ranches were involved.

Politicians quickly learned the power of the conservation idea. Commodity programs, intended to reduce production and increase price, were fashioned on a conservation rationale. In 1936, when the Agricultural Adjustment Act was declared unconstitutional, it was rewritten as the Soil Conservation and Domestic Allotment Act, a facade, since the act had little to do with conservation. The Production and Marketing Administration of the Department of Agriculture, responsible for administering the act, desired to have a conservation arm of its own and succeeded in getting the Agricultural Conservation Program, which doled out money to farmers for draining their fields and applying limestone, practices that contributed little to long-run conservation. In less than a decade, orchestrated by Hugh Bennett, soil conservation had become a leading rationale for farm policy.

Bennett's influence was worldwide. He and his lieutenants traveled the five continents, studying soils and consulting on erosion control. Distinguished visitors from throughout the world came to see him, two-thirds of them from the Eastern Hemisphere.

The soil conservation movement, promoted and undisciplined, had experienced mushroom growth. The country had gone from ignoring the problem to supporting almost any proposal that bore the conservation label. This is a familiar pattern in public policy. Reaction set in.

First, it appeared to the public that the danger had been exaggerated. The Dust Bowl of the Great Plains, supposedly ruined, received rain and produced bumper crops. Instead of running short of food as had been warned, it developed that we had surplus capacity and had to retire some twenty-five to fifty million acres of cropland.

It became evident that some of the recommendations of the Soil Conservation Service were ill-suited to farmers. The conversion of cropland to grass stalled because farmers had no use for the grass unless they shifted from cash crops to grazing animals, which they were reluctant to do. It soon became clear that for most farmers following the recommendations of the Soil Conservation Service would reduce current income.

Kudzu, the wonder plant promoted by the Soil Conservation Service, crawled out of the gullies to invade growing crops and climb trees, choking its hosts. Efforts to graze it and make hay of it proved disappointing.

Terraces, farming on the contour, and strip cropping required small fields, irregular in shape, ill-suited to large modern machinery. Farmers adopted the large new power equipment, pulled out fences, made big rectangular fields, and farmed over the terraces.

Bennett had said in 1950, "It is my belief, given adequate facilities, that we can get the job of applying the basic conservation measures to the land completed by 1970 – around twenty years from now." But it became evident that, contrary to Bennett's prognosis, the conservation job was a continuous one and would never be completed.

Some of the "conservation" programs came into conflict with activities of an opposite sort. While the Soil Conservation Service was channeling streams and draining swamps, other bodies were trying to preserve wetlands. While the service was subsidizing wells for irrigation in the Great Plains, drawing down an irreplaceable water supply, other efforts, public and private, were aimed at checking this practice.

The conservation facade of the efforts to support prices by controlling production became transparent. Crops were divided by law into "soil conserving" and "soil depleting" categories for control purposes. For political reasons soybeans, one of the most erosive of all crops, were put into the "soil conserving" group. Farmers, who knew their crops and land, were quick to see through this pretense. The credibility of the conservation movement eroded along with the soil. Milton Eisenhower, president of Kansas State College, said of the Agricultural Conservation Program on December 15, 1947, "I would say we have achieved perhaps 10 cents worth of conservation for each dollar spent on the program."

Controversy broke out between the "conservationists," who wanted responsible use of our natural resources, including land and water, and "preservationists," who wanted resources set aside, which meant wilderness areas and wild rivers. The united front which once supported the movement became divided.

Originally the conservation drive had been motivated largely by fear that soil loss would jeopardize our future food supply. During recent decades an added concern has arisen: the off-site problem. This term covers sedimentation, siltation, and the deterioration of water quality, including groundwater. Estimates are necessarily crude, but some rough analyses show the off-site damage to be twice as great as damage to the farmers' fields. A new government body, the Environmental Protection Agency, was set up to address off-site concerns, so the Soil Conservation Service no longer had sole custody of the erosion problem. With typical bureaucratic shortsightedness, the Soil Conservation Service looked on the Environmental Protection Agency as a rival rather than as an ally.

The agricultural economists, who with some combination of caution and cowardice had generally held silence, now began to speak up. Economists, like farmers, think of land as being used for profit, while conservationists think of it as a resource to be held in stewardship for future generations. Economists and farmers recognize the claim that the future has on the present but discount the future in accordance with the market rate of interest. For example, the present value of an income of $1,000 to be in hand twenty years from now, discounted at a market rate of 10 percent annually, would be only $385. Thus does the market measure the preference for present over future income. A farmer is disinclined to forgo current income in order to augment future income. The conservationist, in contrast, tries to get the farmer to give up current income in order that future income may be increased. Agreement between the farmer and the conservationist is possible only if conservation tillage is made currently profitable or if the farmer changes his discount for the future.

During the last decade, when the soil conservation movement was in trouble, there came the greatest change of tillage systems in modern times. Innovative farmers, experiment station workers, and pioneering implement companies teamed up to exploit the initiative of the herbicide people, who had made it possible to grow crops without brutalizing the soil. The erosion-deterring effect of an undisturbed surface, protected by vegetation cover, had been known for many years. The problem was that without tillage the weeds took the crop. Now there are controls for weeds and alternatives to the moldboard plow. Conservation tillage systems are available, variously known as chiseling, minimum tillage, no-till, reduced tillage, ridge-till, and till-plant. The rain, striking a field in conservation tillage, spends much of its force on the crop residue. The soil, undistrubed by plowing, stays in place. Last year's vegetation reduces the runoff and feeds the water into the soil. Soil loss is reduced by as much as 80 percent.

Corn yields per acre appear comparable for conventional and conservation tillage methods, with experience varied in accordance with soil type, management system, and operator skills. Costs per acre are also comparable; conservation tillage uses less fuel but more pesticides. Soybeans and small grains are seeded directly into the crop residues of the previous year without plowing. The farmer's interest in current income and the conservationist's interest in future resources may be on the way toward reconciliation.

To one taught to love the appearance of a deep-tilled field with all crop residue buried, a conservation-tilled field is, for a month or more after planting, an ugly sight indeed. But to one who loves the thought of soil kept in place such a field is wonderfully pleasing. In 1981 27 percent of the cropland in the United States was in conservation tillage, up from near zero a few years before. Most of this was chiseled, the soil being worked with narrow teeth that leave much of the trash on the surface. Two and a half percent of our land was in no-till, the most conserving form. In the Great Plains, sowing grain in last year's stubble has partly replaced clean tillage, saving soil, fuel, and moisture.

There is reason to believe that the moldboard plow, perhaps the most lauded farm implement of the nineteenth century, will in time be retired and become a museum piece. It appears that we may, after three centuries, be in a position to curtail the damage to our soils that resulted from the teachings of Jethro Tull, with his "deep tillage" and "iron among the roots."

Hugh Bennett died on July 7, 1960, in his seventy-ninth year. He had led the soil conservation cause from virtually zero to something approaching a passion. He had seen the enthusiasm recede but did not live to see it revive under the new banners and new techniques. Like many another leader, Hugh Bennett generated a movement that had to correct itself before its true and worthy purpose could be satisfactorily addressed. He was a fighter. He identified a crafty enemy and fought it with total commitment. Future generations can thank him for sensitizing America and the world to the dangers of soil erosion.

REFERENCES

Bennett, H. H. 1928. *Soil Erosion, a National Menance.* USDA Circular 33.
_____. 1955. *Elements of Soil Conservation.* 2nd ed. New York: McGraw-Hill.
Brink, Wellington. 1951. *Big Hugh, the Father of Soil Conservation.* New York: Macmillan.
Bunce, Arthur C. 1942. *The Economics of Soil Conservation.* Ames: Iowa State University Press.
Doster, D. H., D. R. Griffith, J. V. Mannering, and S. D. Parsons. 1983. "Economic Returns from Alternative Corn and Soybean Tillage Systems in Indiana." *Journal of Soil and Water Conservation* 38, no. 6 (Nov.-Dec.):504-8.
Eckholm, Eric. 1976. *Losing Ground: Environmental Stress and World Food Prospects.* Worldwatch Institute.
Hardin, Charles M. 1952. *The Politics of Agriculture.* Glencoe, Ill.: Free Press.
Moldenhauer, W. C., et al. 1983. "Conservation Tillage for Erosion Control." *Journal of Soil and Water Conservation* 38, no. 3 (May-June):144-51.
"Resources for the Future." 1984. *Resources* 75 (Winter).
USDA Yearbook. 1938. *Soils and Men.* Washington, D.C.: U.S. Government Printing Office.
_____. 1957. *Soil.* Washington, D.C.: U.S. Government Printing Office.
_____. 1981. *Will There Be Food Enough?* Washington, D.C.: U.S. Government Printing Office.
_____. 1983. *Using Our Natural Resources.* Washington, D.C.: U.S. Government Printing Office.

CHAPTER 20

Nicolas Appert and Food Preservation

FOOD IS PRODUCED SEASONALLY but consumers require it at a fairly constant rate throughout the year. Nature's creatures adjust to this seasonal pattern of abundance and dearth in various ways. The robin flies south for the winter and the bear hibernates. The bob-white neither migrates nor sleeps; it finds what food it can during the bleak winter and the population is reduced to those that survive the time of scarcity.

Mankind has a better plan than does the bob-white. Like the honeybee and the squirrel human beings store food from the season of abundance to the time of shortage. Were it not so their numbers would be limited to those who could be fed during the season of dearth. People have preserved and stored food since early times. We dried it in the sun and put it away in the cool temperature of a cave. We learned to salt, smoke, ferment, spice, and pickle our food. Though we did not understand it, all of these techniques preserved the food by their hostility to the growth of bacteria.

The undoubted founder of food preservation was the Frenchman Nicolas Appert. In 1795, in order to provision the French navy in such a manner as to prevent scurvy, the French government offered a prize of twelve thousand francs for a method of food preservation. Appert, who had already worked for many years in confectionaries, kitchens, distilleries, breweries, and storehouses, went after the prize. Born at Chalons-sur-Marne in 1750, he had no knowledge of bacteriology, the special branch of science on which success depended; that field would not be opened until half a century later. Nor did chemistry afford him much assistance. Gay-Lussac, then the foremost chemist of the world, had little to contribute.

Appert believed that spoilage was caused by the air. If he could cook his food well, he thought, and protect it from the air, it should keep. He did this and his food kept. That his basic assumption was erroneous was not clear until many years later when Pasteur developed the germ theory. Appert thought, like many others, that scurvy, the sailor's plague, was caused by eating salt beef and that perserving food without salt was the remedy. When his preserved food replaced the salt beef, scurvy subsided, though not for the reason he thought. His food carried Vitamin C, which salt beef did not.

Appert partially precooked his foods, which he then put into glass bottles, leaving space for expansion. He corked the filled bottles, wiring the corks into place as is done with some wines to this day. He then placed the bottles in a pressure cooker, which he heated to the boiling point. The time in the cooker depended on the product and was determined experimentally. Appert preserved beef, consommé, poultry, mutton, eggs, and milk as well as a large number of fruits and vegetables. Not only the conventional foods were preserved but also sauces, desserts, and hors d'oeuvres. A catalog of his products looks like a high-class menu, which it was. The success of his system is witnessed by the fact that his method is in use today, with some modification and improvement, by such giants of the food industry as Campbell and Heinz as well as by household canners.

In a critical test eighteen bottles of preserved foods—beef, mutton, fowl, partridge, preserved vegetables, consommé, and milk—were sent to Brest and put to sea for four months and ten days. Tasted, none of them showed any alteration.

By 1810 Appert was sixty years old and had spent forty-five years in the food business, fifteen of them in pursuit of the prize. He demonstrated to the satisfaction of the judges that his method was successful and was awarded the twelve thousand francs, the equivalent of about twenty-five hundred dollars, no small sum in those days. A public-spirited man, he published his work in meticulous detail that same year, readily sharing his system with others. The book, a 113-page classic on food technology, bears the title *The Book for All Households, or The Art of Preserving Animal and Vegetable Substances for Many Years.* This pioneer of food preservation founded the House of Appert in 1812 and remained at its head until the time of his death in 1841. He died a poor man, having exhausted his means in working on his experiments. His family continued the business, improving and refining his techniques.

Appert and the French government thought that the preserved foods would be useful for "sea voyages, hospitals, and the domestic economy." The fact that such food would be useful to the army at first escaped Napoleon, then embarked on his course of conquest.

In 1811 Appert's process crossed the channel to England, where John Hall and Bryan Donkin began producing preserved meats and vegetable soup. The British learned to use tin instead of glass and described the containers as "cans," shortened from "canisters," hence "tin cans." The English navy used the canned products to provision their ships for long voyages. The French influence carried over into naming the new foods. English sailors were fed boiled canned beef; their effort to cope with the French word *bouillir,* "to boil," led to the familiar phrase "bully beef."

The keeping quality of properly canned food is remarkable. Two cans, one pea soup and one beef, were left by Parry on the ice of the Arctic in 1825 when his ship *Fury* was lost. These cans were brought back, unopened, in 1833 and were put into the Museum of Fisheries and Shipping. They were opened in 1911 when eighty-seven years old and found to be in perfect condition; a meal was made of them without ill effects. All one needs to do to appreciate the importance of canning is to walk through the aisles of a supermarket and observe the number of canned food products. The variety of available foods is multiplied by shipping, in canned form, foods that cannot be produced locally.

Jonathan Swift, the eighteenth-century political observer, had written thus in praise of those who till the land: "Whoever could make two ears of corn or two blades of grass to grow upon a spot of ground where only one grew before would deserve better of mankind and do more essential service to this country than the whole race of politicians put together." Swift might have said the same about Appert, a man who would, by food preservation, make possible use of the whole crop rather than only a part thereof.

Other methods of food preservation help to extend the food supply. Refrigeration and freezing are common. Irradiation is less so. Food can be sterilized with heat and kept in low-cost packages, without refrigeration, for about six months by a method known as UHT, ultra-high temperature. Food preservation has permitted the saving and use of a far larger share of our agricultural output than was possible in earlier times.

REFERENCES

Appert, Nicolas. 1810. *The Book for All Households, or The Art of Preserving Animal and Vegetable Substances for Many Years.* Translated from the French by K. G. Bitting, 1920. Paris: Patris.

Connor, John. 1985. *The Food Manufacturing Industry.* Lexington, Mass.: Lexington Books.

International Tin Research and Development Council. 1939. *Historic Tinned Foods.* Publication 85 (2nd ed.). Middlesex, England.

Peterson, M. S., and Donald K. Tressler. 1963. *Food Technology the World Over.* Westport, Conn.: AVI Publishing.

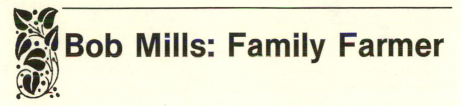# Bob Mills: Family Farmer

DELPHI, INDIANA, November 1982. In the American Midwest, on the tongue of land between the Tippecanoe and the Wabash rivers and in the midst of the Hoosier heartland, is the Mills farm. It consists of 1000 acres, 900 tillable and 100 in rough wooded land known as the Wabash river breaks. Three hundred acres are owned and 700 rented. Products are corn, soybeans, and hogs.

This is a two-generation, three-family farm. Bob Mills and his wife Dorothy, the senior members, are in their fifties. Their daughter Marsha and son-in-law Ed Oilar, together with their son Mark and Mark's wife Michelle, are the oncoming generation. Each family has its own dwelling, near enough to one another to permit ready cooperation and far enough apart to provide privacy.

An appropriate definition of a family farm is that it is one on which most of the management and most of the labor are supplied by the farmer and his family. This definition is silent on whether the land is owned or rented. Traditionalists contend that to be a family farm the land should be owned and the corporate form of organization should be ruled out. The Mills farm is incorporated, primarily to facilitate transfer between generations; all the stock is owned by the family. In every respect except tradition and legal form this is a family farm.

The farm has increased in size. It started in 1953 with Bob and Dorothy renting the home farm, 147 acres, from Bob's ailing and retiring father. It has grown slowly and steadily through rental and purchase, reaching its present size in 1981. The land now farmed as a unit is a consolidation of seven former farms, or parts of farms. What became of the farmers whose land was assimilated? One retired. Several left farming for nonfarm jobs. Two died, leaving the property to heirs who had no wish to farm and so sold or rented out the land.

This is a modern farm, using technology in a solid practical sense. It is of the vanguard but not of the scouting party. It is larger than average but reasonably typical of the modern farms that produce the great bulk of America's food, feed, and fiber.

The Mills farm is a prodigious food producer. In a good year it turns out 2000 tons of corn and 600 tons of soybeans. Part of the corn is fed to hogs, converted to 90 tons of meat, enough pork for twenty-five hundred people. Much of the soybeans and corn go by rail or truck to the Ohio River, then down the Mississippi, out of the the port of New Orleans and to people overseas. The Mills family deals hunger a mighty blow, though the impact is obscured by the impersonal working of the market. (A more extensive treatment of this farm and of eleven other farms throughout the world is to be found in my 1984 book *Farmers of Five Continents* [University of Nebraska Press].)

Consider what the Mills farm uses of the agricultural science described in this book:

Fertilizer: This comes originally from Liebig. The Millses fertilize heavily. Corn gets 500 pounds per acre, plowed down in the fall, plus 150 pounds of nitrogen in the spring. On top of that is 200 pounds of starter. When Bob began farming in 1953 his corn yield was about 70 bushels per acre. Now he gets 150. The doubling of yields in a little over three decades is largely attributable to increased use of fertilizer.

Disease Control: The Millses' hogs stay healthy, a result of preventive as well as remedial medicine. A veterinarian checks them regularly. The Millses wean nine pigs per litter, well above the national average. Swine sanitation is an outgrowth of the work of the first and greatest pathologist, Louis Pasteur, and of the more recent microbiologists, Alexander Fleming and Selman Waksman. Before the development of antibiotics, health problems would have prevented hog farming on the scale now practiced by the Millses.

Machinery: There are three big tractors and two small ones on this farm, a reflection of the mechanical revolution that began late in the nineteenth century. For harvesting corn and beans the Millses have a self-propelled combine, a distant cousin of McCormick's reaper.

Seed and Breeding Stock: The Millses use high-yielding hybrid corn. They buy from Jacques Seed Company, a small rival of Henry Wallace's Pioneer Hi-Bred firm. The Millses produce fast-gaining crossbred hogs, which are more efficient converters of feed into meat than the old-fashioned purebreds. These advances are traceable to a long list of plant and animal breeders beginning with Gregor Mendel.

Institutional Support: Abraham Lincoln's concept of family farming, reflected in the Homestead Act, laid the basis for the Mills farm operation. The two young men took winter courses in agriculture at Purdue University, a land grant college that owes its origin to Justin Morrill. The family uses research results from the agricultural experiment stations fathered by Samuel Johnson. They attend extension meetings, the outgrowth of work initiated by Seaman Knapp. They get useful information from the agribusiness firms that supply seed, machinery, fertilizer, pesticides, and feed supplements. They learn of new practices from the radio, the television, the newspaper, and the farm magazines. Much of this information, privately supplied, originates with the experiment stations.

Economics: The principles of profitable farming come from many economists, including T. W. Schultz, whose work is examined in this book. The Mills family attends extension meetings where they hear analyses and recommendations provided by agricultural economists.

Nutrition: Good nutrition, both in the household and in swine production, is standard at the Mills place. James Lind and Mary Swartz Rose were instrumental in laying a basis for good human nutrition. Animal nutrition stems from chemistry (Liebig) and the work of the experiment stations (Johnson).

The New Biology: Watson and Crick did the basic work that led to gene splicing. Some day the crops and livestock on this farm will show the work of this breakthrough, if not in Bob's time, then during the stewardship of Ed and Mark.

Insecticides: The Millses hold corn rootworm in check with insecticides stemming from the work of Paul Müeller.

Herbicides: Weeds are controlled in corn and soybeans with selective weed killers, thereby reducing the number of needed cultivations. E. J. Kraus did the pioneer work.

Food Preservation: The Millses' hogs reach the consumer either as fresh chilled or as frozen pork. Food preservation grows out of the work of Nicolas Appert.

Visiting the Mills place, one thinks of the pioneers of agricultural science who set in motion the forces that converge at this farm and on millions of others around the globe. For the greater part, the hunger fighters portrayed in this book have no monuments erected to their memories. The growing and evolving advances in food production and human well-being are a living memorial.

The Millses have not gone for every new idea that came over the horizon. They have not adopted conservation tillage nor have they computerized the farm. They have not built costly modern facilities for their hog operation. They have not bought the biggest four-wheel-drive tractor. They may in time do some of these things. The commitment is not to agricultural science as such but to new practices that give promise of paying off.

The Mills farm is an example of the synthesis of agricultural science that has permitted the world to feed its 5 billion people and to feed them better than their parents. Choosing the mix of science that goes into (and is left out of) agricultural production is the key element of good farm management. In entrepreneurial agriculture the reward for choosing well is profit for the farm operator and an abundant supply of low-cost wholesome food for the consumer.

Some people believe that life is a zero-sum game, that what one party wins another loses. There are some zero-sum games, and even some negative-sum games, but agricultural science is not one of them. It yields a positive sum.

The upsurge of agricultural science permitted the world's population to increase by a factor of six during a two hundred–year period and to be better fed. The progression continues. There is new science in use on some farms that is not yet in use on others. There are good new ideas being tested that are not yet in use on any farm. There are worthy new ideas that have not yet been put to the test. There are young men and women being trained in agricultural science who have not yet begun to produce ideas but who will. The pace is accelerating and the end is nowhere in sight.

Food Aid

DESPITE ENORMOUS ADVANCES in agricultural science and farm production want continues in the midst of plenty. Poverty-stricken people are unable to buy enough food for good health even though crops might be abundant. Natural disasters occur: drought, flood, earthquake, and diseases of plants and animals. Wars break out, destroying food and making hungry refugees of millions. Economic depression occurs with resulting unemployment and inability to buy adequate food, however plentiful. Some people, shortchanged at birth and burdened with physical or mental disability, are unable to cope by themselves even in a prosperous economy. Most people are able to meet most of their food needs most of the time. It is by no means true that all people can meet all their food needs all the time.

Agricultural scientists naturally focus on food production, which, while enormously important, is only part of the problem. The other part is distribution. Many people in production agriculture take distribution for granted. Many who are interested in food aid take production for granted, which is at least as great an error.

What should be done for those people who

cannot meet their own food needs? The answer has long been that the family should provide food for those of its number—the young, the old, the infirm—who could not supply food for themselves. But not all families are disposed to help in this fashion. And sometimes, when disaster occurs, even a well-meaning family cannot provide food for its dependent members.

The Christian teaching is plain. "Bear ye one another's burdens" is the precept, and this admonition transcends family, tribal, religious, national, and racial divisions. Non-Christian religions have similar precepts and the concept is not limited to religious teaching. But in practice we fall far short of the ethical ideal.

In the past, for many people the inability to provide their own food meant death by starvation. In a world where class barriers were high, communication was poor, and compassion was underdeveloped, these tragic events were remote from those who were more fortunate. This began to change in recent decades.

It is interesting to speculate as to how the change occurred. There were several causes, of which better communication probably is most important. Widespread starvation occurred in Africa during the nineteenth century but few people in Europe or America knew about it. Today television brings the tragedy into the living room. There is something within us that is wrenched by the sight of starving people. This anguish is greater in our day than it was in former times. In the nineteenth century it was possible for well-fed people of the Western world to say of the hungry man in India: "It is better that he starve. If we fed him he probably would have children and a few years from now the problem would be worse. Let the death rate balance the population with the food supply as it has for all species since life began." That cannot be said in today's world of awareness and concern.

There are other reasons for the growth of food aid. Greater affluence no doubt has its effect. The abundance of food in the developed nations makes food aid more easily possible. Public-supported food-aid institutions provide the means by which food may be distributed. Their very existence encourages their use. Weakening of the family increases the need for alternative means of providing food security. The lengthening radius of human concern is a factor. What once was almost exclusively a matter for the family became, with the passage of time, also a concern for the tribe, the city-state, the nation, and now, in some measure, the world. Food aid is riding a trend of broader social awareness.

Like any other innovative venture food aid experiences both success and disappointment. Much has been learned about how to administer food aid. Some who have done it, including this writer, are convinced that it is harder to give food away helpfully than it is to sell it.

Part III relates the stories of six people who have been involved in food aid:

Joseph Smith, the Mormon church leader who laid the basis for private, voluntary mutual aid within a religious group.

Herbert Hoover, who devised and administered a program to provide food aid at public cost to the people of Europe after World War I.

Hubert Humphrey, who was the key figure in public-supported programs to feed the poor at home and abroad.

Anthony Dias, civil servant in India, who administered food aid in the province of Bihar during the 1960s and so averted famine.

Pastor Ludwig Stumpf, who organized food

aid for the refugees in Hong Kong and steered thousands of derelicts into self-reliance.

Madame Wang Shun Ying, who shares responsibility for food security on Evergreen Commune near Beijing, China.

We hope to learn what we can from the experiences of these people, all pioneers in the trend that has moved food aid into the public domain.

CHAPTER 22

Joseph Smith: The Church and Food Security

IN THIS CHAPTER WE INQUIRE whether food aid can be provided to needy people in a satisfactory manner by private charity without government help. We review a successful system of this kind, the welfare program of the Mormon church, based on principles laid down 150 years ago by the founder, Joseph Smith. We conclude that such a plan cannot be generalized. We then see how it is that government must provide food aid if hunger is to be alleviated.

Joseph Smith, religious leader, colonizer, and architect of a unique social system, was born into a farm family in Vermont in 1805, the fourth of ten children. Smith founded the Church of Jesus Christ of Latter-Day Saints, known as the LDS or Mormon church, in Fayette, New York in 1830.

The church drew its doctrines from the Bible and the Book of Mormon, both of which were considered sacred. The ethical standard was the teaching of Jesus. The civil code was based on the Constitution. Economic practice was entrepreneurial, relying heavily on the work ethic. The family was the basic social unit. Responsibility for meeting food needs rested first on the family, and then, if the family could not cope, on the church. Church organization was authoritative and the church was the center of social as well as religious activity. The system thus had the motive of compassion, the incentive of individual enterprise, the safety net of group responsibility, and the organizing power of central authority. So deeply were these principles ingrained that they remain little changed to the present day. The Mormons took as their token the honeybee, a hard-working, productive, well-disciplined creature, an apt symbol.

Presently the church has more than 5 million members, many of them in the western states with others throughout the nation and the world. Most members give one-tenth of their earnings to the church. Mormons are anxious to share their faith; many young men and young women give eighteen to thirty months of their lives to a worldwide mission, without pay.

Our interest here is not so much in the church as such but in its program to meet the food requirements of its needy members. For many years the Mormon church placed responsibility primarily on the family, where it was borne with love and charity as well as with a sense of duty.

During the 1930s, when the Great Depression struck, many breadwinners lost their incomes and could no longer meet family food needs. The federal government responded to this national emergency with its relief programs: food donation, cash welfare, and make-work enterprises like the Civil Works Administration. But the Mormon church had a deep commitment to individual enterprise and a feeling for family and church obligations. It was wary of federal aid, concerned that people would be deprived of responsibility and that they would look to the government rather than to the church for food security and other things. So in 1936, mindful of Jesus' admonition to bear one another's burdens and to feed the hungry, the church set up its own welfare system, of which food security was central. The church would take care of its own. The welfare program is limited to members of the church. The Mormon ethic of hard work and interdependence reduces the number of needy below what it would be in other circumstances. Mormon food aid thus took on a problem of tractable dimensions.

The Mormon program consists of three parts: prevention, temporary assistance, and rehabilitation, which are here described briefly.

Prevention. Emphasis is on avoiding dependency. Literacy and education are pushed and career development is encouraged. People are counseled to avoid debt, to build financial resources, and to pay tithes. Those who can do so are urged to have gardens and are taught how to preserve food. People are told to keep a year's supply of food on hand, preferably in the form of wheat. Physical fitness is urged. Social, emotional, and spiritual strength are built through worship, temperance, and self-mastery.

Temporary Assistance. Crises can occur, despite efforts to prevent them. When such times come and personal or family resources are exhausted, the church steps in with direct help. A team of two lay members has responsibility for a certain number of families whom they visit each month, on the alert for evidence of need. When a needy family is found, assistance is provided, whether food, clothing, fuel, or medical help. The women of the church have a relief society which also visits each woman once a month. Employment specialists help find jobs for the unemployed and better jobs for those whose capabilities are being underutilized. There are production projects and processing facilities, using surplus commodities and voluntary labor. Fruits and vegetables are canned and dried. Food products are saved and stored. There are about one hundred storehouses in various parts of the United States. The worthy poor receive these products, not as a dole but as deserved assistance, the help merited by their membership in the group, their own contribution in better times, or their current labor on one of the projects. Job assistance and counseling help the troubled family to again become self-supporting; the system of monthly visits is intended to assure that assistance is terminated as soon as the family is again able to meet its own needs.

There are retail thrift stores similar to those of the Salvation Army and Goodwill Industries. There are fast offerings; church members are asked to abstain from two meals a month and contribute the equivalent sum to the church. Social services are provided: adoptions, help for unwed parents, foster home care, and clinical services.

Rehabilitation. Job retraining is provided. Training in sign language is available for the deaf. For the blind there are Braille readings in addition to records and cassettes as well as suitable job opportunities. Elderly people receive social contacts, transportation, proper nutrition, and useful work. Admittedly, not all these services are available in all areas. Sparsely populated rural regions cannot be supplied as well as the cities.

After World War II, when much of Europe was devastated, large quantities of food were sent to hungry church members in the war-torn areas. Experienced administrators were sent to help set up the distribution system. One such person was Ezra Taft Benson, member of the Council of Twelve, later to become secretary of agriculture and in 1985 president of the church.

Such are the consequences of Joseph Smith's vision a century and a half ago, faithfully transmitted to the present day by a series of devoted leaders held on course by a set of principles highly resistant to change.

This system not only meets material needs like food; it provides respect, fellowship, spiritual support, and a feeling of identity within a group. For some people the system calls on them to concede too much of their individuality to the group. Some members leave the church for this reason. But apparently more people welcome the group orientation than dislike it; the church is one of the fastest growing within the Christian community. This system of food aid, coupled with help of other kinds, is acknowledged by virtually all observers, Mormon or otherwise, to be exemplary by almost any criterion: religious, social, or economic.

Mormons constitute only about 1 or 2 percent of the American population. Could this system be generalized for the others? Regrettably the answer must be "no." As a result of their culture the Mormons have attributes that are found to only a limited degree among other groups in America. Faith, commitment, discipline, group entity, a work ethic, and an effective way of raising money all contribute to success of the program. The rank and file of America can no more succeed with the Mormon system than a sandlot team could win the Super Bowl by using the playbook of the New York Giants.

The other Christian churches, mostly less authoritarian and less group-minded than the Mormons, are nevertheless aware of Jesus' commission to love one another, feed the hungry, heal the sick, and bear each other's burdens. Limited as they are in their resources and in influence over their members, how can they carry out this mission? Most of them have voluntary programs of direct assistance to needy families in the community and overseas, some of these efforts being of significant size and others being little more than tokens.

For the greater part church involvement in programs of food aid has taken the same form as it has in education and medical assistance. The churches pioneered schools and hospitals but the need grew beyond church resources. Strength was unequal to the task. The government moved in, taking over the major share of the load. Private nonchurch philanthropy and entrepreneurial capital supplemented what was done by church and government. Many of the churches maintain their involvement in health and education, which is sometimes substantial but often little more than evidence of their continuing good will. A similar trend is found in food aid. Pioneered by the churches, it has gradually moved into the public sector.

What we have here is the secularization of American society. There are two views of this trend. One view is that the decline in the church role evidences a waning of the spirit and so is regrettable. The other view is that the churches supplied the yeast which leavened the lump and so produced a more caring society, which is laudable. Mormons incline toward the first view and hold out against tax-supported welfare programs. Most liberal church people and many of the unchurched incline toward the latter view and encourage more government assistance in the social area.

Non-Christian religious groups, similarly inclined by their doctrines toward charity and facing similar handicaps—how can they cope? And secular movements, motivated by humanitarian concern—what can they do? These disparate groups, associated by their mutual concern for the hungry, have lobbied hard for larger federal food aid programs, domestic and foreign, about which we will read in the chapter on Hubert Humphrey.

The interdependence of individual and group envisioned by Joseph Smith and his followers has shown its merit. But most citizens lack the necessary charitable commitment. Government food aid programs may be second best but when the first best is inadequate the second best must move up.

REFERENCES

Benson, Ezra Taft. 1984. Personal correspondence with the author.
Clark, J. Reuben, Jr. 1944. "Fundamentals of the Church Welfare Plan." General Conference, Salt Lake City, Utah.
Monson, Thomas S. Undated. " 'Mormon' Church Welfare Services." Prepared for the President's Task Force on Private Sector Initiatives. The Church of Jesus Christ of Latter-Day Saints, Salt Lake City, Utah.
USDA. 1979. *Food for Peace.* 1978 Annual Report on PL 480. Washington, D.C.
Wittwer, Sylvan. 1984. Personal correspondence with the author.

CHAPTER 23

Herbert Hoover: Pioneer in Food Aid

ASK THE AVERAGE PERSON what he associates with the name of Herbert Hoover and he may respond, "The Great Depression and Hoover's unwillingness to help the poor." Yet Hoover is the humanitarian who developed and administered the program that brought food to hungry people during and after World War I, a program that saved millions of lives. Herbert Hoover may be the most misunderstood man in the history of American public life.

Herbert Clark Hoover was born of poor parents at West Branch, Iowa on August 10, 1874. He was of the Quaker faith, as were his forebears. To understand Herbert Hoover one must understand the Quakers, more accurately known as the Religious Society of Friends. Friends reject war, work at reconciliation, oppose barriers to race equality, stress humanitarian activities, and foster education. They protest religious rote and until recent times dressed in "plain clothes" and used "plain language." They witness what they call the Inner Light, a manifestation of the Spirit which they believe dwells in the hearts of ordinary people. Herbert Hoover was brought up in the nurture of these beliefs.

Hoover's father died when the boy was six years old, and his mother died three years later. The future president was raised by his Quaker relatives, first in Iowa and then in Oregon. When he was about fifteen years old he chanced to meet an engineer from the East, a Robert Brown, was impressed by Brown's tales, and resolved to be an engineer, with which purpose he entered newly founded Leland Stanford University. Part-time work and a summer job with the Geological Survey kept him solvent.

The new Stanford graduate started work in the gold-mining districts of Nevada City and Grass Valley in northern California, pushing a car in the lower level of the Reward Mine at two dollars a day on a ten-hour night shift and a seven-day week.

His rise was rapid. He met and impressed favorably Louis Janin, an outstanding mining engineer, who sent him to the Australian gold mines to work for the British mining firm Bewick, Moreing and Company. Hoover, twenty-three years old, learned of a small gold mine 150 miles inland from the coast, inspected it, and was impressed with its prospect. He recommended that Moreing buy a two-thirds interest in the mine for $250,000, which was done. During the next fifty years the mine produced $10 million in dividends. Hoover's position with his firm was solid.

Hoover quickly became an international mining engineer. He ricocheted around the world as a successful "doctor of sick mines." His wealth and his reputation both grew. In 1899 he worked in China; in 1901, Japan; in 1902, New Zealand; in 1903, India; in 1904, Rhodesia and the Transvaal; in 1905, Egypt. In 1907 he went to Burma, where he opened one of the largest and richest lead-zinc-silver ore bodies ever discovered and made himself a fortune. In 1908 he engineered and managed mines in Italy. In 1909 he went to the Urals in Russia where he established new plants for iron, steel, coal, coke, lumber, sulfuric acid, and copper, together with railroads and ships to serve them. In 1911 he went to Siberia, south of Omsk, to build railroads and river steamers for bringing in American mining machinery.

At the culmination of his mining career Hoover, still a young man, was world renowned, the director of more than a score of mining companies and the chief executive of half a dozen of them. A hundred and fifty thousand men were drawing pay in his various mining works. He was rich. He mused with his friend, Will Irwin, "I'll soon have an independent income—big enough. . . . I'm interested in some job of public service." He was ready for the challenge soon to come.

World War I broke out on July 28, 1914. On August 3 Germany declared war on France and the following day invaded Belgium, quickly overrunning that small country. Belgium produced only 30 percent of its food, much of which was destroyed or seized by the Germans. The Allies imposed a blockade, cutting off the flow of food to the Continent. Northern France was in similar straits. Ten million people were in danger of starvation.

Hoover, forty years old, was then in London trying to adapt his mining, smelting, and shipping operations first to the prospects and then to the fact of war.

The American ambassador to Great Britain, Walter Hines Page, invited Hoover to a meeting at the embassy on October 18 to consider what might be done to prevent starvation in Belgium. Ambassador Page said he had received word from U.S. Secretary of State William Jennings Bryan stating that the American government, then neutral, would provide its good offices in meeting the Belgian food problem but would undertake no obligations. Emile Francqui, a Belgian banker who had differed with Hoover on a number of points in China fourteen years earlier, asked Hoover to take on the relief job. Hoover took a day to decide. He would have to locate the food supply for a whole nation, find the money to pay for it, get it past the German navy and the occupying armies, and set up a distribution system. Acceptance would mean terminating his career as mining engineer.

Hoover, who had an abhorrence of committees and organizational charts, accepted on the condition that he be given absolute command, which was agreed to. Thus was born the Commission for Relief of Belgium. Hoover saw the need for wheat to feed the Belgians and the prospect that the price would rise. Despite the lack of program funds, he at once called a broker and gave a personal order to buy 10 million bushels of wheat. The prevailing view was that the war might last eight months. Hidden was the fact that it would last four years.

Hoover, reflecting his Quaker upbringing, was appalled by the war. Most people in the Allied nations attributed the beginning of hostilities to acts of the German and Austrian chancellors and of the Russian czar. Hoover's perceptions were deeper. He attributed hostilities to "the combative nature of man, the forces of aggressive nationalism, and the human yearning of men for the adventure and glory of war." Hoover saw the war not only as a result of past hatred but as a cause of future animosity. Again and again in his memoirs, written at the time and a resource for this chapter, are forebodings about the deepening hatreds fed by the war and the danger that there would be future hostilities.

Hoover's visit to occupied Belgium gave him a measure of the problem. His comment: "Half the population were unemployed and destitute. Before we got into action prices of food rose stupendously. The rich obtained enough. The farmers hoarded for their families. The middle class got something. The unemployed and destitute got little but soup. . . . People do not lie down and die of sheer starvation; they don't have a chance. They lose resistance to contagious disease, which does the rest."

For the relief program to operate at all, agreement had to be obtained from the belligerents. There was a legal obstacle. The Logan Act, put on the books one hundred years earlier, made it a crime for a private American citizen to negotiate with a foreign government. Senator Lodge of Massachusetts prepared an attack on Hoover for allegedly violating this law, but former President Theodore Roosevelt came to Hoover's rescue and the issue subsided.

Hoover started his negotiations with the British government. He asked that the naval blockade be relaxed in order to permit the passage of food-laden ships to Belgium and that financial support be provided. Lord Kitchener, minister of war, and Winston Churchill, first lord of the Admiralty, were strongly opposed. The military leaders considered that starving Belgians would make trouble for the Germans and help the Allies win the war. They contended that it is the responsibility of an occupying army to provision the civil population. Lloyd George, chancellor of the Exchequer and somewhat less adamant, was instrumental in helping reach a tentative agreement that the blockade would be opened for a regular advance program of food shipments. No hope was given for financial help. All was contingent on securing from the Germans more effective food control in Belgium.

With this conditional agreement in his pocket, Hoover approached the Germans. The United States was then still neutral, so Hoover had little difficulty in arranging a meeting in Berlin. He noted the total dedication of the German officials to the war effort and lengthened his estimate of the duration of the war. The Germans agreed to stop taking food from Belgium and northern France, to give instructions to submarine commanders to respect the markings on ships bearing food to Belgium, and to provide sailing instructions on mine-free sea routes to Rotterdam. Chancellor Bethmann-Hollweg's promise that the German submarine commanders would spare the food supply ships was not enough for Hoover. He said it reminded him of an old American story, the case of a man who demanded that a neighbor keep his bulldog in better control. The neighbor replied, "Oh, he won't bite." The man observed, "You may know he won't bite. I may know he won't bite. But does the dog know it?" Hoover, generally believed to be a mirthless man, drew the only laugh of the meeting.

The German assurances were not honored. Unlimited submarine warfare was declared in February 1917. Two food aid ships were sunk, the *Euphrates* on February 3 and the *Lars Kruse* on February 6, with loss of life and cargo. Nevertheless, much food got through.

How could the relief operation be financed and administered? The combatants felt no responsibility. Public funds were unavailable. Private donations were then the only credible source of food aid. A program was launched to sensitize world opinion and organize charity. The estimate was that $12 million a month would be needed. Belgian relief committees were set up all around the world. Money flowed in but it was not enough. Hoover, who served without pay as chairman of the commission, personally incurred a debt of $12 million to keep the food moving.

Private charity brought in $52 million, enough for only four months. As the need became more urgent and under pressure from Hoover, governments finally contributed: the British $109 million, the French $205 million, and the United States $387 million. Not only was the need met, but an important precedent was established. Thereafter government funding of international food aid would be debated case by case, not rejected outright on the basis that there was no precedent for it.

In setting up the machinery for food aid, Hoover had no established experience as a guide. He settled on a system having these attributes.

1. *Centralize policy but decentralize execution.* Hoover took major decision making for himself but the final stage of distribution was in the hands of burgomasters and mayors, with ex officio Americans on all committees. Much of the distribution work was done by unpaid volunteers.

2. *Financial support.* Private charity alone was not sufficient; government appropriations were needed.

3. *Rationing for the entire population.* Normal food intake was reduced by one-third. So great a reduction was acceptable only if it was shared in a fashion that was deemed equitable. Bread was rationed first but other commodities followed as supplies shortened.

4. *Prices were fixed.* Official prices were established for the rationed commodities at retail and farm levels. Originally maximum retail prices were set for unrationed commodities but black markets negated this effort.

5. *Requisitioned supplies.* As the situation became more difficult, all surplus production was requisitioned from the farms and rationed out, as was imported food.

6. *The destitute were treated separately.* Indigents were given free ration cards. Fuel, clothes, rent, and medical care were provided. The program for the destitute was kept distinct from the regular program.

7. *Distribution was on the basis of need.* Political and religious affiliation were not criteria for providing or denying food aid.

8. *A special child feeding program was developed.* Two and a half million children and expectant mothers were fed daily in schoolhouses and public buildings. Soup and a cracker were the standard fare. When the war ended it was found that child mortality and morbidity were lower than before the war.

9. *Strict accounting was maintained.* Credibility and public acceptance were deemed essential. Scandal was not tolerated.

10. *The program was terminated when the emergency passed.* When peace came the normal channels of trade were reopened. Belgian agricul-

ture revived with surprising speed. The program was ended on July 1, 1919, eight months after the armistice.

These principles, with some modification, have been followed in virtually all subsequent emergency programs of international food aid.

During the four years of the program, two thousand cargoes or part cargoes of food reached Belgium. Altogether more than 5 million tons of food were distributed. Wheat and flour accounted for about two-thirds of the total.

The destitute received not only food but also clothing. Some 55 million pounds of new and second-hand clothes were distributed. Women all over the world started knitting wool garments for the Belgians, mostly sweaters. The Belgian women carefully unravelled these sweaters and knitted them over again into shawls—their idea of a knitted garment.

When the Belgian Relief Program was terminated, in mid-1919, the auditors gave their accounting. The overhead expenditures of the commission were $4 million, less than half of 1 percent of the value of commodities supplied. Despite this remarkable record, Hoover and others were accused of grafting money from the Belgian relief. Senator James Reed of Missouri led this attack.

How many lives were saved? There is no way of knowing. One thing is clear: the Commission on Relief of Belgium demonstrated man's humanity to man alongside the contrary evidence of a war that took the lives of millions.

The United States entered the war on April 6, 1917. President Wilson asked Hoover to serve as United States food administrator, organizing food for the war effort. This Hoover agreed to do, subject to the stipulation that he continue to conduct the Belgian relief effort and that he receive no salary. Hoover's chief purpose was to see that the American agricultural plant produced sufficient food for our domestic requirements and for the needs of Europe. "Food Will Win the War" became the slogan.

The American situation was radically different from that of Belgium. American food supplies were generally abundant throughout the war. Encouragement to farmers, campaigns of food conservation, limited intervention in markets, avoidance of general rationing, and focus on staples rather than on the whole grocery list were the major features of Hoover's program. If Hoover was a "food czar," as some claimed, he was a benevolent despot.

The armistice came on November 11, 1918. Hoover was given the task of administering the relief and economic rehabilitation of Europe, heading the European Relief Council. This was in addition to his duties as head of the Commission on Relief of Belgium and his responsibility as United States food administrator.

This new task completely overshadowed the Belgian relief program in magnitude.

	Commission on Relief of Belgium	Relief and Reconstruction of Europe
Dates	1914–20	1918–20
Number of nations involved	2	30
Number of people concerned	10 million	400 million
Tons of supplies distributed	5 million	19 million
Financial commitment	$928 million	$3937 million

Source: *Hoover Memoirs*

Immediately after the armistice, when the reconnaissance men assessed conditions within Europe, they reported the gravest chaos and suffering. Hoover tells it in his memoirs:

the world began to survey the wreckage. Ten million men were dead or maimed. Ten million men, women, and children had died of starvation and disease. It was the worst European famine since the Thirty Years War, three centuries earlier. Towns, cities, ships, railways were destroyed. Governments had gone $250 billion in debt which, in Europe, they could never pay. Currencies, credit and prices were inflated. There were no jobs ready in industry for the soldiers and munition workers.

Here is Hoover's description of famine: "It is impossible for one who has never seen real famine to picture it – the pallid faces; the unsmiling eyes; the thin anemic and bloated children; the dead pall over towns where the children no longer play in the streets; the empty shops; the dull, listless movements and dumb grief of the women; the sweep of contagious diseases and the unending procession of funerals."

Agriculture had been hard hit. Men had been taken from the fields and put into the army. Nitrogen had been diverted from fertilizer to explosives. Steel had been used for swords instead of plowshares. Cattle numbers had dropped from a prewar level of 93 million to 18 million. Hog numbers had been cut almost in half. Draft horses had been reduced in number, a critical loss in the days before tractors. Planted acreage in 1918 was 60 percent of normal.

There were six to seven hundred thousand Russian prisoners of war in Germany and a like number of German prisoners in Russia. A prisoner of war is the last and least of claimants on a limited food supply. These prisoners, said Hoover, were "dying wholesale from neglect." French army leaders thought the Russian prisoners should be held in Germany to keep them from joining the Communist armies in Russia. Hoover's men finally got some food through to these prisoners. After the peace treaty they were gradually repatriated.

Prior to the armistice there had been political discipline and food rationing. With the end of the war everyone grabbed for food. Revolutionary governments came and went. Hungary went through four revolutions during the year the relief commission was in operation. Communists took advantage of the chaos. Here is Hoover's description of Hungary:

Hungary in the year 1919 presented a sort of unending, formless procession of tragedies, with occasional comic relief. Across our reconstruction stage there marched liberalism, revolution, socialism, communism, imperialism, terror, wanton executions, murder, suicide, falling ministries, invading armies, looted hospitals, conspirators, soldiers, kings and queens—all with a constant background of starving women and children. Defeat in a modern war means much more than surrender of a general's sword.

The first thing Hoover and his lieutenants did was to divide the thirty political units of Europe with their four hundred million people into five groups.

The Allies. Five countries: Britain, France, Italy, Portugal, and Greece. 135 million people. They had ships and needed credit; their situation was difficult but not critical.

The Neutrals. Six countries: Holland, Denmark, Norway, Sweden, Switzerland, and Spain. 42 million people. They had made money out of the war, had ships and credit, and could fend for themselves.

The Liberated Countries. Thirteen countries: Belgium, Poland, Yugoslavia, Albania, Czechoslovakia, Rumania, Finland, Estonia, Latvia, Lithuania, Armenia, Georgia, and Azerbaijan. 110 million people. They had new inexperienced governments and were mostly destitute.

Enemy Countries. Five countries: Germany, Austria, Hungary, Bulgaria, and Turkey. 110 million people. They had governments which were weak and inexperienced. They had some gold resources but no ships. They were threatened by communism and unemployment.

Soviet Russia. 170 million people. Starving, yet its agents were everywhere stirring up trouble.

For a time the Allies maintained their blockade of food and other supplies against the neutral, liberated, and enemy countries and against Russia. The Allied reasoning was that the situation was one of armistice, not surrender, and that pressure should be kept on Germany in order to set the stage for "favorable" peace terms. Hoover had opposed the food blockade from the first. He said that with short supplies the military, the munitions workers, the elite, and the governing classes would get food; the blockade was a campaign against the women, the children, and the destitute. At one negotiation after the armistice, Admiral Sir Rosslyn Wemyss, head of the British delegation, thus addressed Hoover: "Young man, I don't see why you Americans want to feed these Germans." To this the feisty Hoover responded, "Old man, I don't understand why you British wish to starve women and children after they are licked." The blockade was maintained for four months after the armistice while the Continent starved.

The organizational setup was like that pioneered in Belgium. Similar principles were followed. Logistical problems were incredibly difficult. Communication had been interrupted. Ports were damaged, railroads were torn up, rolling stock was scarce, and truck transport was crippled.

There was corruption. Some thousands of tons of food, clothing, and medicine, intended for Armenia, had been landed at Batum on the Black Sea. Only a part ever reached the Armenians. Thousands of tons had been sold in Georgia and Azerbaijan, where there was no need for relief. Hoover instantly removed the local American director of the committee and had nearly every member of the business staff arrested. This was all done "with no public remark" lest the credibility of the relief mission be damaged. As for the Armenian people themselves, from whom food had been diverted for the profit of the administering officials, there is this excerpt from a field report: "In the larger towns the dead and the dying are everywhere in the streets, children wandering about like dogs looking through the offal. I have seen women stripping flesh from dead horses with their bare hands. There is abundant evidence of cannibalism. Typhus is rampant."

A typhus epidemic began in Eastern Europe in April 1919. Short rations, debilitation, and filth resulting from lack of sanitary facilities all contributed to the spread of this louse-carried disease. At its peak there were possibly a million cases. The death rate was about 25 percent. The commission took on this adversary, threw up a sanitary cordon, deloused and reclad people village by village, and so checked the pestilence.

The Child Feeding Program, fashioned after the Belgian model, probably gave Hoover more satisfaction than anything else the commission did. The Friends Service Committee asked Hoover what they could do to help and he told them they could take on a very big job, the Child Feeding Program in Germany, which they did. The general plan in all countries was to set up local committees which would gather up waifs and orphans and take them into established institutions, where the commission would supply food, three meals a day. Infant children and their mothers also came under the system. In addition to food, clothing and medical supplies were provided. As fast as the children were restored to health and there was reasonable assurance that they would be cared for they were discharged and others were picked up.

The overwhelming share of the relief and rehabilitation effort was provided by the United States and most of the financing was in the form of credit. The European Allies had nearly exhausted their resources. They insisted that they had borne heavy loss of life and destruction of property while America had lost relatively few men and had experienced no property damage, so, they said, America should bear the burden of rehabilitation. This was acceptable to American voters only with the facade of loans, which were ultimately to be wiped out by default. The United States provided 93 percent of the supplies and 96 percent of the financing. Hoover knew there was small likelihood that these loans would be repaid (only about 5 percent were recovered). He was torn between his code of forthright dealing and his Quaker commitment to the value of human life. His humanitarian urge triumphed over his business principles.

The European crop of 1919 was good; agriculture has remarkable recuperative powers. On July 1, 1919, the program was officially terminated, though child feeding continued longer. From the start the intention had been to close out the program as soon as the worst of the crisis had passed.

Hoover thus appraised the postarmistice relief operation: "This operation saved the Allies millions of human lives; it saved the peace-making; it saved large parts of Europe from Communism; it saved millions from starvation, and restored at least 15 million children to health." But this was too glowing an assessment; his relief effort did not save the peace. Later, after World War II, when he updated his memoirs, he wrote of the Allies and their harsh treatment of postwar Germany: "the mine they had planted blew up in the faces of these world peace-makers."

Hoover was involved in famine relief in the Ukraine during 1921 to 1923, a controversial undertaking because the United States viewed the Soviet Union as a threat to the free world. True to his Quaker faith he believed that human lives were worth saving regardless of the political system by which people are governed.

Hoover served one term as president of the United States from 1929 to 1932, a period which coincided with the Great Depression, giving him an adverse image that would last for decades. The first part of his career reads like a book by Horatio Alger; the last part reads like the Book of Job.

The Second World War, more terrible than the First, began twenty years after the armistice. In 1946 the world again suffered postwar

famine. Hoover again was involved. Though seventy-two years old he
visited thirty-seven countries, helping to organize the food supply and
establishing feeding programs for 6 million children. He headed a campaign on behalf of the United Nations International Children's Emergency
Fund (UNICEF), rallying help for undernourished children the world
over. His Quaker values persisted throughout his life.

In 1960, when he was eighty-six years old and had only four more
years to live, Hoover spoke in Washington at the dedication of the memorial to President William Howard Taft. He stood erect and spoke briefly,
his voice somewhat reedy but earnest with praise of former President
Taft and the traditional American virtues. When he finished the large
audience stood and gave him prolonged applause. It was a fitting tribute
to a great man.

REFERENCES

Bane, Suda Lorena, and Ralph Haswell Lutz. 1943. *Organization of American
Relief in Europe, 1918–1919.* Stanford: Stanford Univ. Press.
Comfort, Mildred Houghton. 1960. *Herbert Hoover: Humanitarian.* Minneapolis:
Denison.
Dalrymple, Dana G. 1975. "Review of Weissman's 'Herbert Hoover and Famine
Relief in Soviet Russia.' " *Soviet Studies* (July):504–8.
Hard, William. 1928. *Who's Hoover?* New York: Dodd, Mead and Company.
Hoover, Herbert. 1951. *The Memoirs of Herbert Hoover, Years of Adventure 1874–
1920.* New York: Macmillan.
Irwin, Will. 1928. *Herbert Hoover, a Reminiscent Biography.* New York: Century.
Lyons: Eugene. 1948. *Herbert Hoover, a Biography.* Garden City, N.Y.: Doubleday.
Weissman, Benjamin M. 1974. *Herbert Hoover and Famine Relief to Soviet Russia,
1921–1923.* Stanford: Hoover Institution Press, Stanford Univ.

CHAPTER 24

Hubert Humphrey and the Hunger Lobby

FROM THE MID-1940s TO THE MID-1970s American food aid programs, both foreign and domestic, went through a transformation. Before those years food aid was small scale, intermittent, emergency oriented, and had a large element of private charity. At the end of the thirty-year period food aid had been federalized, institutionalized, and increased by several orders of magnitude. Leadership in this change was shared by a large number of people, most notably by Hubert Humphrey, variously Democratic senator from Minnesota, vice-president of the United States, and member of the Senate Committee on Agriculture.

The basic change was really an alteration in the concept of social justice. For long years equality of opportunity was thought to be the paradigm for social justice, with economic rewards bestowed through the market in accordance with an individual's contribution, government being held to a minimal role. The doctrines of John Locke and Adam Smith were dominant in this view. The concept fell into disfavor during the Great Depression, when the judgment emerged that minimal government could not provide equality of opportunity and that some people could not live decently on the meager rewards this system provided them.

The opposite view of social justice was egalitarianism, the idea that the economic dividend should be shared equally or nearly so. This view is of ancient origin; it is found in the Bible (Acts 4: 33–37). It was given a theoretical underpinning by the socialist writers of the nineteenth century. The concept is faulted by its critics primarily because it takes production for granted and provides insufficient incentives to work and save.

The third view of what constitutes social justice lies between these two extremes. Known as the welfare state, it was implicit in Roosevelt's

New Deal and was embraced by Senator Humphrey. In this concept the government provides a safety net to protect the individual from disaster whatever his or her economic or social performance. Above that level people are generally to be rewarded in proportion to their contributions as determined in the market while bearing the tax load required to care for the less fortunate. This altered view of social justice affected almost every issue put on the public policy agenda from the time of Roosevelt onward: civil rights, education, health, Social Security, housing, labor, law, tax policy, regulation of industry, and much more. The issue came late to food aid, probably because food availability was not thought to be a big problem. In this chapter we shall see how the new ethic was applied to food aid and try to interpret its consequences for the alleviation of hunger.

Hubert Horatio Humphrey, Jr., was born in Wallace, South Dakota in 1911, the son of a small-town druggist. His early years were spent in Doland, a town of five hundred people in that state. The young man received a degree from the Denver College of Pharmacy in 1933 after which he worked for four years in his father's drugstore. But filling prescriptions was not for him. He entered the University of Minnesota and earned membership in Phi Beta Kappa, graduating with highest honors in 1939. The following year he received a master's degree from Louisiana State University. He taught political science briefly at Macalester College in St. Paul.

Politics was in his blood. He ran unsuccessfully for mayor of Minneapolis in 1943 when he was thirty-two years old and only three years out of college. In 1945 Humphrey ran for mayor again. This time he won and was reelected two years later.

In 1948 the Democratic party met in national convention in Philadelphia, deeply divided over civil rights. Humphrey, a delegate, electrified the convention (and helped split the party) with a rousing speech favoring and winning a strong plank on civil rights. His thrust: "There are those who say to you we are rushing the issue of civil rights. I say we are 172 years late." A bitter fight developed within the Democratic party, but their underdog candidate, Harry Truman, won the election. Humphrey had carried his point on civil rights and helped his party win this unexpected victory. He was elected to the Senate that same year, the first Democrat ever sent to the upper house from Minnesota. He went to Washington flushed with victory and aglow with liberal causes. For thirty years Washington would be his base. He was elected to the vice-presidency in 1964, his Senate seat going to Walter Mondale, cut from the same cloth and advocate of the same causes. Humphrey was his party's nominee for the presidency (unsuccessful) in 1968 and was twice an unsuccessful candidate for his party's presidential nomination. He was known for his eloquence, his garrulous style, his congeniality, his advocacy of costly programs, and his predictable position as a liberal. He was a Democrat in the New Deal mode. Franklin Roosevelt was his hero. He was a strong believer in Social Security, health programs, price support for farmers, collective bargaining for hired labor, civil rights, foreign aid, federal support for education, the War on Poverty, the Great Society, and food aid, both domestic and foreign.

DOMESTIC FOOD AID

Until recent times federal domestic food aid was small scale and of low priority. Private charity and local governments were expected to carry most of the load. During the hard times and huge food stocks of the 1930s a program of direct donation was set up. A complicated food stamp program was put in place, providing subsidized food for the poor, but it was closed out when World War II began. A new food stamp plan was inaugurated in 1961, but it was of rather small dimensions. The essential idea of the food stamp plan is that poor people receive stamps with which they can buy food. The degree of subsidy depends on the income of the recipient.

Hunger was "discovered" in the United States during the 1960s. The Hunger Lobby emerged and everything changed. Shortly after the assassination of President John Kennedy, new president Lyndon Johnson announced his War on Poverty and launched the Great Society. In April 1967 a Senate Subcommittee on Employment, Manpower, and Poverty held hearings in Mississippi to study poverty programs. Among those present were Democrats Robert Kennedy of New York, candidate for his party's presidential nomination, and Joe Clark of Pennsylvania, candidate to succeed himself as United States senator. One of the witnesses was Marian Wright, a twenty-seven-year-old civil rights worker and attorney for the NAACP Legal Defense Fund. She testified that people were starving and urged the senators to investigate. This they did.

At Cleveland, a small Delta town, they found Annie White, mother of six children, all obviously malnourished. The youngest, two years old, was underweight, listless, and unresponsive. The mother told the senators she had no money and so could not afford to buy food stamps, even with the subsidy. She was feeding her family only some rice and biscuits made from leftover surplus commodities.

The senators, authentically and visibly moved, visited other homes. They saw more hungry children. The press, following these candidates for public office, recorded the events with pen and camera. The papers carried the story in full, nationwide, with pictures. Hunger had been discovered.

Two organizations, involved in projects to help the poor, saw this as an opportune moment. One, the Field Foundation of New York, had been set up by the Marshall Field family, owners of the famous Chicago department store. The other, the Citizen's Crusade against Poverty, was backed by the United Auto Workers, the National Council of Churches, the United Presbyterian Church, and the Ford Foundation. In July 1967, the two organizations set up a Citizens' Board of Inquiry into Hunger and Malnutrition in the United States, with membership of twenty-three people from various social action groups. Agriculture, agribusiness, and the Congress were not represented. Thus the Hunger Lobby was born.

The movement attracted activists from diverse backgrounds: religious, humanitarian, labor, civil rights, and health. There were social reformers and dissidents. People who were themselves hungry were a small part of the movement. They lacked the resources and the political acumen needed to push the issue.

On April 22, 1968, the Citizens' Board of Inquiry released its report, a 96-page document of narrative and pictures. Leslie Dunbar, the director, said: "We have found concrete evidence of chronic hunger and malnutrition in every part of the United States where we have held hearings or conducted field trips." He stated that at least ten million Americans suffered from hunger and malnutrition.

In May 1968 the Columbia Broadcasting System showed a television documentary titled "Hunger in America," based on the report of the board of inquiry. It was a sensation, portraying hunger in all its cruelty. The hunger issue was on the public policy agenda.

The central factual question concerned the actual state of nutrition and health. Most of the evidence was anecdotal; scientific studies were slow in coming. Early in the Nixon administration Dr. Arnold Schaefer, director of the Department of Health, Education and Welfare's National Survey, reported: "Our studies to date clearly indicate that there is malnutrition—and in our opinion it occurs in an unexpectedly large proportion of our sample population."

In 1971–72 a deeper inquiry, the HANES study (Health and Nutrition Examination Survey), also done by the Department of Health, Education and Welfare, revealed that on the average the diets of those in poverty were marginally inferior to the diets of those above the poverty line. On the average the wealthy buy more prestigious, tasty, and expensive foods than do the poor, and they buy more service with their food. The weight of the evidence is that they also buy somewhat better nutrition. Similar findings came from the 1972 Ten-State Nutrition Survey, also done by the

Department of Health, Education and Welfare. More recent studies generally corroborate these findings, but there is little evidence that many minds have been changed. The Hunger Lobby insists that the problem is immense and the hard-liners maintain that it is small.

The gross evidence is that hunger and malnutrition, whatever their incidence, are on the retreat in the United States. At least one-third of Americans, including substantial numbers of the poor, are overweight. This may be an evidence of poor diets but not of hunger. The average life span is increasing and the height of the new generation exceeds that of the parents. The nutritionally related diseases—rickets, beri-beri, goiter, anemia, scurvy, and night-blindness—are becoming rare.

Two pieces of popular evidence need to be excluded in the search for generalized truth. One is the starving family, such as found by senators Kennedy and Clark, cited as evidence of widespread malnutrition among the poor. The other is the brawny heavyweight boxing champion coming from a background of poverty, cited as an indication that dietary problems among the poor are a myth. There are such individual cases but neither is typical. It is human nature to observe and generalize from the unusual. Pockets of poverty exist but the condition is not as general as the Hunger Lobby insists.

The agitation about hunger was deeply offensive to the agricultural establishment. First of all there was disbelief in the allegation that hunger was widespread. On a deeper level, the presence of hunger challenged basic agricultural premises: (1) that America is a well-fed nation; (2) that the real problem is the low income of the farmer who produces food, not the inability of the consumer to buy it; (3) that farm programs to limit food production and increase its price are in the public interest; (4) that food aid programs of the Agricultural Department are adequate; and (5) that a person should work for what he or she gets.

So a great battle arose. The more extreme activists, arguing from their concept of social justice, contended that adequate food was an entitlement regardless of individual effort, that the diets of the poor should be not only ample in amount but also nutritious and aesthetically pleasing and that no onus should be associated with receiving food aid. The more adamant opponents argued that hunger and malnutrition occurred only rarely, that the existing food aid programs were adequate, that hunger was largely the result of ignorance or laziness, and that those who can work must do so if they are to eat.

President Johnson, during whose term the issue reached its apogee, held firm against increasing food aid. The Hunger Lobby, knowing Humphrey's sympathy, went to him for help. Humphrey tried his private judicious best to get the president to increase food aid, but to no avail. Humphrey's loyalty to the president on Vietnam, food aid, and other matters cost him liberal support and very likely contributed to his defeat as his party's nominee for the presidency in 1968.

A stalemate had developed. The agricultural committees of the Congress, dubious about the hunger issue as was the president, had control of the food programs and would not move. But with the dwindling size of the farm population, the committees needed urban help in passing farm price support programs. The Hunger Lobby disliked the supply-restricting price-raising farm programs but needed help in liberalizing food aid. Hubert Humphrey, a political realist as well as a liberal ideologue, helped the agricultural committees and the Hunger Lobby to see the merits of cooperation. So rural southern and midwestern congressmen made a deal with urban congressmen from the East and North. A bargain was struck; the agricultural committees would increase food aid and the Hunger Lobby would deliver the urban vote needed to pass the farm price support legislation.

Humphrey promoted and relished this deal. He won on both counts. He favored both increased food aid and high farm price supports. The liberalization of food aid and the passage of farm legislation in recent years are in large part explained by the coalition of the Hunger Lobby and the Farm Lobby. It was an unpublicized agreement. The Farm Lobby said nothing to their constituents nor the Hunger Lobby to theirs.

As food aid matured it developed a supportive cast of special interests, which is true of all government programs. The food programs marginally increase food consumption and so raise gross farm income by 1 or 2 percent; propagation of this fact helped neutralize farm opposition. The grocery chains found it more congenial to accept food stamps than to turn beggars away. Support for the school lunch program came from venders of refrigerators, stoves, and cafeteria equipment. Support for food aid programs became a litmus test for liberals. The administering bureaucracy of course supported the programs.

During these years of controversy the food stamp program, the main but by no means the only domestic food aid venture, grew (see Tables 24.1 and 24.2).

From January 1982 through fiscal 1985 the federal government, burdened by surplus stocks of food accumulated under price support programs, released 2.5 billion pounds of food, most of it butter and cheese, valued at $3 billion. Lipsky and Thibodeau report that this food, targeted to needy persons, went to as many as 20 million people in a loosely structured program that operated through some twenty thousand church groups, food banks, community action programs, soup kitchens, food pantries, and civic clubs across the country. It was a remarkable example of cooperation between government and voluntary private groups. How

Table 24.1   Food Stamp Program Growth

	Participants (millions)	Cost (millions of dollars)
1961	—	1
1962	.1	14
1963	.2	20
1964	.4	30
1965	.4	35
1966	.9	70
1967	1.4	115
1968	2.2	187
1969	2.9	229
1970	4.3	550
1971	9.4	1,523
1972	11.1	1,797
1973	12.2	2,131
1974	12.9	2,718
1975	17.1	4,386
1976	18.5	5,327
1977	17.1	5,067
1978	16.0	5,139
1979	17.7	6,480
1980	21.1	8,685
1981	22.4	10,630
1982	22.1	10,409
1983	21.6	11,152

Source: USDA.

much of this food went to the truly needy and how much of it went to displace what would otherwise have been bought are pertinent but un-answered questions.

A public policy issue has a life cycle similar to that of a biological specimen: conception, birth, adolescence, maturity, senility, death (and possibly reincarnation). The duration of the cycle may be days, decades, or centuries, depending on circumstances. The domestic food programs appear to be on this path and seem to be maturing. Food aid in America declined as an issue and stabilized as a program in the early 1980s. The

Table 24.2   Complexion of 1983 Domestic Food Aid Programs

	Millions of Dollars
Food stamp program (low cost food for families in poverty)	11,152
Direct donation (surplus food commodities to needy families)	2,067
School lunch program (low cost food in the schools)	2,402
Women, Infants and Children (supplemental food for the vulnerable)	902
Other (school breakfast, summer feeding, special milk, child care, food for the elderly)	746
Total	17,269

Source: USDA.

nature of bureaucracy is such that the program congeals and continues after the issue has subsided.

There were several reasons for abatement of the issue. When food stamp recipients reached about 20 million (around 8 percent of the population), the consensus arose that authentic needs had been met, perhaps more than met. Evidence emerged that food stamps were going to ineligible recipients. The various welfare programs came under criticism, particularly when their disincentive effect was demonstrated; in some areas welfare dependence continued into the third or fourth generation.

It was once felt that food aid was not only laudable from a humanitarian standpoint but that it would be politically rewarding. This appraisal underwent revision. Three Democratics who were strong supporters of food aid received their party's nomination for president: Humphrey in 1968, McGovern in 1972, and Mondale in 1984. All were defeated.

The earlier ethic of reward in accordance with economic contribution could not be sustained and the egalitarian principle could not be established. What emerged was the concept of social justice implicit in the welfare state – a publicly provided floor over the pit of disaster, with rewards above that level generally in accordance with contribution as measured by the market. The new idea became generally endorsed. The existence of hunger and malnutrition became accepted as a fact and the need to relieve them was established. Present arguments concern the level of the floor and the identification of persons in need. A conservative administration has not been able to reduce food aid in any major way and the Hunger Lobby, somewhat jaded, has not been able to raise it significantly.

INTERNATIONAL FOOD AID

We have seen how Herbert Hoover won an American commitment to help relieve postwar famine. There were other examples of federal food aid but these were mostly episodic and of an emergency nature.

International food aid was institutionalized in 1954 with the passage of Public Law 480, the Agricultural Trade Development and Assistance Act, sometimes known as Food-For-Peace. In its origin it was primarily a surplus disposal operation; the initiative came from agriculture. Huge stocks of farm products had been accumulated which could not be sold because by law they were priced out of the market. They could not be donated abroad because the public was against "giveaways." They could not be destroyed; this was politically unacceptable. They could not be held for an overlong period; in about six years the cost of storage equalled

the value of the product. The Congress would not cut the acreage enough
to make room in the market for this accumulated hoard. The surpluses
hung over the market like a cloud, depressing the agricultural economy.
What to do?

Early in the Eisenhower administration Gwynn Garnett, staff man
with the American Farm Bureau Federation, called on True Morse, under
secretary of Agriculture. Garnett had assisted in the feeding of postwar
Europe and had innovative ideas about the use of food. Waving his notorious cigar in crisp circles, Garnett revealed his idea. Here it is, condensed
and paraphrased:

Sell the stocks to the poor and hungry nations, not for dollars because they don't
have dollars but for their own currencies. There is no shortage of such currencies.
We can say to the public at home and abroad that we are not giving food away, we
are selling it. Use some of the national currencies to support the American em-
bassies in the receiving countries. Hold the rest and decide later what to do with
them. Channel the operation through the private commercial trade, thus winning
agribusiness support and avoiding the charge that a huge new government initiative is being launched. Assure that what moves through this new mechanism will
be in addition to normal purchases so regular commercial sales will not be displaced. With this device introduce American farm products to nations not yet
familiar with them and so in time develop a new commercial market. Parallel
these sales with donations through the charitable agencies, giving the operation a
clearly visible aspect of combatting hunger. Thus move out the stocks and give
American farmers some breathing room.

It was an escape hatch for a drowning agricultural policy. But it was
an institutional invention of the first order. The Eisenhower administration bought the idea and the Agriculture Department drafted legislation.
Strongly aided by Senator Humphrey, it sailed through the Congress with
bipartisan support. Public Law 480 was the child of a shotgun wedding —
a pregnant Department of Agriculture and a reluctant State Department.
It was a live birth, with little midwifery. The child grew up to have a
career not contemplated by the parents. Begun as a surplus disposal
program, PL 480 evolved into a multipurpose instrument. In addition to
surplus disposal were relief of hunger, a diplomatic tool, and, it was
hoped, an aid to economic development. Humanitarians, concerned with
the relief of hunger, resented the servicing of some of these other goals.
But there was not enough political support to sustain the program based
on alleviation of hunger alone.

Initially, opposition came from other food-exporting countries who
saw a threat to their sales and from the State Department, reflecting the
interest of the rival exporting countries. But the State Department found

that PL 480 grain could be used in support of American diplomatic initiatives and rival exporters came to see that it was in their interest that the American surplus be moved into use through additional outlets. Significantly, the receiving foreign nations were doubtful about the new arrangements. This was in part the result of American heavy-handedness in disposing of the government stocks; some foreign nations were strongarmed into taking American surpluses that they did not want.

The largest component of Public Law 480 has long been Title I, sales for foreign currency or on very favorable dollar credit terms. Though it has strong concessional elements the greater part of the food thus supplied moves through the commercial market. It is a near form of food aid. In 1985 it totaled $1.1 billion. Our concern in this chapter is with Title II, which involves food donation directly to needy individuals, without pay, outside the regular market, through the private voluntary organizations. In 1985 it moved commodities worth $1 billion.

The voluntary agencies, which include both religious and secular groups, have deep concern for hungry people abroad. But they lack the resources, the diplomatic credentials, and the logistic support needed for overseas donation. These capabilities are uniquely possessed by government. Public Law 480 with its Title II provided an ideal opportunity for cooperation between the private voluntary organizations and the government. No one saw this more clearly than Hubert Humphrey. He and the Hunger Lobby joined forces to make the most of the opportunity.

Among the church organizations now prominent in this cooperative effort are Catholic Relief Service, Church World Service, Lutheran World Relief, and Seventh Day Adventist Welfare Service. Secular agencies like CARE, UNICEF, American Joint Distribution Committee, and the Cooperative League of the United States are involved. A list of participating agencies is shown in the appendix to this chapter. These organizations raise money chiefly from private contributions. The government supplies the food, free of charge, processes and packages it if need be, and pays freight to the receiving country. Distribution is to persons approved as needy by the government of the receiving country, the food typically going for in-clinic feeding of mothers and infants and to school children. Wheat and wheat products are the major donated commodities, followed by nonfat dry milk and vegetable oil. The receiving country assists with the distribution. Food must be provided without discrimination as to the political, racial, or religious affiliation of the recipient; proselytizing is not allowed. The donated food is supplemental; it meets only a small part of individual need.

The program provides enormous leverage for the voluntary agencies. The overwhelming share of the cost is borne by government. For example, in a 1980 program in Togo, a small West African country, the costs were divided thus: U.S. government, 91 percent; government of Togo, 5 percent; voluntary agencies, 4 percent. A dollar contributed to the voluntary agency helped move twenty-five dollars worth of food.

How much of the hunger problem is alleviated by this food aid? The Food and Agriculture Organization (FAO) of the United Nations has estimated the number of malnourished people at about 450 million. The operation we have been describing reaches about 75 million people with an average of around 60 pounds of food apiece. If the FAO is right in its assessment and if all this food goes to the right people (which it does not), we would be supplying about 15 percent of the world's hungry with about 10 percent of their total food needs. This is the most generous assessment of which a supporter of the program is capable. Commendable and helpful though the program is it cannot in itself be a solution to the world food problem.

Can the direct overseas food donation programs be expanded in a helpful fashion? These are the constraints: (1) the financial and administrative capabilities of the charitable agencies; (2) the amount of food the American people were willing to make available; and (3) the danger of making recipients continuously dependent on the program.

The relationship between the volume of food aid and the general well-being is not linear; it is curvilinear. Some is good, but it does not follow that more is better or that the maximum amount is the best possible. There is some point at which benefits are greatest. Pushed beyond that point benefits diminish and if pushed still further harm results. Excessive amounts of donated food drive down prices in the receiving country, inhibiting agricultural development and building a bond of dependency that both giver and receiver find difficult to break. Friends of food aid emphasize the part of the curve that is positive and rising; opponents look at the part that is falling and negative.

Where are we on the curve? There is no way of answering with assurance. Judgment is needed, case by case. In the opinion of this writer we have sometimes gone too far, as in Egypt, where reliance on food aid has become so great that the Egyptian government has lost control of food policy. We have sometimes not gone far enough, as in the case of the famine on the island of Timor in southeast Asia some years ago. And we have sometimes been at or near the optimum point, as with India in 1966–67, a case we shall examine in the next chapter.

Senator Humphrey consistently supported all aspects of Public Law 480. The Hunger Lobby converged on him like iron filings on a magnet. For food aid Humphrey was both advocate and symbol. During the terrible Indian drought of 1966–67, Humphrey, then vice-president, was influential in using Public Law 480 to supply 14.5 million tons of grain, amounting to one-fifth of the U.S. wheat crop, thus averting disaster in the Asian subcontinent.

In 1963 Humphrey was helpful in using Public Law 480 as a means of supporting the World Food Program, the multilateral food aid initiative launched by the United Nations through the Food and Agricultural Organization.

In 1974, at the height of concern about the ability of the world to feed itself, came the World Food Conference in Rome. There were proposals for action, old and new. Senator Humphrey supported food aid, economic development, and technical assistance in agriculture but stayed clear of the radical reformers who wished to pull down the existing trade system and supplant it with a new international economic order.

The U.S. government, which has only recently and after great controversy accepted responsibility for the alleviation of hunger within the United States, is now testing the much deeper principle of responsibility beyond our borders. This testing process is under way both in the public forum and in private deliberations, in sacred and in secular settings.

Has the attitude toward international food aid changed during the life of Public Law 480? It has, with Humphrey's help. During the tight food situation of the mid-1970s the United States continued to supply food aid abroad, though in diminished volume. Most architects of Public Law 480 had little awareness that it would become the means of institutionalizing international food aid.

What do we learn from examining this thirty-year confrontation on food aid, foreign and domestic? We see an affirmation that in the years ahead when the cry of hunger is heard it will fall on attentive ears; we have been sensitized. Response is more likely because a new ethic has emerged and the institutional machinery has been put in place. A measure of success is more probable as a consequence of experience gained. The conquest of hunger has advanced a step or two through the mingled motives of self-interest and humanitarian concern. This change is attributable to Hubert Humphrey more than to anyone else.

Hubert Humphrey died in 1978 of cancer after a long courageous fight. Compassion, zeal, prudence, and pragmatism were so mingled in him as to gladden his friends, confound his adversaries, and baffle any who sought to explain him by one attribute only.

REFERENCES

Amrine, Michael. 1960. *This is Humphrey.* Garden City, N.Y.: Doubleday.
Aziz, Sartaj. 1975. *Hunger, Politics, and Markets.* New York: New York Univ. Press.
Berry, Jeffrey M. 1982. "Consumers and the Hunger Lobby." In Don F. Hadwiger and Ross B. Talbot, *Food Policy and Farm Programs,* pp. 68–78. Academy of Political Science.
Citizen's Board of Inquiry. 1968. *Hunger USA.* Boston: Beacon Press.
Food and Agriculture Organization of the UN. 1963. *Man's Right to Freedom from Hunger.* Special Assembly, Rome.
Guither, Harold D. 1980. *The Food Lobbyists.* Lexington, Mass.: D. C. Heath.
Harris, Charles E., Jr. 1984. "Capitalism and Social Justice." *Intercollegiate Review* 20, no. 1 (Spring–Summer):35–49.
Humphrey, Hubert H. 1964. *War on Poverty.* New York: McGraw Hill.
Kotz, Nick. 1969. *Let Them Eat Promises: The Politics of Hunger in America.* Englewood Cliffs, N.J.: Prentice Hall.
Lipsky, Michael, and Marc A. Thibodeau. 1985. *Food in the Warehouse, Hunger in the Streets.* Cambridge, Mass.: Department of Political Science, MIT.
Nelson, Jack A. 1980. *Hunger for Justice.* Maryknoll, N.Y.: Orbis Books.
Poppendieck, Janet. 1986. *Breadlines Kneedeep in Wheat: Food Assistance in the Great Depression.* New Brunswick, N.J.: Rutgers Univ. Press.
Rawls, John. 1971. *A Theory of Justice.* Cambridge, Mass.: Harvard University Press.
USDA. 1982. *Food for Peace: 1981 Annual Report on Public Law 480.* Foreign Agricultural Service, Washington, D.C.
U.S. Agency for International Development. "Outreach Grant Project Assessment – Togo and Benin." Prepared by International Science and Technology Institute, Washington, D.C.

APPENDIX.   A Partial List of Organizations That Are or Have Been Active in Food Aid

Organizations Mostly Interested in International Food Aid

Africare; Adventist Development and Relief Agency; The American Council of Voluntary Agencies for Foreign Service; American Council for Judaism Philanthropic Fund, Inc.; American Council for Nationalities Service; American Friends Service Committee, Inc.; American Foundation for Overseas Blind; American Fund for Czechoslovak Refugees, Inc.; American Mizachi Women; American National Committee to Aid Homeless Armenians (ANCAHA); American ORT Federation, Inc.; Assemblies of God, Foreign Service Committee; Baptist World Alliance; CARE, Inc. (Cooperative for American Relief Everywhere); Catholic Relief Services, U.S. Catholic Conference; Christian Reformed World Relief Committee; Church World Service; CODEL, Inc. (Cooperation in Development); Community Development Foundation, Inc.; Direct Relief International; Foster Parents Plan, Inc.; Foundation for the Peoples of the South Pacific, Inc.; Grassroots International; Hadassah, the Women's Zionist Organization of

America, Inc.; Heifer Project International; HIAS, Inc. (Holt International Children's Service); Interchurch Medical Assistance, Inc.; International Rescue Committee, Inc.; Lutheran Immigration and Refugee Service; Lutheran World Relief, Inc.; MAP, Inc. (Medical Assistance Programs); Mennonite Central Committee, Inc.; Migration and Refugee Service, U.S. Catholic Conference; Near East Foundation; Operation California; Oxfam America: Africa Crisis; PACT, Inc. (Private Agencies Collaborating Together); Presiding Bishops Fund for World Relief; Project Concern, Inc.; The Salvation Army; Save the Children Foundation, Inc.; Seventh-Day Adventist World Service, Inc.; Tolstoy Foundation, Inc.; Travelers Aid—International Social Service of America; United Israel Appeal, Inc.; Unitarian Universalist Service Committee; United Lithuanian Relief Fund of America, Inc.; UMCOR (United Methodist Committee on Relief); U.S. Committee for UNICEF; United Ukranian American Relief Committee, Inc.; World Concern Development Organization; World Relief Corporation; World Vision Relief Organization; World University Service; Young Men's Christian Association, International Division; Young Women's Christian Association of the U.S.A, National Board, World Relations.

Organizations Mostly Interested in Domestic Food Aid

Children's Foundation; Food Research and Action Center; Community Nutrition Institute; Consumer Federation of America; National Child Nutrition Project; National Urban League; National Council of Senior Citizens; League of Women Voters of the United States; Women's Lobby; American Association of Retired Persons; Migrant Legal Action Program; National Association of Farm Worker Organizations; Amalgamated Meat Cutters and Butcher Workers of America; Industrial Union Department of AFL-CIO; United Automobile, Aerospace, and Agricultural Implement Workers of America.

Organizations Interested in Both Domestic and International Food Aid

Interreligious Task Force on U.S. Food Policy; American Baptist Churches, U.S.A.; American Jewish Committee; American Lutheran Church; Christian Church (Disciples of Christ); Church of the Brethren; Episcopal Church; Friends Committee on National Legislation; Jesuit Conference; Lutheran Church in America; Lutheran Church–Missouri Synod; Moravian Church in America; National Council of Churches; Presbyterian Church in the U.S.; Reformed Church in America; Union of American Hebrew Congregations; Unitarian Universalist Association; Unitarian Universalist Service Committee; United Church of Christ; United Methodist Church; United Presbyterian Church in the U.S.A.; Bread for the World; Center of Concern Network.

Source: Mostly from Guither, *The Food Lobbyists*.

CHAPTER 25

Anthony Dias and the Famine that Didn't Happen

BOMBAY, August 1982. Things can be learned from events that don't occur as well as from those that do. It is thus possible to learn from the Bihar famine of 1967, the one that didn't happen.

Famines have been intermittent throughout India's history. The Rig Veda, many centuries before Christ, has this prayer to Indra, the raingiver:

From this our misery and famine set us free,
From this dire curse deliver us.
Succor us with thine help and with thy wondrous thought,
Most Mighty, finder of the way.

In 1769–70 an estimated one-third of Bengal's population of 30 million perished of famine. W. W. Hunter's *Annals of Rural India* contains this vivid passage describing that famine: "All through the stifling summer the people went on dying. The husbandmen sold their cattle; they sold their implements of agriculture; they devoured their seed grain; they sold their sons and daughters, till at length no buyer of children could be found." In 1837–38, in the northwest provinces, a famine took eight hundred thousand lives; another famine in the same region in 1860–61 took the lives of two hundred thousand people. The famine of the 1865–66 in Orissa wiped out whole villages; a million people starved. During the Bengal famine of 1943 deaths were variously estimated from one and a half to as many as three or four million. This famine was partly a matter of bad weather and in part a result of World War II, which cut off rice supplies from Burma.

The British, while they held India, had a threefold policy regarding famine relief, explicit in the Famine Code:

1. Indian famines were considered to result from a lack of buying power, not from a lack of food. Therefore the appropriate remedy was work projects.

2. Famine relief was to be related to circumstances as perceived, not launched from a preplanned base.

3. A huge commitment to famine relief was thought to be potentially more hurtful than the famine itself.

Famine relief under the British therefore consisted chiefly of work projects for the poor, providing them with the means to buy food. Relief wages were kept low to avoid attracting people from their customary work.

The years between independence and 1965 showed a dangerous pattern: food production fluctuating around a slowly rising trend, accompanied by a rapid increase in population, 2.4 percent per year. The sluggish agricultural performance was a cause of warranted concern. The years 1962–63 and 1963–64 showed an ominous deficiency in food grain production. Imports increased, chiefly from the United States under a four-year Public Law 480 program involving 16 million tons of grain. The year 1964–65 produced a recovery and a record 89.4 million tons of food grain, but not enough to overcome the disappointment during the previous two years. On August 25, 1964, A. L. Dias took charge as secretary to the government of India in the Department of Food. Dias would therefore be the man in charge when the Bihar famine struck.

Anthony Lancelot Dias (pronounced DY-us) is a native of India, one of eight children born to a medical doctor in Poona, a university town east of Bombay. He and his family are Christian; his ancestors were converted by the Portuguese in Goa 450 years ago. The converts were given new names – Portuguese ones – which accounts for the Iberian name in a land of Guptas and Mehtas. Dias took his bachelor's degree in economics, with honors, from the University of Bombay. He went to England, where he received his bachelor of science degree from the London School of Economics. In 1933 Dias entered the Indian Civil Service, detailed to his hometown area, Bombay. His outstanding performance came to the attention of C. Subramaniam, then food minister, who asked him to come in as secretary, and Dias agreed. Then fifty-four years old, seasoned in a variety of posts, administratively tough but personally gentle, imbued with a sense of mission and concern for the poor, Dias was the man for the job.

He barely got his chair warm before famine conditions began to develop.

The year 1965 was marked by a delayed and erratic monsoon. The deficiency in rainfall which characterized the summer persisted through September and October, blighting the prospects for the *kharif* crop (spring planted, chiefly rice) throughout much of India. The *rabi* crop (fall planted, chiefly wheat) was sown in dry conditions and showed poor prospects. When the 1965–66 crop of food grains was tallied it came to 72.3 million tons, compared with 89.4 million tons for 1964–65, a shortfall of 17.1 million tons or 19 percent. In the production of food grains, where there is limited inventory and where consumption cannot be postponed, a decline of this magnitude is grave indeed. This is particularly true in India, where the population presses heavily on the food supply and there is little cushion to absorb a shock.

Hopes were high that the new year, 1966–67, would show a recovery. But hopes were blasted. The monsoon was again deficient. This was the one-in-a-hundred event: two disastrous monsoons back to back. The drought struck with particular ferocity in the state of Bihar, northwest of Calcutta. *Kharif* rice, the main crop of the state, turned out at 1.2 million tons as against a normal 4.4 million tons, making only one-fourth of a crop. The population of the areas seriously affected by the drought in Bihar came to nearly 30 million. Other provinces were affected, though less seriously than Bihar. For India as a whole, food grain production in 1966–67 totaled 74.2 million tons, only slightly above the disaster of 1965–66 and 15.2 million tons below the 1964–65 level.

As is generally the case in famines, the greatest difficulty came when the supply from the previous poor crops had been depleted and the new crop was not yet ready for harvest. This occurred during the spring and summer of 1967. The severity was the greatest in the state of Bihar. Within that state the crisis was most critical, locally, in the district of Palamau, northwest of Calcutta, in the Gangetic Plain. This district had a population of 12 million people, 95 percent of whom were rural. Historically the land and the people had both been poor. In Palamau the staple *kharif* rice crop was virtually lost; drought burned it up. It was the worst drought since 1884. It was in Palamau that most of the stories were written and the pictures taken that appeared in the foreign press.

One of the first actions of the Indian government was to revise the policy toward famine that had prevailed during colonial times. That policy had treated famine as a deplorable but more or less natural condition, to be alleviated as much as possible without impairing the ongoing productive efforts of the society. Under the new policy the government considered that people afflicted by famine had a natural right to food and that this right took precedence over the normal activities of the country. Dias, the new secretary of the Department of Food, strongly pushed this view.

The idea was that people severely injured by a drought—a force beyond their control—should be assisted and that such assistance was a matter of entitlement. Help was obligatory, not optional. This policy position prevailed throughout the government from Prime Minister Indira Gandhi, through Food Minister Subramaniam, through Dias, and on down to the workers at the district level. There thus was harmony in the famine relief effort springing from singleness of purpose.

Importation of food grain was essential, as much and as soon as possible. Food grains are the mainstay of the Indian food supply and are ideally suited to famine relief. Of the cereal grains, wheat is preeminent. The chief source of imported wheat obviously was the United States. Dias and Subramaniam worked closely with Chester Bowles, the American ambassador to India. They went to Washington to request help from Vice-President Hubert Humphrey and Secretary of Agriculture Orville Freeman, who received them well and provided the needed help. During the two years 1966 and 1967 the United States supplied 14.5 million tons of grain, almost entirely on concessional terms. Most of this went to the drought-stricken rural areas but some of it was distributed in the cities. Other sources were solicited and responded in lesser degree, chiefly Canada, Australia, and the World Food Program of the United Nations.

The private voluntary agencies were enlisted, among them CARE, Catholic Relief Service, CORAGS (Committee on Relief and Gift Supplements of the National Christian Council of India), and the Indian Red Cross. These agencies supplied a variety of American foods, among them nonfat dry milk, soybean meal, vegetable oil, and cereal grain.

Administrative machinery had to be set up where it did not exist and strengthened where it was already in being. Volunteers had to be recruited; there were four thousand of these in Bihar alone.

Arrangements had to be made for procurement of domestically produced grain, chiefly by purchase at official (low) prices, from those Indian farmers who had escaped the worst ravages of drought. Facilities had to be augmented for receiving and unloading cargoes of grain from overseas. During the height of the crisis, ships docked at a rate of three a day. Food had to be transported to the point of need, seven trains a day, fifty cars per train, an average distance of 550 miles. Altogether, 20 million tons of food grain were distributed in the drought areas, most of it imported.

The ultimate focus of all this effort was individual need. If the effort bogged down at the final distribution point all was lost.

The main means of distribution were the fair price shops. These were retail food outlets through which subsidized food was sold at official (low) prices in rationed amounts to holders of identification cards. During 1967, at the height of the famine, there were 153,000 such shops operating in the country. Twenty thousand of these were in Bihar, benefiting 47 million Biharis.

In the absence of assistance many of the poor were unable to buy food even at the official low price. For the able-bodied poor, work projects were developed, involving heavy manual labor such as digging wells, cleaning irrigation canals, and repairing roads. Wages were paid for this work which made food purchase possible. Those less strong were employed at light manual labor such as rope and basket making and spinning. Some who could not work at all were given small outright grants. Substantial numbers of small consumption loans were made. In Palamau loans and relief work provided by the government accounted for 70 percent of the assistance. Thus buying power was transferred to the drought-striken people with which food could be bought at the fair price shops. These methods made modified use of the conventional food market economy. In addition there were free food kitchens. There was food distribution for pregnant and nursing mothers and for infants and children. Government and the private charitable agencies worked together in this massive feeding effort.

Wells went dry; drinking water was a problem. Old wells were deepened and new ones were dug. Well-drilling rigs were put into operation; Canada flew in some of these. Twelve thousand tube wells were put down. Bullock carts hauled water to thirsty people. In previous famines cholera and smallpox had taken a dreadful toll. In Bihar state, six million cholera vaccinations were administered and a like number for smallpox. Four million wells were disinfected.

Through these troubled times news of the food situation in India moved onto the front pages of the world press. Television cameras were focused on Bihar; the Bihar famine was the first to be brought into the American living room. The *Reader's Digest* stated that in early 1967, fifteen million people were threatened with starvation. Garrett Hardin came up with his famous lifeboat illustration, arguing against food aid to India. In many countries, Hardin said, population was outrunning the food supply. The ship had gone down, the lifeboats were filled, and if others were allowed aboard all would be lost.

The myth, prevalent in much of the world outside of India, was that Indian officals couldn't administer anything. Conventional wisodm had it that all they had learned from the British was the ability to follow orders, adhere to procedures, and bind up old documents with red tape. With the British no longer in control, everything would bog down. But the Indian officials broke the pattern, scrapped the rules, and gave authority to the people at the operating level.

Dias took strong hold of famine relief. He streamlined the operation at the policy level, reaching decisions quickly by short daily conferences with his top men. Committees, reports, files, endorsements, verifications, and certifications were minimized; policy making was speeded up and food delivery was expedited.

At the operational level decisions were decentralized. Eligibility for assistance, authorization of work projects, logistical decisions as to transportation and warehousing, drafting of officials for special duty—these matters were pushed onto the district level administrators. Speed was essential. In dealing with the threat of famine, delay meant death.

Whether Dias knew of the famine relief principles laid down by Herbert Hoover half a century earlier is not clear. His operations were similar, whether borrowed or rediscovered.

What was the result of this prodigious and complex effort? The famine didn't happen. Some five years after the crisis had passed, an assessment was made by Dr. K. Suresh Singh, who had been in Palamau in Bihar state during the drought years. Singh reported that the death rate in Bihar as a whole declined in 1967 during the height of the famine. This probably resulted from the health measures that accompanied the food relief as well as from the food relief itself. If famine is defined as an increase in the death rate resulting from a lack of food, there was no famine in Bihar. In Palamau, the worst affected area, for reasons that were obscure the birth rate rose. A high protein food named Bal Ahar was made available. CARE distributed a gruel called CSM (corn–soybean meal–milk powder) supplemented with salad oil, perhaps the best food the recipients had ever eaten. In ordinary times poverty-stricken people ate poorly; during the Bihar famine their diets improved.

Migration, which had been feared, was not important. Only 5 percent of the households reported migration. The cattle population decreased. During the height of the famine the number of cattle hides sold was twice the normal level. The mortgaging of land doubled during the famine. Thus current buying power of farm people was augmented. Caste structure did not impede relief efforts. People from many castes and faiths ate together at common kitchens and free feeding centers. Lack of food was a leveler. But the social changes that came about under conditions of stress proved to be largely temporary, as had been true in former crises.

Economic development took place, concurrent with the famine and subsequent thereto. Irrigation ditches, wells, and reservoirs had deteriorated prior to the famine; work projects helped to restore these and to construct new ones. The famine brought fresh attention to a fact that previously had been known but not much exploited; Bihar state sat over a vast supply of underground water, recharged annually by outflow from the Himalayas. The obvious need for more food stimulated the sinking of tube wells.

Some negative social results were associated with the famine. Crime increased. There was greed, graft, and callousness. The crisis was accompanied by some regression in values and a measure of deterioration in the standards of public morality. People overstated family numbers; thus came the "ghost ration cards." Some undeserving people got food from the free kitchens. Drinking and drug use increased. But by any measure, not only was an increase in the death rate averted, but there was also less social disruption than was the case with any previous food crisis of which there is public knowledge.

The food crisis convinced the government that increased food production was essential and led to endorsement of the new high-yielding wheat and rice, together with the associated inputs of credit, fertilizer, and pesticides. While Dias, the food secretary, was dispensing famine relief, Subramaniam, the food minister, was pushing agricultural development, and Swaminathan, the scientist, was laying the basis for the Green Revolution. Without the Green Revolution to increase food production the extension of life provided by famine relief could have been only temporary.

The rains returned during the 1967–68 crop year. Food grain production surged upward to 95.1 million tons, a 28 percent jump from the year before and a new record. The Green Revolution took hold and India terminated its reliance on the United States for concessional imports of food grain.

Emergence of self-reliance was one of the most noteworthy achievements of the famine relief effort. Other countries have built themselves into continuing dependence on outside food aid. To its lasting credit, India escaped that trap. Probably no better use of Public Law 480 was ever achieved than the relief of hunger and the reprieve from death during the Indian food crisis.

Anthony Dias is asked, Who were the heroes in the fight to overcome the Bihar famine? Without hesitation he says the heroes were the district officers working in the villages and the thousands of civil servants on the firing line. They met daily crises of all kinds, large and small, each with its personal and emotional dimension. They had to allocate scarce supplies among overstated demands. They had to say "no" when a negative answer wiped out the hopes of desperate people.

Mrs. Gandhi was one of Mr. Dias's heroes. Jagjivan Ram, "a very able administrator," rates high. So does Subramaniam. And Chester Bowles, the American ambassador. And Orville Freeman, U.S. secretary of agriculture. Especially U.S. Vice-President Hubert Humphrey. "President Johnson?" Dias hesitated. Then, "He came through. But as we say in India, he sat too long on the file!" "Any villians?" If there were villians Dias either has forgotten or will not recall them.

What was learned in the Bihar famine? That famine can be avoided if there is the will to do so and if outside help is forthcoming. That strong action by government is necessary. That Indian officials can act with dispatch when the need arises. That India has friends in the world. That India must be ready to act if there should again be a food crisis. And that the effort to meet the Bihar famine is a better model than the performance during the Bengal famine a quarter of a century earlier.

In 1982, when my wife and I saw him, Dias was retired, living in Bombay, enjoying his home, his family, his friends, his golf, his dog, and his memories. He was a champion famine fighter and he retired undefeated.

REFERENCES

Berg, Alan. 1971. *Famine Contained: Notes and Lessons from the Bihar Experience.* Reprint 211. Washington, D.C.: Brookings Institution.

Chopra, R. N. 1981. *Evolution of Food Policy in India.* New Delhi: Macmillan.

Dias, A. L. 1982. Personal interview with the author, Bombay.

Ministry of Food and Agriculture. 1963–64 through 1968–69. *Annual Report.* New Delhi: Department of Food.

_____. Various issues, 1964 through 1966. *Review of the Food Situation.* New Delhi: Government of India.

_____. Various issues, 1966 through 1967. *Review of the Scarcity Situation and Measures Taken to Meet It.* New Delhi: Government of India.

Rowan, Carl T., and David Maize. 1968. "The Great Grim Famine That Wasn't." *Reader's Digest* (Aug.).

Sen, Amartya. 1981. *Poverty and Famines. An Essay on Entitlement and Deprivation.* Oxford: Clarendon Press.

_____. 1986. "Food, Economics, and Entitlements." Elmhirst Memorial Lecture, Proceedings, International Conference of Agricultural Economists, held at Málaga, Spain, August 26–September 4, 1985. Institute of Agricultural Economics, University of Oxford.

Singh, K. Suresh. 1975. *The Indian Famine, 1967, a Study in Crisis and Change.* New Delhi: People's Publishing House.

Verghese, B. G. 1967. *Beyond the Famine, an Approach to Regional Planning for Bihar.* Published by Super Bazaar under the auspices of the Bihar Relief Committee.

CHAPTER 26

Pastor Ludwig Stumpf: Good Samaritan

THERE IS HUNGER that comes from drought, from flood, and from the breakdown of law and order. But of all its forms, the most poignant hunger is that of the homeless, for this is a hunger of the heart as well as of the body.

In 1985 the United Nations high commissioner on refugees estimated the world refugee population at 10 million. This chapter examines a small part of that huge problem, a unit small enough to be understandable. But it is large enough to reveal the complexity, the tragedy, and the sometime triumph of those categorized by the colorless phrase "displaced persons." Hunger is an important dimension of the refugee problem.

On the east coast of Asia is a small complex of rugged islands and mainland, altogether comprising an area smaller than an average American county, wrung from the Chinese by the British in a series of negotiations beginning in 1841. Together, Hong Kong Island, the tip of Kowloon Peninsula, and the New Territories are known as Hong Kong. When the British came nearly a century and a half ago Hong Kong was little more than a fishing vilage. Under the British Hong Kong became a bridgehead for trade with China. It was capitalistic and competitive.

As it was open to trade so it was open to people. When the Communist upheaval struck, refugees converged on Hong Kong. There were four waves, each related to the revolutions of East and Southeast Asia.

First were the White Russians, defeated defenders of the czar who had fled from Russia to China during and after the Russian Revolution and could not return. They were called "stateless Europeans." As the Chinese Communists gained strength these people came under political suspicion and were forced out of China. They had no country to which they could go and converged on Hong Kong. Their overriding need was for a new country in which they could reestablish themselves.

In 1949 came the ill, the disabled, the deserters, and the camp followers of Chiang Kaishek's defeated Nationalist army. Unable to make their homes in China and unwilling to follow Chiang to Taiwan, they remained in Hong Kong. Most were destitute. Some were on drugs. Their major need was rehabilitation.

The third wave and the largest was the inflex into Hong Kong of Chinese people from the mainland following the Chinese Revolution of 1949. They were a mixed lot: defeated political adversaries of the triumphant People's Republic; wealthy landlords and industrialists who fled to escape expropriation or execution or both; free spirits who were uncomfortable in the lock-step culture of the People's Republic; and adventurers who saw that opportunities in Hong Kong were greater than those on the mainland. From 1958 to 1961 the flow was swollen by refugees from the famine that accompanied Chairman Mao's Great Leap Forward. These refugees were resourceful and ambitious. Given some temporary help they could and did establish themselves in Hong Kong in a competitive setting among people of their own language and culture.

The fourth wave was the boat people from Vietnam and Cambodia following the Communist triumph there. This began in the late 1970s and continued into the 1980s. The categories of refugees were similar to those that flowed from mainland China: political, philosophical, religious, and economic. Many were people whose ancestors had come from China and had established themselves in Southeast Asia. They were not welcome in nearby Malaysia, Thailand, the Philippines, or Indonesia. Hong Kong was the most open of available destinations.

In the midst of these human tides was a benign and energetic cleric, Pastor Karl Ludwig Stumpf, head of the Hong Kong Christian Service. He not only helped provide the refugees with food, he also supplied counseling, health service, and vocational training. He sought out visas and sponsorships that helped the holders to become established in some new country. Most important, he provided understanding and hope.

Stumpf was born in 1913 in Mannheim, West Germany, the son of a printer. His parents were Social Democrats, socialists but neither communists nor Nazis. He grew up among people who "thought otherwise." His parents were unbelievers. The boy was baptized in the Lutheran church as a concession to convention but he received no religious training and was not confirmed in the Christian faith. He studied Marx, Engels, and Lenin and was an unbeliever with a strong sense of social justice.

By the time Stumpf reached young manhood Hitler was mobilizing Germany for World War II. Stumpf was opposed both to war and to Hitler. So in 1937, a week before he was scheduled for induction into

Hitler's army and with his parents' protests ringing in his ears, he left for Shanghai. He was employed by the pharmaceutical firm C. F. Boehringer and Soehne GmbH and promised his family to "return in three years." The three years went by and many more before he again saw Germany.

Arrived in Shanghai, Stumpf plunged into the sale of pharmaceutical materials for his firm, demonstrating an aptitude for business. But he was appalled at the poverty and degradation of the Shanghai slums. His sense of justice was deeply offended. He read a book that influenced him greatly, *The Social Pathology of Shanghai.* He wrote: "I had searched but not found anything which seemed to me of absolute value. I was still loyal to certain philosophical and ethical values and hoped that an attitude of tolerance, emancipation, and common sense would bring me satisfaction, possibly even happiness. But they did not. Life, somehow, left me dispirited, discontented."

At about this time he met Professor Maas, an intellectual and a Christian. The two of them, one a believer and the other not, had long discussions that at first seemed to lead nowhere. Maas contended that Jesus was the greatest revolutionary of all time. The professor's perception of the Christian life was that of activism. "Life has a claim on us, not we on life," said Maas. "Incorporate in a creative way the things imposed by fate. Get involved; get into life. There is no safe place. One cannot withdraw from life." This was an interpretation of Christianity that was new to Stumpf; his perception had been that of the conservative established church and a Jesus meek and mild.

So Stumpf was converted. It changed his life and the lives of thousands. He immersed himself in the needs of his fellows. Nearest at hand and most responsive to help were the white émigrés from Russia, many of whom had gathered in Shanghai, a somewhat Westernized city which they found less hostile than other places in China. They were a tragic group, many of them destitute and some despondent. Stumpf plunged into service to this group and became chairman of a coordinating committee for foreign refugees. He quickly demonstrated the administrative skills that he would exercise for the rest of his life.

For a time Stumpf held his own with the Chinese Communists. As a result of his early reading he could quote Marx, Engels, and Lenin better than most of them. He knew both the strengths and weaknesses of the agruments. The Communists decided he was a "progressive capitalist."

The Chinese Communists considered Christianity a foreign capitalist influence and thus subversive. After the Revolution Christian ministers were driven out of Shanghai or were put under house arrest. To Stumpf, the newly converted businessman, fell the lot of providing Christian baptism, marriage, and burial for the remaining believers.

"You marry, bury, and preach," said the church fathers. "You should be a pastor." So, upon the request of the foreign office of the Evangelical church in Germany and despite his lack of formal Christian education, Stumpf was ordained the full-time pastor of two churches. Shortly after he became a pastor he and his family were evicted from Shanghai and went to Hong Kong.

At Hong Kong there was a better chance to provide homes for the White Russians. Letters asking for help poured in at a rate of three thousand per week. Stumpf asked for and obtained the support of the Evangelical church and of the World Council of Churches. With this help he traveled throughout Europe, Latin America, and the United States, asking that visas be granted to the White Russians. One country after another opened its doors to these refugees. They scattered themselves around the world. Purposeful, industrious, and welcomed, they quickly adapted themselves to their new homes.

As the problems of the White Russian refugees faded those of the Chinese refugees increased. Stumpf was quick to see that food from the newly enacted Public Law 480 could be a great help in feeding the growing flood of Chinese refugees.

My wife and I visited Hong Kong in 1958 when this program was at its height. Refugees from mainland China were streaming into the city, living on sidewalks and huddled under packing crates, tin, or canvas. They clung to hillsides outside the city, exposed to storms and mudslides. They swam the river, they came by boat and on foot, eluding the border guards. Some carried valuables and pictures of family members; others had nothing but the clothes they wore. The more fortunate ones had relatives in Hong Kong who could give them help.

The first need was food. Pastor Stumpf had managed to obtain American wheat under the PL 480 Food-For-Peace program. He set up a factory to make the wheat into noodles, relished by the refugees. He organized seventeen kitchens, strategically located and staffed by volunteers. We saw long lines of refugees, stretching the length of the block and around the corner, each with a bowl to be filled with noodles. At the peak of the program, Stumpf was feeding 100,000 people.

While the immediate need was food the longer-term needs were health service, counseling, rehabilitation, and job training. All of these Stumpf organized and provided with the help of financial contributions and volunteers. Awareness of need and appreciation for what Stumpf was doing became widely known. The organized church supplied help. Money flowed in from Germany, the United States, and other countries.

The enterprising Chinese refugees, given temporary help, soon integrated themselves into the Hong Kong population. They found jobs and began small enterprises. Stumpf estimated that 90 percent of them became self-reliant. Every now and then he met, in a business transaction, someone who stood in his food lines twenty-five years earlier.

The Hong Kong government organized itself to deal with the refugee problem. When we visited Hong Kong again in 1982 the government, now more affluent and dealing with a more manageable problem, had institutionalized its refugee program and was assisting with housing, medical services, and education. Small cash grants had replaced the food lines. Stumpf had been appointed consultant to the government and was working with the city officials. He had been awarded a CBE (Commander of the British Empire) by Her Majesty the Queen.

The use of Public Law 480 in Hong Kong under Stumpf's direction was admirable. The food was there when needed, it was distributed fairly, and it was tapered off as the caseload diminished. Local officials took over when the problem was so reduced that they could cope, whereupon the American food donation program was closed out.

Stumpf had mellowed a bit when we last saw him but still was full of spirit. He had an office in a nine-story building in the heart of the city. We visited him in his home, a pleasant apartment overlooking the harbor. He took pride in the first title that came to him, won by Christian service rather than by formal study.

We sounded him out on matters of refugees, food help, and assistance programs. Here are some quotes:

In helping refugees food is first. But it is not enough. People must be helped to become self-reliant.

When I see poverty and hardship I am not discouraged; I am energized.

Most people want to be self-reliant. In my experience helping them rightly does not deprive them of the desire to help themselves.

Private and public assistance programs are not adversaries; they are complementary.

There are some questions to which we can have no answers. Why should thousands of people perish in a typhoon? No one can say. We must go on doing our best despite lack of understanding.

I lose patience with people who are bored or passive.

Stumpf died in the spring of 1987, a fulfilled person. It is wonderful when a sense of fulfillment can come from feeding hungry people rather than from the pursuit of purely selfish goals.

REFERENCES

Stumpf, Pastor K. L. 1958. Personal interview with author. Hong Kong.
_____. 1968. The Methods and Techniques of Social Work and Social Welfare and the Safeguarding of Human Rights. Hong Kong Christian Service. Mimeo.
_____. 1968. Human Welfare and the Faces of Dehumanization. Speech at Rotary Club. Hong Kong Christian Service. Mimeo.
_____. 1969. Sharing a Christian Approach to Social Change and Social Justice. Hong Kong: Lutheran World Federation. Hong Kong Christian Service. Mimeo.
_____. 1976. Primary Prevention of Juvenile Deliquency. Hong Kong. Hong Kong Council of Social Service. Mimeo.
_____. 1980. Untitled. Speech at the First Pan-Pacific Conference on Drugs and Alcohol, Canberra. Hong Kong Christian Service. Mimeo.
_____. 1980. Meeting the Needs of Refugees in Countries of First Asylum. Twentieth International Conference on Social Welfare. Hong Kong Christian Service. Mimeo.
_____. 1980. Preventive Education and Rehabilitation. World Health Organization Training Course II. Hong Kong Christian Service. Mimeo.
_____. 1981. Getting Jobs for the Disabled. World Trade Center Club. Hong Kong Christian Service. Mimeo.
_____. 1982. The Role of Philanthropy in Resource Mobilization, San Francisco. Hong Kong Christian Service. Mimeo.
_____. 1982. Personal interview with author. Hong Kong.
_____. Undated. Risk and Hope. Hong Kong Community Council for the Resettlement of Vietnam Refugees.

CHAPTER 27

Madame Wang Shun Ying of Evergreen Commune

HEBEI PROVINCE, September 1982. We have looked at the food security systems of the United States, India, and Hong Kong. Though their economies have differently mixed proportions of enterpreneurship and regulation they are all considered to be within the free world. What of the centrally directed countries in which now live nearly one-third of the world's people? What kind of food aid systems do they have? Madame Wang Shun Ying, vice-chairman of the managing committee of the Evergreen People's Commune in north China, showed my wife and me about and described the food security system of her commune.

But first some background. For many centuries the Chinese economy was essentially feudal. Then as now, the great majority of the people lived on the land. The social system was the extended family, three or four generations living together with lines of interdependence sometimes reaching out to uncles, aunts, and cousins, linking the productive workers with the dependent elderly, the children, and the handicapped. A food need on the part of any individual within this extended family was seen as a group responsibility.

Zealots for individual entrepreneurship deplore the extended family because of its socializing principle. They contend that a farmer is disinclined to work hard or to adopt new methods if the increased output will be shared with uncles, aunts, and cousins. Whether this is indeed true and if so to what degree are unanswered questions. In any case, the extended family is the world's oldest food aid institution. In China the system worked fairly well in supplying intergenerational support and coping with the needs of dependent individuals within a family. It socialized supplies and needs within a relatively small unit but could not deal adequately with widespread disasters such as war, drought, flood, and civil unrest.

In 1949 China experienced a political upheaval that must have registered at least 9.0 on the agrarian reform scale. The government expropriated all the land in the country. Landlords and rich peasants were executed, "reconstructed," or driven into exile. The land was distributed to the peasants for their use, an average of less than an acre per farm worker, deemed too small for effective individual operation.

This was merely the first jolt of the earthquake; there were aftershocks. En route to a socialized agriculture farmers were first put into "mutual aid teams," then "lower stage producer cooperatives," and then "advanced producer cooperatives."

In 1958 Chairman Mao launched his Great Leap Forward, a push toward utopian socialism. Income distribution approached equality, incentives practically disappeared, private plots were abolished, eating was in community mess halls, and family institutions were upended. Catastrophe ensued. Food production fell and famine struck. An economist writing in the December 1984 issue of *Population and Development Review* under the pseudonym of Basil Ashton reports that it resulted in about 30 million deaths in excess of normal mortality. Other estimates place the death loss at half that number. The Great Leap was rescinded and from 1961 to 1966 agriculture made considerable progress.

But the agrarian earthquake produced yet another shock, the Great Proletarian Cultural Revolution of 1966 to 1969. The purpose of this undertaking was to rekindle revolutionary enthusiasm and "destroy outdated counterrevolutionary symbols." Groups of young activists called Red Guards disrupted town and country. The resulting chaos wiped out the gains of the previous five years. The Cultural Revolution was conceded a failure and was countermanded.

Chairman Mao died in 1976. Gradually there came a counterrevolution, a reaction to earlier excesses. By 1982, when we met Madame Wang, farming had been transformed to the "responsibility system." A surprising degree of individual decision making had been restored. The family had regained something of the social and economic status it had lost. A farmer negotiated a contract to grow a certain amount of a particular crop for the official price. He was given custody (but not ownership) of an identified piece of land. If he overfulfilled his contract he was paid 50 percent above the official price for the excess. He had use of a small plot of land on which he could produce crops or livestock for his family or for sale in a free market. In addition he and his family could engage, for profit, in a sideline activity like producing handicraft objects. He could do additional work for compensation on the land or in one of the commune's off-farm enterprises. It was a mixed system.

Evergreen People's Commune was so named because it had greenhouses and produced vegetables year-round for sale in Beijing. In 1982 it had forty-four thousand people and occupied 5,500 acres. Chief crops were Chinese cabbage, pole beans, maize, wheat, castor beans, eggplant, and sweet potatoes. Fruits were apples, pears, peaches, and grapes. Crops looked good. Livestock production was chiefly pigs and poultry. There was an aura of discipline, thrift, and hard work.

Madame Wang, fifty years old, was dressed in a plain blue uniform as befitted her party membership. She explained the organization of the commune. There were 362 delegates among the members. Twenty-two were elected from these to form the governing body. There were ten vice-chairmen, of whom Madame Wang was one. There was an elected overall chairman. The commune was divided into about ten brigades and these were in turn divided into production teams of about thirty families each.

Madame Wang, the child of a soldier father and a peasant mother, was one of four children. She worked in the fields as soon as she was old enough to pull weeds. As a child she had no schooling. She was fifteen years old when the Revolution came; she joined it as soon as she was old enough. She then received eight months of intensive schooling, much of it political. Natural gifts, deep commitment, and party loyalty, all of which were obvious, had carried her to the upper echelons of this huge operation. The fact that she was a woman had neither helped nor hurt her career.

Madame Wang was married and had two children. There were nine people in her "family": herself, her husband, her twenty-year-old son, her mother and father (each of whom was seventy-four years old), her sister and her sister's husband and that couple's two young children, who were cared for by the grandparents. The son was a tractor driver. This "family" had five workers and four dependents, two of whom were old and two young. They had met the dependency problem within the family without need for food aid from the commune. In this case the extended family system persisted despite the wrenching changes of past decades.

In this huge commune, much of the food was consumed by the families that grew it. Some was sold, and the families that grew these products received the income from such sales. Labor in behalf of the commune was paid for on the basis of "work points," scaled according to the skill and physical effort required. Thus a farm family had food from its own production plus cash income which could be used to purchase additional food or for other purposes.

China was operating a dual food system. Quantities rationed by the government were retailed at official prices and excess amounts were on the free market. The free market price was about 30 percent above the official price. Food was acquired from the farmers at official prices intended to encourage production and sold below cost to help meet the needs of low-income consumers. The difference was the government subsidy, which was enormous. In addition input items like fertilizer were supplied at artificially low prices. The economist An Xi-Ji, in a paper at the 1985 Conference of International Economists at Málaga, Spain, reported that government budgetary subsidies in the food area accounted for more than 30 percent of the government budgetary revenue.

There was a safety net. If crop production fell below the contracted amount through no fault of the farmer, the deficiency was forgiven and if the crop failed badly food was supplied. On the other hand, if performance was above the contracted level most of the excess accrued to the farmer but a part went to provide for the welfare needs, including food, of less fortunate members.

The difficulty with early feudal China so far as food security was concerned was that the family socialized supplies and needs within so small a unit there was no way to cope with generalized disaster. The difficulty with the Great Leap Forward was that it socialized supplies and needs on so broad a basis that the individual saw no link between his performance and the well-being of himself and his family. Hence he did not perform and supply was reduced.

The present Chinese system is intent on increasing the food supply, socializing the dividend within a group bound together by kinship, and providing assistance to those who are beyond family help. The food security principle is as follows: First responsibility for sharing is within the family. That failing, responsibility moves progressively to the production team, then to the brigade, then to the entire commune. If widespread drought or flood should devastate the commune, help would be sought from distant communes, a difficult thing logistically because transportation is inadequate. And it would be difficult also for other reasons; such entitlements have not been fully accepted.

At Evergreen Commune there is a day school–nursery–kindergarten for young children which starts the young on the path of education. It involves political indoctrination and releases the parents for work in field or factory. There is an official retirement age, fifty-five years for women and sixty for men. By that age many of these hard-working people have worn themselves out. Here at Evergreen Commune retired people receive small pensions, but this is somewhat of a rarity, not general throughout the country.

Population control, a priority in China, has as its objective the one-child family. This weakens the security in late years that was provided for by the younger generation within the extended family system. Consequently the state has announced guarantees for the dependent elderly:

guaranteed food, housing, medical care, cash income, and burial expenses. These promises have been only partially fulfilled.

We saw a Respectful Home for the Elderly intended to make good on some of these guarantees. It was a new brick building housing about fifty men and women, some of whom were more than eighty years old, one of them ninety-three. The grounds were well tended by the residents, with flowers in abundance. There were rooms for visiting and a dining room for group meals. Sleeping rooms were small, two beds in each. In the kitchen were huge pots of steaming rice and chopped-up Chinese cabbage, no doubt the staple foods. The residents seemed happy. But we were told that if there are children and grandchidlren with whom they can live most of the elders prefer the old system.

During the years since 1978, when incentives were brought into the system, the Chinese food economy appears to have done well. The crude death rate, which stood at about twenty-five per thousand in 1953, was reduced to seven per thousand in 1982, lower than the nine per thousand in the United States. Obviously the larger numbers of surviving people are getting food, chiefly by their own efforts but with help in the various forms of food aid. How the present Chinese food aid system would bear up in the event of widespread natural disaster remains untested. The commitment to agricultural betterment and to family planning seems likely long-term, to ease what would otherwise be an enormous food aid burden.

This writer is impressed by the similarity of food aid in a centrally directed country like China and in a free economy like the United States. Both try for an adequate overall supply of food. Each has institutionalized a safety net for the unfortunate. In each country, those productive people who are above the margin of want, help bear the burden of food aid for the poor. Though there are marked differences, each has found a middle ground between egalitarian sharing and unbridled individualism.

Certainly in recent years the Chinese food system has moved closer to the enterprise model and, as we have seen, the American food aid system has become more socialized. This is in accordance with the concept known as "convergence theory," which postulates that with the passage of time differences between the free and the centrally directed worlds will diminish. This trend is deplored by ideologues of both camps. But in food aid, convergence appears to be under way.

REFERENCES

An Xi-Ji. 1986. *Pricing System Reform for Agricultural Products and Price Policy in China (1979–1984).* Proceedings, Nineteenth Conference of International Economists, Institute of Agricultural Economics, Oxford.

Ashton, Basil, Kenneth Hill, Alan Piazza, and Robin Zeitz. 1984. "Famine in China, 1958–61." *Population and Development Review* 10, no. 4 (Dec.):613–45.

Banister, Judith. 1984. "Analysis of Recent Data on the Population of China." *Population and Development Review* 10, no. 2 (June):241–71.

Luo Hanxian. 1985. *Economic Changes in Rural China.* China Studies Series. Beijing: New World Press.

U.S. Department of the Army. 1981. *China, a Country Study.* Area Handbook Series. Washington, D.C.: American University.

Wang, Shun Ying. 1982. Interview with the author, Evergreen People's Commune, China.

World Bank. 1984. *World Development Report 1984.* Published for the World Bank. New York: Oxford Univ. Press.

IV Family Planning

DURING THE LONG YEARS when high birthrates were balanced by high death rates and populations were relatively stable, it was possible for food strategists to concentrate on improved agriculture and on food aid as adequate answers to the hunger problem. No more.

The change began in the nineteenth century. During the hundred years from 1820 to 1920 medical advances reduced the crude death rate in Europe from about thirty per thousand to something like half that level. Since 1920 improved sanitation and antibiotics have cut the death rate in the developed countries almost in half again to an average of about nine per thousand. In the Third World the reduction in the death rate began later and has been even more dramatic. In 1950 the death rate in the developing countries averaged twenty-six per thousand; by 1982 it was about eleven. The death rates in China, Taiwan, Korea, and Hong Kong are now lower than in the United States.

Meanwhile, the birthrate in many Third World countries, conditioned by centuries of tradition and religious belief, continues high. The result is an upsurge in population numbers. Improved agricultural production and food aid are no longer sufficient answers to world food needs, but for many people the historic mindset continues. This section of the book will focus on the need for family planning, the blind spot in food strategy.

The world population in 1980 was almost ten times as great as it had been in 1650:

Estimates of the Population of the World	
Year	Millions
1650	465
1750	660
1800	836
1850	1,098
1900	1,551
1950	2,504
1980	4,453

Source: 1650–1900, Carr Saunders, p. 30 from W. F. Willcox; 1950–1980, World Bank, quoted by Demeny, *Population and Development Review* 10, no. 1, 110.

Robert McNamara, former president of the World Bank, sets forth the arithmetic in startling fashion: "Whereas it had taken mankind more than a million years to reach a population of one billion, the second billion required only 120 years, the third billion 32 years, and the fourth billion 15 years."

All kinds of frightening scenarios come from projecting this trend. Suffice it to say that unless birthrates come down substantially or unless unprecedented disaster wipes out a large share of the human race, the population graph will run off the edge of the chart. Unless the birthrate is brought down there is no solution to the world food problem or, for that matter, the ecological problem, the resource problem, or the problem of social stress.

Food strategists must now focus on the people side of the equation that balances population with sustenance. But such a change takes place slowly. Family planning is made difficult by historic attitudes, taboos, and ignorance. It is further complicated by the divergence between the perceived private gain and the real social cost of having large families. To many people the population problem is so remote in time and so vague in dimension that it is simply dismissed.

There is a persistent minority view that a high birthrate is desirable. In 1978 the United Nations inquired of 158 countries as to their population policy. One hundred twenty indicated support for family planning, sixty-two considered their fertility rates satisfactory, and eight replied that their birthrates were too low. The categories of opposition to family planning are religious, military, and economic, the latter a reflection of the feeling that the earth is capable of supporting more people, as indeed some areas are. It is significant, however, that in the quoted United Nations survey, fifteen nations would like to reduce the birthrate for every one that would like to increase it. This book is written in support of the majority point of view.

If we interfere massively in the processes associated with death we are compelled to interfere also in matters related to birth.

In this section of the book we look at four pioneers in family planning. In the United States, Margaret Sanger broke the legal and cultural barriers that forbade birth control and demonstrated to the world that this could be done. In India, Sanjay Gandhi, the impulsive heir apparent, imposed a strong-armed birth control program on a country whose political system was democratic socialism and engendered a backlash. In the People's Republic of China, Ma Yen Chu, a persistent demographer, persuaded Chairman Mao to adopt an authoritarian family-planning program that made a deep cut in the birthrate. In Taiwan, Chiang Mon Lin, a strong-willed sage, pressured

Chiang Kaishek into launching a voluntary family-planning program that is making visible progress.

In the long chronicle of people and their food, these innovators with their successes and failures, may take their places along with the scientists and the providers of food aid as pioneers on the way toward a well-fed world.

CHAPTER 28

United States:
The Margaret Sanger Story

In 1910, before Margaret Sanger began her work, the crude birthrate in the United States stood at twenty-seven per thousand. By 1983, after her life had ended, it had been cut almost in half, to sixteen per thousand. Some share of the decline must result from the work of this remarkable woman.

Margaret Sanger showed the world that the long-established custom and tradition associated with human procreation could be changed. That was her main contribution. Before Margaret Sanger it was a pronatal world. Frank Notestein, the eminent demographer, describes it thus:

Marriage customs, family organizations, property systems, the means of attaining status, the systems of community rewards and sanctions, educational processes and religious doctrines all were organized in ways that promoted nearly universal and fairly early marriage and high rates of reproduction. These institutions, customs and beliefs were deeply rooted in long traditions. They represented the moral code, the normative order, which provided the non-rational cement of loyalty that bound the individuals into groups and bound the past to the present.

It is not hard to see how this body of belief arose. In the days before science and sanitation, the death rate was frightfully high. It took an average of six or eight births to bring two of the offspring to adulthood and so replace the parents. In addition, children were an asset. In that rural day a child became useful at about age six or eight; he or she could then gather firewood, pull weeds, carry water, tend cattle, and care for younger siblings. In that early time parents asked not what they could do for their children, they asked what their children could do for them.

Not only was it a pronatal world, it was also promale. The male was physically stronger and dominated the institutional arrangement. Sexual intercourse was initiated by the male and it was the woman's part to accept pregnancy and childbearing as her duty. In the Victorian model of society males masked this exploitation by conferring empty honors on their womenfolk.

A few quotations will serve to document this characterization of earlier society. Here is the military man Napoleon Bonaparte: "Woman is given us to bear children. She is our property. . . . Because she produces children for us, we yield none to her. She is our possession, as the fruit tree is that of the gardener." This is from a churchman of Margaret Sanger's time, Patrick J. Hayes, archbishop of New York: "Children troop down from Heaven because God wills it. . . . To take life after its inception is a horrible crime; but to prevent human life that the Creator is about to bring is Satanic." In 1873 the so-called Comstock Laws were passed, prohibiting the use of the mails for transmitting obscene material and giving authority to open any letter or package. Contraceptive information was declared to be obscene and its dissemination therefore effectively blocked. So the pronatal promale bias was locked in, endorsed by the law and the prophets.

During the nineteenth century these things began to change. Vaccination and sanitation cut the death rate so that it was no longer necessary to bring six or eight children into the world to have progency surviving to adulthood. Industrialization began to replace agriculture; people trooped to the cities where children were an economic liability rather than an asset. Parents, moving out of poverty, began asking themselves what they could do for their children and the obvious answer was that the fewer children they had the more could be done for each.

Contraception, though still under strong social disapproval, gradually came into greater use. In the eighteenth century an English Colonel Cundom, developed and advertised a sheath made from sheep gut. The condom, as it became known, was apparently legal because its purpose was to protect the male from venereal disease, not the female from conception. In France the Napoleonic code required property to be divided equally among the children and the astute French people saw that the fewer the children the better the prospect of keeping the patrimony intact. French women prided themselves on their suppositories and douches. The people of Ireland, remembering vividly the Great Famine of the mid–nineteenth century, were aware of the dangers of overpopulation and limited the number of their children, in part by late marriage.

A forerunner of Margaret Sanger was Annie Besant, an Englishwoman. She, with a publisher named Charles Bradlaugh, brought out a book on contraception. The two were arrested and brought to trial in London where, in 1877, they were both found guilty and sentenced to six months in jail, a sentence that was later dismissed on a technicality. The court proved more sympathetic than the law.

Promale bias was also coming under attack. Susan B. Anthony (1820–1906) and Elizabeth Cady Stanton (1815–1902) worked together for half a century in behalf of women's rights, an effort that culminated in the Nineteenth Amendment to the Constitution (women's suffrage) in 1920. Women were breaking the barrier against higher education. Increasingly they were entering the labor force, first as teachers, nurses, and stenographers, then more generally.

Into this kind of world Margaret Higgins (later Margaret Sanger) was born, reportedly in 1879, in Corning, New York, the sixth of eleven children. Her father, Michael, was a red-haired free-thinking Irish-born sculptor of tombstone angels. Her mother, Anne, was a self-sacrificing woman, raised in the Catholic faith, who capitulated to her husband's steellike domination. The mother died of tuberculosis at age forty-eight.

Margaret's rebel spirit, courage, and tenacity were evident early. When she was in the eighth grade she arrived at school minutes late. The teacher, a domineering person, snapped at her, "So your ladyship has arrived." Margaret sat down, hoping the teacher would forget her, but the taunting continued. Suddenly Margaret stood up, tucked her books under her arm, and walked out, never to return. Her later comment: "Nothing on earth or heaven could change me. I'd go to jail, I'd go to work, I'd starve and die; but back to that school and teacher I would never go."

Margaret had sought unsuccessfully to get into Cornell University and become a doctor. Her fallback position was nursing; she became a probationary nurse at White Plains Hospital, just north of New York City. The illness, misery, and malnutrition of the numerous children from large families of poverty-stricken people came into sharp focus at her hospital. Especially wrenching to her was the parade of women who came under her care made weak and ill by unwanted pregnancies. Infections from self-induced or illegal abortions stirred her anger.

The case of Sadie Sachs set Margaret on her career. In July 1912 Margaret took on the case of this woman, still in her twenties, already the mother of three tiny children, near death from blood poisoning caused by self-induced abortion. The husband, Jake, a truck driver, was distraught. After three weeks the crisis passed. The doctor told the woman that another pregnancy would finish her. "What can I do to prevent it?" she asked. The doctor said, "Tell Jake to sleep on the roof!" Four months later the woman was pregnant again; this time she died.

With all her mental toughness, Margaret was convinced that there should be a better answer to this woman's question than to have her husband sleep on the roof. From the moment of Sadie Sachs's death she devoted her life to birth control. She committed to this endeavor all the unwavering purpose of her indomitable spirit.

Margaret's motivation for contraception came primarily from her feeling for women's rights, improved health, and the alleviation of poverty. She later became aware of the Malthusian problem (a major concern of this book) and used it as a makeweight argument for contraception. But it was never central to her concern. She learned, too, mostly from the Englishman Havelock Ellis, about the psychology of sex, which she discreetly built into her cause. Others charged her with promoting free love by removing the fear of pregnancy. She dismissed the religious case against contraception, an understandable position; she was a nonbeliever.

In 1902 Margaret Higgins married Bill Sanger, an artist and an architect. She took his name and thereafter was Margaret Sanger. The New York into which the newly married Sangers plunged was astir with rebel causes. Her husband, a socialist, was a friend of Eugene V. Debs, the perennial party leader. Bill Haywood, leader of the International Workers of the World (IWW, or Wobblies) was a frequent guest in the Sanger home, as was John Reed, the left-leaning journalist who wrote *Ten Days that Shook the World.*

From this background and with this support Margaret Sanger pushed her campaign for family planning. At various points in her career she issued a magazine, *The Woman Rebel* (later entitled *Birth Control Review*), and distributed a pamphlet, *Family Limitation.* She wrote books: *Woman and the New Race* (1920), *Motherhood in Bondage* (1928), *My Fight for Birth Control* (1931), and *Margaret Sanger: An Autobiography* (1938).

Her biographer, Emily Taft Douglas, says this of Sanger:

Not only was Margaret a prolific writer, she fought her battle on all fronts. She founded clinics, organized societies, made speeches, raised money, lobbied in the Congress and the New York State legislature, fought in the courts, and courted the press. She fought any challenge to her leadership. Her life was exhilarating, hectic, and beset by deadlines. Eight times she went to jail. The medical profession denounced her, the churches excoriated her, the press condemned her, and even the liberal reformers shunned her. She entered the fight alone, a frail young woman without much education, with no social or financial backing and with nothing but conviction. Yet, step by step she made her points and won her battles.

In 1914 two agents of the Department of Justice appeared at Margaret's door with a warrant for her arrest. As a result of her publication *The Woman Rebel* she was indicted by the grand jury on nine counts for alleged violation of the Comstock laws against obscenity. Sanger, faced with a court appearance, had studied the case of Annie Besant in England and decided to dispense with counsel. At her trial she spoke softly and persuasively in support of her movement. After a dramatic hearing the judge granted the request of the district attorney to adjourn the session. The *New York Sun* said that the Sanger case presented "the anomaly of a prosecutor loath to prosecute and a defendent anxious to be tried."

In part because of what she had learned on a visit to England, Sanger adopted new tactics. She became convinced that her movement would catch on if it won the support of the well-to-do and the socially elite. These were the pattern setters, the English had told her. So she dropped her left-leaning agitating friends and cultivated the people of the upper classes, many of whom accepted her with remarkably alacrity. Her goal remained the same but strategy and tactics were changed. Among her new friends was the wealthy Mrs. Stanley McCormick, wife of the youngest son of Cyrus McCormick, founder of International Harvester. Mrs. McCormick donated large sums to the movement and persuaded others to do likewise.

Sanger's fame had spread to other lands. First in 1922 and then on numerous other occasions she visited the populous countries of Asia, mostly encountering popular acclaim and official diffidence. Noteworthy were her trips to Japan, India, China, Russia, Korea, Hong Kong, and Singapore. The Japanese visits were a particular triumph. Several times she visited that country and was received with great warmth. The American embassy in Japan sought to downplay her visit but the public thronged to hear her.

In 1936 she visited India and called on the saintly Mohandas K. Gandhi, called the Mahatma (Great Soul). In two long talks they agreed on the need for family limitation but could not agree on how to achieve it. To Gandhi sexual union was merely lust. Total abstinence was the only moral way. Wives should resist their husbands and, if need be, separate from them to avoid sexual relations. Gandhi deplored the fact that in his youth he had desired his wife, and he now included celibacy as a cardinal virtue along with truth, nonviolence, fearlessness, and self-control. Sanger, who was not a saint, could not accept Gandhi's view of relations between the sexes. More congenial was Rabindranath Tagore, the poet, who wrote Sanger thus: "I am of the opinion that the Birth Control Movement is a great movement." Madame Pandit, sister of Jawaharlal Nehru, gave active sympathy and suggested future cooperation.

Sanger visited China in 1922. The enormous crowds and the evidence of poverty weighed her down. She spoke at the University of Peking to two thousand students. Within twenty-four hours her publication *Family Limitation* had been translated into Chinese and five thousand printed copies were distributed. Lawrence Lader, one of Margaret Sanger's biographers, calls it the first flame of birth control in China.

The Soviet Union was another story. In 1934 she visited that country, intent on learning whether the Soviets had really developed a contraceptive in the form of spermatoxin, as claimed. She did not find the answer to her question but she did learn what was then the official Communist line regarding limitation of birth. Malthus was wrong, said Dr. Kaminsky of the Commissariat of Health. The difficulty was not excessive numbers of people, it was the unfair distribution of the factors of production. The Soviet Union needed all the workers it could get. In capitalistic societies the Malthusian theory might be valid, but not in a communistic country. If the world would accept communism it could forget about birth control.

Sanger admired the high regard in which children were held in the Soviet Union, the health care, and the general availability of education. But she experienced a shock. She met her old friend Bill Haywood, former leader of the Wobblies, who had made his way to Russia where he hoped to help usher in the brave new world. He reported to her his observations of the "Workers Republic." Shock troops were used to speed up production. The meal with Sanger was the best he had eaten since he left home. Sanger asked, "Why not return to the United States?" He assured her he would grab the chance but could not get in.

Not only did Sanger change from supporting the rebels to cultivating the elite; she also changed from trying to rewrite the laws to winning liberalized interpretation from the courts. This course proved fruitful and yielded, in 1937, what probably was her greatest success. At issue was the seizure of contraceptive materials sent from abroad two years earlier to Dr. Stone, Sanger's colleague. The importation of such articles was illegal under Section 305 of the Revenue Act. Judge Moscowitz accepted medical testimony that contraceptives could save the lives of mothers and children and ruled for the defense. Dr. Stone wrote for *The Nation,* "It [the decision] established contraception as a recognized part of medical practice and removes the last barriers to the dissemination of contraceptive knowledge."

The movement was now an acknowledged success and Margaret Sanger was famous at home and abroad. She had set up the first International Birth Control Conference at Geneva. At the sixth International Conference, held in New York in 1925, there were eight hundred delegates from eighteen countries. The churches were being won over. Such influential clergymen as Rabbi Stephen Wise, Reverend Karl Reiland, and Dr. Charles Francis Potter supported the conference. Sanger set up the International Planned Parenthood Federation in 1952 and served as its president for six years. These activities served to institutionalize the birth control movement in various countries.

International interest in family planning led to assistance in such efforts provided by the U.S. government. Since 1966 the Agency for

International Development has been providing assistance, on request, in the form of basic research, contraceptive devices, and administrative support. The program grew rapidly. In 1985 the U.S. government contributed $290 million to international population assistance, nearly half the amount provided by all donors. The Reagan administration's opposition to international family planning was more rhetorical than substantive. Abortion was disapproved but other means of averting birth were supported. The program provides not only supplies, including oral contraceptives, intrauterine devices, condoms, aerosol foam, diaphragms, creams, and gels, but also medical kits for family-planning purposes. These instruments are used to perform pelvic examinations, insert IUDs, take Pap smears, and perform tubal ligations, uterine aspirations, and vasectomies. The developing countries themselves have increased their national expenditures in support of family-planning programs to the range of $1.5 billion annually, up from zero before Margaret Sanger.

Margaret Sanger helped bring down the average birthrate in the United States. The adoption of family planning came at different rates for the different groups within the society, a subject which is beyond the scope of this book.

In the United States the work of Margaret Sanger must be reckoned a gain for women's liberation, health, material well-being, and social justice. It does not represent an escape from the Malthusian threat, because the wealthy United States, with abundant agricultural resources and a relatively low population, is not within the Malthusian shadow. But in the poor, hungry, and heavily populated Third World countries, where the Malthusian threat is real, Margaret Sanger's ideas are taking hold and may prove decisive in the move toward a well-fed world.

Margaret Sanger died in a Tucson nursing home of arteriosclerosis on September 14, 1966, a few days short of her eighty-seventh birthday. The ultimate accolade, perhaps more a testimony of friendship than an objective appraisal, came from her friend H. G. Wells: "When the history of our civilization is written, it will be a biological history and Margaret Sanger will be its heroine."

REFERENCES

Bogue, Donald J. 1959. *The Population of the United States.* Glencoe: Free Press.

Carr-Saunders, A. M. 1936. *World Population, Past Growth and Present Trends.* Oxford: Clarendon Press.

Dash, Joan. 1973. *A Life of One's Own.* New York: Harper and Row.

Douglas, Emily Taft. 1970. *Margaret Sanger, Pioneer of the Future.* New York: Holt, Rinehart and Winston.

Lader, Lawrence. 1955. *The Margaret Sanger Story.* Westport, Conn.: Greenwood Press.

Notestein, Frank. 1983. "Population Growth and Economic Development." *Population and Development Review* 9, no. 2 (June):345–61.

Sanger, Margaret. 1920. *Woman and The New Race.* New York: Truth Publishing.

_____. 1928. *Motherhood in Bondage.* New York: Brentano's.

_____. 1938. *Margaret Sanger: An Autobiography.* New York: W. W. Norton.

U.S. Agency for International Development. 1972. *Population Program Assistance,* Bureau of Population and Humanitarian Assistance, Office of Population, Washington, D.C.

CHAPTER 29

India: Sanjay Gandhi—Compulsion and Rebuff

WHEN DEMOGRAPHIC PROBLEMS ARE DISCUSSED two nations immediately come to mind, India and China, by far the most populous countries in the world. We consider them both in this section of the book.

The population of India has trebled during the past century. Population growth could be considered moderate until after World War II. Then, with widespread use of modern medicine, the death rate plummeted. Sustained by the momentum of centuries, the birthrate stayed high and numbers of people spiraled upward. Each year India adds more people than live in all Australia. The average Indian woman produces five surviving children. At present rates of growth population numbers will double in thirty-three years. According to estimates of the World Bank, India is expected to have more than a billion people by the turn of the century; one-third of the way through the twenty-first century it is expected to exceed China and become the world's most populous country.

India seems to be coping, just barely. The proportion of India's population which is malnourished, huge though it is, may be marginally less than it was in time past. With admirable initiative and to the amazement of the pessimists, Indian farmers have kept a half-step ahead of surging population growth. The average life span has increased and infant mortality has diminished, events reflective of increased food availability. The Green Revolution and the general awakening of agriculture have staved off disaster.

Optimists say that agricultural production can continue to keep ahead of population growth and that natural social and economic forces will in time reduce the birthrate, averting starvation. Pessimists say that Malthusian limits on population growth will discipline numbers of people unless Draconian measures are taken. Those torn between worry and hope, of whom the writer is one, believe that agricultural advance has won time—a decade or two or three—within which to reduce the rate of population growth. If that hard-won time is used wisely the optimistic scenario can occur; if not, the pessimists will be right.

Family planning in India is divided into three periods: 1952 to 1976, a time of voluntarism, experimentation, and modest accomplishment; 1976 to 1977, during the Emergency Rule when the New National Population Policy was announced and Sanjay Gandhi took aggressive control of the movement; 1977 to the present, when voluntary programs were reinstated.

During the first phase primary reliance was placed on male and female sterilization, the condom, and the intrauterine device (IUD). The condom proved acceptable, but there was difficulty with distribution problems and pregnancies resulting from irregularities in its use. The IUD proved to be of limited usefulness. Retention rates averaged only about 60 percent at the end of two years. The Pill was not used extensively, apparently because of the difficulty Indian women had with keeping up the regimen. Abortion was officially available but was not actually promoted or offered on a large scale until 1975. Legal abortions in 1974–75 were on the order of 97,000 per year. The number of illegal abortions is estimated by Casson at 2 to 4 million a year, compared with more than 20 million births, making abortion the leading means of limiting family size. Prolonged lactation, which inhibits ovulation, has long been an effective method of contraception in India.

India's voluntary family-planning program showed modest achievement in the early years. But after 1972–73 there came a downturn in accomplishment. The census showed an unexpectedly sharp rise in population. Other events collaborated to heighten the country's concern. In 1974 India had a poor crop. The complacency which had surrounded the Indian family-planning program was shattered.

On June 25, 1975 Prime Minister Indira Gandhi, beset by political foes, declared a state of emergency. She arrested her major opponents and imposed press censorship. It was a major departure from the tradition of democracy that had characterized India since independence. With normal democratic processes suspended there was opportunity to use strong measures in an effort to achieve objectives unattainable by voluntary methods. Family planning, in the new setting of urgency, was one of these. On April 16, 1976 a New National Population Policy was announced, the essence of which was coercion. The legal age of marriage was raised. Family-planning performance would become one of the criteria for allocating funds to states, which were given authority to make sterilization mandatory.

We now introduce Sanjay Gandhi (no relation to Mahatma Gandhi), younger son of the then Prime Minister Indira Gandhi, grandson of Jawaharlal Nehru, and younger brother of the present Prime Minister Rajiv Gandhi. Sanjay was a handsome, charismatic impulsive, undisciplined, ambitious twenty-eight-year-old man with strong political instincts. It was commonly believed that Mrs. Gandhi was grooming him to be her successor.

Sanjay Gandhi was highly controversial. His support was chiefly in the Youth Congress while opposition came mostly from his mother's adversaries. Almost no one was indifferent to him. He quickly seized the opportunity provided by the emergency. The new tough family-planning program appealed to him and though he had no official responsibility he immersed himself in it. With the support of the Youth Congress he made it the first plank of his personal five-point program. His mother gave him near-total liberty in pursuing his initiatives.

Operational details of the new family-planning program included a combination of inducements, edicts, threats, and punishments. Main reliance was on sterilization, the surest method. Payments, the equivalent of about twelve dollars, were made to men who accepted sterilization. Commisions were paid to "motivators" who brought men in for vasectomies. Sterilization was required of government servants after the birth of the third child. Farmers were refused credit, tube wells, and fertilizers unless they consented to vasectomy. State employees were deprived of benefits — loans, subsidized housing, travel allowances, hospital treatment — if they refused sterilization after having three children.

Regulations were imposed with a stern hand, and sometimes practice went beyond the regulations. Often it was inept. Among the volunteers attracted by the cash payment were men who were old, unmarried, impotent, or had sterile wives. Operatives, anxious to show a good record, accepted patients more or less indiscriminately. A headman might be offered some sought service for his village if he "delivered" fifty clients. Those with low social and economic status and those whose potential for procreation was minimal were chief among the ones brought forward. Motivators used bullying and blackmail in rounding up their droves of "volunteers." There was straightforward collection of sterilization patients, willing and unwilling, by the police. In Delhi, applicants for driver's licenses, telephones, and school placement were told that a certificate of sterilization was necessary. Houses were raided and men were taken away for vasectomy. In 1977 8 million sterilizations were performed compared with an earlier peak of 1.8 million in 1967–68. There were problems with postoperative pain and illness.

Rumor was rife and fear arose. Genocide was suspected. The Moslems thought their numbers were being restrained so they would be outnumbered by the Hindus; the Hindus thought the exact opposite. Men stayed away from nutrition centers, afraid that these were connected with the sterilization program. Cholera inoculators were unable to approach men for the same reason. Parents kept their children home from school, confusing the school-based vaccination program with sterilization. Family planning was imposed on the humble by the elite. With the crippling of civil rights resistance was suppressed.

Public reaction to sterilization became deeply antagonistic. The obvious prosperity of the "motivators," with their commissions for bringing people in, was offensive to the poor. A stigma was associated with sterilization. Those who had submitted to the operation were looked down on as eunuchs. Ridicule was heaped on a sterilized man if his wife became pregnant. The sterilization program was seen as immoral, permitting sexual license without fear of consequences. An aroused public resisted. In Muzaffarnagar in western Utter Pradesh a confrontation between people and police resulted in an unknown number of deaths, estimated at from 50 to 150.

Amidst this seething tumult careened Sanjay Gandhi, the unofficial official with limited administrative experience and no training in medicine or demography, giving orders, issuing statements, hiring, firing, dispensing favors, receiving honors, claiming successes, denying failure, and presenting himself as defender of the poor. When family planning faltered he shifted his advocacy to tree planting and other initiatives of his five-point program. All of this frenetic activity was carried on seemingly without restraint or guidance from the prime minister, his mother. What share of the excess was attributable to the basic law, what part to Mrs. Gandhi, how much to Sanjay's lurching style, and what portion to overzealous local officials is impossible to determine.

Sanjay's supporters considered him a political genius. One must have doubts about the political judgment of one who would base the prospects for his career on an authoritarian family-planning program in a free country, a position avoided by every knowledgeable politician of record.

On January 18, 1977 Mrs. Gandhi announced an election for March and so a return to representative government. This decision must have come from a desire to be vindicated at the polls and from an anticipation of success. Instead came defeat. Mrs. Gandhi, her son Sanjay, and a number of her ministers were voted out of office. Her Congress party, for the first time since independence, became a minority. Excess zeal in implementing the sterilization program is believed to have been a major contributor to the defeat. Mrs. Gandhi herself acknowledged this.

Out of office, Mrs. Gandhi, resolute and resourceful, organized the Congress-I party (the I stands for Indira). In January 1980, two years after her defeat, Mrs. Gandhi won a seat in Parliament and her party gained control. She again became prime minister. On September 24, 1980 Mrs. Gandhi, chastened by the lost election of 1977, the language a politician understands best, spoke on the radio about the family-planning policies of her new administration. Her position sounded much like that before the emergency and indeed like that of the rival party during 1976 to 1980, while she was out of office. It was vastly different from the authorization program of 1975–76. Its essence: "We do not believe in coercion; we think there should be persuasion. But this must be done on a massive educational scale and unless everyone is in favor, it will take a very long time and may defeat the whole purpose of it." The World Bank, which rates the family-planning programs of twenty-six Third World countries, considers India's present effort to be one of the eight strongest.

There are three models for dealing with population problems in heavily peopled Third World countries.

1. *The development model.* In this view, economic development is the key. With economic development come rising income, urbanization, education, and cultural change, all of which result in a naturally declinnig birthrate. This is how Western Europe, the United States, and Japan restrained the rate of population growth. It is seen as the pattern to be emulated by Third World countries. Those who fault this model point out that it took 150 years for the Western world to discipline population numbers by following this pattern and the Third World countries do not have that much time.

2. *The strong antinatal model.* According to this concept, economic development takes too long; the country can't wait. Effective contraceptive measures must be invoked. Given the pronatal tradition, authoritarian measures must be undertaken. The People's Republic of China is the leading example of this model. Political leaders contend that authoritarian measures cannot survive an open election and point to the experience of India in 1977.

3. *The two-track model.* Advocates of the two-track strategy contend that it is inappropriate to force a choice between development and antinatal policies. Everything that can reasonably be done to promote development should be undertaken, supplemented by education to change people's attitudes and such contraceptive initiatives as the people can be persuaded to accept. Taiwan is cited as an example of this model. Detractors of one kind say that it is too slow and of another kind that it is too authoritarian.

India has at various times accepted and followed each of these three models. At the 1974 World Population Conference in Bucharest, the Indian delegate, Health Minister K. Suresh Singh, endorsed economic growth as the proper policy alternative. He said, "Development is the best contraceptive."

In 1976 India's New National Population Policy was announced, based on antinatal thinking. It declared: "To wait for education and economic development to bring about a drop in fertility is not a practical solution. The very increase in population makes economic development slow and more difficult of achievement. The time factor is so pressing and the population growth so formidable that we have to get out of this vicious circle through a direct assault on this problem as a national commitment."

In 1980 Mrs. Gandhi, chastened by the 1976–77 experience, accepted the two-track model and said: "Ultimately, of course, size of population has to be tackled at various levels, not just through development but through persuasion of the people."

To this course, which conforms to her democratic tradition, India now seems committed. The crude birthrate has come down but in 1982 still stood at a high thirty-four per thousand. The annual population increase is 2.1 percent. Whether, in such conditions, this moderate course will hold hunger in check awaits the judgment of history.

Sanjay Gandhi, that impulsive young man, performed a service in demonstrating, for his time and place, the limits to family planning which, if exceeded, lead to political disaster.

REFERENCES

Agency for International Development. 1972. *Population Program Assistance.* Bureau for Population and Humanitarian Assistance, Office of Population, Washington, D.C.

Cassen, R. H. 1978. *India: Population, Economy, Society.* New York: Holmes and Meier.

Chhabra, Rami, and Ashish Bose. 1981. "Population Policy in India: Two Comments." *Population and Development Review* 7, no. 1 (Mar.):168–71.

Demeny, Paul. 1984. "A Perspective on Long Term Population Growth." *Population and Development Review* 10, no. 1 (Mar.):103–26.

Leach, Gerald. 1970. *The Biocrats.* New York: McGraw Hill.

Nagarajan, S. 1977. *Sanjay Gandhi Exposed.* Bangalore: New Book.

Population Crisis Committee. 1981. *Status Report on Population Problems and Programs in India.* Washington, D.C.

Rao, M. J. 1976. *Youth Resurgence.* New Delhi: Progressive Writers and Publishers.

Sharma, Piare Lal. 1977. *World's Wisest Wizard—A Psychography of Sanjay Gandhi's Cosmic Mind.* New Delhi: Sagar Publications.

Singh, Jagat. 1977. *The Rise and Fall of the Sanjay Empire.* New Delhi: Pankaj Publications, Cambridge Book and Stationery Store.

CHAPTER 30

China: Ma Yen Chu and the One-Child Family

DURING THE PAST HUNDRED YEARS China has gone from something like feudalism to a special form of socialism and from a strong pronatal tradition to the strictest birth control program anywhere in the world. Witness to the political revolution and architect of the demographic reversal was Dr. Ma Yen Chu, an American-trained economist and educator who survived jail and disgrace, dying in 1981 at the age of ninety-six. Dr. Ma, a professional man who held politics at arm's length, advised Chiang Kaishek on economics and later counselled Mao Zedong on family planning, offending both. He was jailed by Chiang and anathematized by Mao.

The chief contribution of this remarkable scholar was his reformulation of communist theory in a fashion that made family planning acceptable to the communist world. Malthus was, in communist eyes, the archetype of capitalist thinkers, accepting starvation as the discipline for population numbers, rationalizing a system that exploited workers by holding them at subsistence levels, and skimming off the surplus that came from their labor. The communist belief was that hunger resulted from unfair distribution of the means of production, as Marx had said, not from population outrunning the food supply, as Malthus claimed. Friedrich Engels, co-founder with Marx of revolutionary communism, had rejected Malthus's theory. He had written that in a communist country an excessive population was only an abstract possibility. Chairman Mao Zedong had said that a large and growing population was in no way disadvantageous in the context of the Chinese revolutionary regime. Until Dr. Ma came forward there was no way a communist country could initiate a family-planning program without seeming to accept the hated Malthusian theory. Ma made an end run around the communist objection.

Dr. Ma Yen Chu was president of Peiping University and a man of great courage. For years he had been studying Chinese demographics, reading party dogma, testing public attitudes. Against the counsel of his more cautious colleagues Ma made a speech in the Fourth Session of the First National People's Congress. This speech, published in the *People's Daily* of July 5, 1957, recommended family planning, offering a new construction of communist thought. He said: "The purpose of Malthus is to cover up mistakes of capitalist government policies. My purpose, on the contrary, is to raise the peasants' productivity and thus to raise their living standard."

Dr. Ma, the economist, said that capital investment was necessary if productivity was to be increased, and investment could come only from savings. China could not accumulate sufficient savings if it had to pour so much of its resources into caring for excessive numbers of children, whose needs for housing, education, health care, food, and clothing siphoned off resources that should go into capital formation with consequent increased productivity and improved living levels for all. In economic terms his case was airtight.

Despite the care with which he crafted his speech, Dr. Ma stirred up heated controversy. He had offended tradition as old as history, confronted a century of communist dogma, and challenged the seemingly immutable statements of the party chairman. He was castigated by spokesmen for the party who accused him of being arrogant, obstinant, and ignorant of Marxism. Ma was removed from the presidency of Peiping University in 1960 and was stigmatized for fifteen years. The caliber of the man is clear from this statement: "Though I am nearly 80 and am aware that I am outnumbered I will accept the challenge single handedly and fight until I die. I will never capitulate to those critics who are bent on bringing others to submission by force and not by reasoning."

Not long after Ma spoke out Malthusian reality arose. The Great Leap Forward of 1958 to 1960 was a disaster. Estimated food output dropped 25 percent in 1960–61. Starvation became a fact, not an "abstract possibility," causing millions of deaths. A runaway rate of population growth and a severe famine persuaded Mao to reverse himself and five thousand years of pronatal policy. According to Liu Yu Liang, family-planning officer, Mao said: "We cannot allow population to grow in a blind way. It would interfere with the economy."

Dr. Ma's rationale for family planning in a communist state gave the party a politically credible basis for needed policy change. After Dr. Ma's recommendation for family planning had been accepted, after initial results had proved successful, and after the scholar had spent fifteen years in disgrace, the denunciation was lifted and the persecuted doctor was

restored to respectability. The year was 1975. Dr. Ma was ninety years old. He had six honored years of life remaining.

Family-planning efforts, begun in low-key fashion in the 1950s, lapsed during the Great Leap Forward, were reinstated thereafter, lapsed again during the Cultural Revolution, and were reinvoked with vigor during the 1970s.

Ma Yen Chu was born in Shanshing, Chekiang, China, in May 1885, the son of a silk merchant. He studied at Tientsin University and the Anglo-Chinese College at Shanghai. He came to the United States for advanced work, studying at Yale University, receiving his bachelor's degree in 1910. He received his master's and his doctorate from Columbia University, concentrating on economics.

Dr. Ma returned to China to become a teacher, a respected economist, and an occasional advisor to Chiang Kaishek, then the Nationalist leader. Although a member of no political party, Dr. Ma's conscience compelled him to denounce publicly the "profiteering and corruption" that was "injuring China's war effort" against the Japanese. He was immediately imprisoned by Chiang Kaishek's Nationalists. After the revolution Zhou Enlai, aware of the potential usefulness of an able economist who had stood up to the Nationalists, sent him a cable asking him to join the new regime. Dr. Ma worked with the communists but did not join the party. He was made president of Peiping University, the country's largest and most prestigious institution of higher learning. It was from this post that he was deposed after the speech that was initially so disastrous and ultimately so effective.

We encounter again and again the importance of ideas, be they right or wrong. Someone has said, "There is nothing more powerful than an idea whose time has come." The time had not come for Sanjay Gandhi's idea. It had come for Margaret Sanger's idea, and for the idea of Dr. Ma Yen Chu.

China had excellent reason for implementing a family-planning program. From the time of the Revolution, 1949, to the 1982 census, a period of thirty-three years, the population increased by 85 percent to 1.008 billion. The evolving pattern of thought is clear from changes in slogans and official pronouncements: "Live together with five generations, having children everywhere in the house," "One added mouth means two more arms" (folk sayings before the Revolution); "Promote the one-child fami-

lies, reasonably arrange for a second parity birth, eradicate the third birth" (1983, after the Revolution).

Thought control is China's first line of defense against an excessive population. The state has control of the press, radio, television, schools, movies, film strips, the theater, songs, posters, lectures, and discussion groups. The family-planning program is constantly before the people in strong advocacy terms. Nothing contrary to it is said. The educational campaign is total, operating at national, provincial, and local levels, directed at men as well as women. There are discussion groups in the workplace and medical corpsmen who visit each family. There are neighborhood medical clinics with female technicians who keep track of individual menstrual cycles. Peer pressure is used to change the minds of recalcitrant women. The theory and to some extent the fact is that after years of this single-voiced propaganda the citizen not only comes to believe the message but also gradually forgets that there is any other possible case.

Within its state-imposed antinatal mindset, China's second line of defense is delayed marriage. In former times the Chinese married early, often in their teens. In 1982 the legal marriageable age for males was twenty-two years and for females twenty.

The next buttress and the main one is contraception. Almost all forms are used in what amounts to a free-choice supermarket system. In September 1982 a sample study of 120,000 married women under fifty years of age showed that 69 percent were using methods of fertility control. One reason this number is no higher is that some couples do not ordinarily use contraception prior to the first birth. Most popular were the one-time methods, sterilization (of male or female) and the intrauterine device. Contraceptive materials are provided free of charge, together with counseling from "barefoot doctors" as to their use. China does research on new methods of contraception, including spermicides, injectible steroids, a paper pill, a male pill, a postcoital "vacation pill" for married couples who live apart for extended periods.

If unwanted pregnancies occur despite thought control, late marriage, and contraceptives, abortion is available. Dr. Ma warned against it, saying, "Abortion is equal to killing a life." He said, "It should be prohibited unless the mother is in poor health." Nevertheless, abortion is available free of charge at health clinics and is often urged. Asked about this, a local official says, "It is like medicine. Prevention is best but if it fails treatment is necessary." Being atheists, the Chinese leaders feel no religous compunction about abortion. According to Liu Zheng, Chinese population official, induced abortion accounted in 1977 for 22 percent of births averted by the family-planning program. Lucien Bianco of the School of Advanced Studies in Social Sciences of Paris, France, reported in No-

vember 1985 that in 1978 in Szechwan there were 850,000 abortions, a ratio of 67 abortions for every 100 births.

The final bulwark against excessive population growth, repugnant and illegal but an ancient practice, is infanticide, especially of girl babies. It appears to persist. In November 1982 the *China Youth News* reported that in rural areas three out of five surviving babies were male. The 1982 census reports 106.3 males per 100 females.

To the greatest possible extent the family-planning program is administered locally. Saturated with propaganda and caught up by the zeal of participatory authoritarianism, local groups hold meetings, make lists, set goals, keep records, allocate pregnancies, call on recalcitrant couples, threaten, cajole, harass, educate, and plead. The psychological mechanism of group dynamics is invoked.

Incentives are used. Each couple is urged to sign a certificate, pledging to be a one-child family. Cooperating families receive preference in housing. Nursery care and kindergarten are provided free of charge. Extra food rations are available. Private plots are larger for one-child families and job preferences are given. In some communities there are cash allowances for one-child families. A mother who signs a certificate to have only one child is given maternity leave up to six months, meanwhile drawing the normal work points and earning the normal income. If additional children are born the benefits are withdrawn. Admittedly these program elements are applied unevenly in various regions of the country.

Matters of sex are not flaunted. There are no erotic movies, magazines, or books. Dress is plain. Activities of the young are so planned as to be group centered; young people are discouraged from pairing off. Courtship in the Western sense seems not to exist. By all reports teenage pregnancies are few. But with the greater freedom of recent years these things are changing.

How are these measures received by the people? In a centrally directed country it is hard to know. How can one tell what mood lies behind that expressionless face? Is it unquestioned acceptance? Is it suppressed resentment? Undoubtedly there are vast numbers of people who practice family planning voluntarily. But not all. An account is given in a Beijing newspaper of December 1978: "Some localities popularizing birth control have dispatched 'militia propaganda teams' to those households that did not practice birth control to 'propagandize' them and exercise control over their food, drinking water and workpoints. These local laws have caused great dissatisfaction among the people."

Resistance is greater in the rural areas where children work in the fields and so are an asset. There is still preference for male children partly as a matter of tradition, partly because boys, being stronger, can earn more work points, and partly because there is still life in the idea that name and property should descend through the male line. If the first child is a girl, a couple often is strongly motivated to have another child. A couple's parents, desirous of grandchildren, counter the influence of government propaganda.

China's family-planning program is, at the time of writing, thirty years old. The first twenty of these were mild and intermittent; since 1973 the program has been bold. How reads the record?

Analyses show that from 1953 to 1982 the crude birthrate had been cut in half, from well over forty per thousand to 21.1. In 1953 the average woman produced 6 children; by 1982 this had been cut to 2.7. The crude death rate, meanwhile, had been reduced to one-third of its former level, from about twenty-five per thousand to about eight. Putting this together, the annual rate of population increase, which had been fluctuating around 2 percent, had been pushed down to 1.3. But still, working on a higher base, China was adding about twelve or thirteen million people a year, almost the same number as thirty years earlier, before the program began. China's prodigious effort at family planning had served to hold the annual increase in numbers to about the same level as before the program began. Such is the inertia, the momentum, of a young population in a country with a pronatal history and a falling death rate. What China has done is to transform a geometric rate of increase into an arithmetic rate. As anyone knows who has studied mathematics, this is a great change, with enormous portent for distant years.

The one-child family was far from realization. In 1981, countrywide, 47 percent of the births were first children. Twenty six percent were second children and 27 percent were in excess of two. There was great variation by province. In Shanghai 87 percent of the births were first children; in Guangxi province in the south only 31 percent were first births. China was moving toward the one-child family but the process was uneven and it had a long way to go.

A good test for the program is to ask what China's population would have been had the rate of population increase continued at 2.1 percent as it was when the program began in earnest in 1973. The 1982 population would then have been 1.064 billion instead of 1.008 billion, 6 percent greater than in fact occurred.

Population dynamics are such that a family-planning program, painful in its imposition, is rewarding only in the long run. The momentum of an established high natal pattern is like that of a ship; the forward motion continues, little diminished, long after the power has been cut. The leverage of family planning is so little and the desired result so long delayed that only a leader with extraordinary vision and power will commit himself and his country to it.

Dr. Ma was such a leader and helped produce a program that has slowed runaway numbers of people in the world's most populous nation. Does the Chinese experience hold promise for other Third World nations? It is too stern for any country with an open political system.

REFERENCES

Djerassi, Carl. 1981. *The Politics of Contraception, the Present and Future.* San Francisco: W. H. Freeman.

Draper Fund Report. 1980. *Birth Planning in China,* Number 8. Washington, D.C.

Liu Yu Liang. September 11, 1982. Interview with the author, Beijing.

Liu Zheng. 1981. "Population Planning in China." Asian Conference of Parliamentarians on Population and Development, Beijing.

Liu Zheng, Song Jian, et al. 1981. *China's Population: Problems and Prospects.* China Studies Series. Beijing: New World Press.

Ma Yen Chu. 1957. "A New Essay on the Principle of Population." *People's Daily,* July 5, Beijing. Translated from the Chinese by Mao Xing Ran.

Population Council. June 1978, March 1981, June 1982, June 1983, December 1983, March 1984, June 1984. *Population and Development Review.*

Population Crisis Committee. 1981. *Status Report on Population Problems and Programs of the People's Republic of China.* Limited circulation, Washington, D.C.

"Red China Foe Gets Muzzle." *Wichita* (Kansas) *Eagle,* April 17, 1960.

Sen, Samar. 1983. Personal correspondence with the author on his trip to China in 1956.

U.S. Department of the Army. 1981. *China, a Country Study.* Area Handbook Series. Washington, D.C.: American University.

Yale University. April 1944. "Professor Ma Yen Chu, 1910." *The Graduate Fence.*

CHAPTER 31

Taiwan: Friendly Persuasion

TAICHUNG CITY, October 1982. Taiwan is an island about 230 miles long and 90 miles wide, lying astride the Tropic of Cancer, 90 miles off the Asian coast. Aprons of gently rolling hills and level land border the mountains, supporting an agriculture that is mostly small scale, modern, and productive. Population per square mile is twenty times as great as in the United States.

For generations past, the birthrate, though high, was only slightly in excess of the death rate, so that the population moved slowly upward. About 1920 the death rate began to fall, the result of improved medical care, stable social life, better nutrition, and a rising level of living. The decline was one of the most dramatic on record:

Historic	30 (±5)	per	thousand
1943	20	"	"
1947	18	"	"
1956	8	"	"
1983	5	"	"

Source: Liu and Sun.

The birthrate was slow to come down, reflecting tradition and Confucian thought. It fluctuated wildly, responsive to social and economic conditions and to conscious government policies. In 1983 it stood at twenty-one per thousand. In the early postwar years these patterns produced a surge of population that frightened the country's leaders. Numbers were increasing at a rate of 3.8 percent annually. If continued this would double the population in less than twenty years.

In 1949 Chiang Kaishek moved his troops and his government to

Taiwan, adding a million and a half people to the already crowded island, increasing the population by one-fifth. A small island, limited tillable land, a large population, a growing rate of natural increase, an influx of new people, and a precarious food supply set the stage for a family-planning program.

Promoter, architect, and moving spirit of Taiwan's family-planning program was Chiang Mon Lin, Chinese educator and public official who convinced his principal, Chiang Kaishek, head of state and head of government, that the island needed to curb its population growth. It was a long and difficult campaign, encountering as it did age-old cultural, ethical, and traditional barriers. Military leaders opposed family planning because they wanted more men for the army. But Chiang Mon Lin persisted. "You can kill me," said he, "but I won't stop talking." Finally Chiang Kaishek agreed to tolerate the program if it were done "in a silent way."

The government of Taiwan was not as authoritarian as the government of the People's Republic. It could tolerate some experimentation and could countenance private activity that lacked official approval. There was no political dogma to be overcome as was the case in the People's Republic. It could thus float a trial balloon without jeopardy.

The first activity was in 1954 with the China Family Planning Association, a "private" organization. Training in "first aid" was offered to women in military dependents' villages and in some rural areas. There was a degree of success and official fears were somewhat allayed.

In 1959 the first official steps were taken. The Taiwan Provincial Health Department started to provide services called "prepregnancy health," a euphemism for family planning. This was offered in one of the island's twenty-two counties as part of the government's Maternal and Child Care Program, a wondrous redirection of a government bureau; the original purpose had been to accommodate birth and the new purpose was to prevent it. No major problems were encountered and in 1963 the program was expanded. Conventional contraceptive methods were used.

In 1964, after an experimental project in Taichung City, the program was strengthened with the introduction of an intrauterine device, the Lippes Loop. A five-year family-planning program was begun. In 1968 the government issued "Regulations Governing the Implementation of Family Planning in Taiwan Area." All facades were stripped away and the program had full government support, verbal, financial, and bureaucratic. It took ten years to lay the groundwork.

There is an astounding parallel between family-planning architects Chiang Mon Lin in Taiwan and Ma Yen Chu in mainland China. The men were contemporaries, Chaing born in Yuyao, Chekiang in 1886 and Ma in Shanshing of the same province a year earlier. Both did advanced study in the United States and both finished their work at Columbia University.

Both were associated with Nationalist leader Chiang Kaishek as councillors, and each became chancellor of Peiping University. When the Revolution reached its climax in 1949, Chiang Mon Lin remained faithful to Chiang Kaishek and moved with his chief to Taiwan; Ma Yen Chu made conditional peace with the victors. Chiang designed for Taiwan a successful voluntary family-planning program; Ma Yen Chu laid the basis, in the People's Republic, for a successful centrally directed effort. Both died rich with honors, Chiang Mon Lin in 1964 at age seventy-eight and Ma Yen Chu in 1981 at age ninety-six. They developed differing programs that averted millions of births. They must be acknowledged as pioneers of family planning for their respective systems.

The setting for family planning in Taiwan was especially favorable, such as would have produced a decline in the birthrate even without an organized effort: increased urbanization, a rising level of living, broad-based education, weakened commitment to things past, and an economy conducive to enterprise.

We visited with Dr. T. H. Sun, director of the Taiwan Provincial Institute of Family Planning at Taichung. Dr. Sun, a thorough-going and dedicated professional, is heard and respected in international circles as well as at home. He described his program for us.

First, its principles. It is voluntary, based on education and inducement rather than on compulsion. It is aimed especially at poorly educated low-income people in the rural areas. Unlike the program in Mainland China, achievement is more noteworthy in the countryside than in the cities. By 1980, five of six uneducated women were practicing contraception. Focus is greatest on young women who have long years of potential fertility ahead of them rather than on older women who already have families of desired size and so readily consent to family limitation. Greatest reliance is on the intrauterine device, chiefly the Lippes Loop, with limited help from the Pill, the condom, and sterilization.

Friendly persuasion in the Taiwan family-planning program takes these forms:

Postpartum mailing. After a woman has a baby and when she is therefore likely to be most receptive to family planning, she receives a congratulatory letter with a coupon for a free intrauterine device.

Telephone services. Women are called on the phone and encouraged to practice family planning.

Newsletters for physicians. Six newsletters go out each year to doctors and local planning personnel, featuring new contraceptive technology and program activities.

The media. Half-minute television commercials appear advocating the concept of "3321" (first child three years after marriage, second child three years later, two children are enough, boy and girl are the same).

Family-planning month. Each November there is a focus on family planning, featuring posters, banners, exhibits, mobile vans, slide shows in local theaters, cartoon contests, and debates.

Military reserve training. Young men are reached through the military reserve's regular refresher training.

Family-planning education for factory workers. Fieldworkers from the Family Planning Institute visit factories and talk to the young people.

Wedding gifts. Newlyweds receive, through local health stations, gift packages containing condoms and educational materials.

Leaflets, booklets, and comic books. These low-cost items are distributed through home visits, group meetings, and mailings.

There are intensive training programs. New fieldworkers receive supervision on the job under a senior person and attend a two-week preservice training course at the institute. Doctors and nurses attend training sessions on the insertion of the intrauterine device, and public health nurses, midwives, clerks, and laboratory technicians are given special training. Government officials at all levels are given two hours of family-planning education in the form of films and lectures. In 1980, 1,700 officials attended thirty-five such classes. Community workers for farmers' associations, women's clubs, fishermen's organizations, and other voluntary groups attend educational programs on family planning. Home economists in the aboriginal areas are given subsidies to run courses on family planning for their class members. Junior high school teachers are brought into the program, providing educational material on population problems, program activities, and contraceptive methods. Voluntary workers are brought together for seminars.

Fieldworkers are the heart of the program. They are provided with bicycles and motorcycles. Bonuses in cash are provided based on performance. These are paid three times a year, according to (1) number of couples contacted as a percent of total eligible couples; (2) number of families home visited as a percent of the number of couples contacted; (3) number of women under age twenty-five contacted as a percentage of total eligible women; (4) proportion of remote areas contacted; and (5) average individual monthly achievement. The system carries inducements to bring the message to the people and the areas that need it most and the results indicate that this is achieved. A point system is used to scale the bonuses, which are earned by 90 percent of the workers, averaging fifty dollars (U.S.) per person each of the three payment periods. Supervisors spot-check the activities of these fieldworkers. None of this appears to be offensive to the public. No compulsion is involved. By the end of 1976, after twelve years of the program, 69 percent of the eligible couples were practicing relatively effective contraceptive methods.

Family-planning programs are demanding in terms of skills, ideas, initiative, and persistence. Financially, the burden is modest. Cost of the program in 1976 was about $2.5 million (U.S.) or about fifteen cents for each person in Taiwan.

From its beginning in 1964 through the year 1977 the program averted, by Dr. Sun's calculations, 1,212,000 births. In 1977 alone, the program was calculated to prevent 184,000 births. This may be judged against 428,000 actual births in 1976. Altogether, during the period 1964 to 1977, births were 2.7 million below the preprogram trend. Dr. Sun claims credit in the name of his program for less than half of this reduction; most of the averted births, he says, were attributable to causes outside the program such as urbanization and industrialization. Bianco estimates the proportion of births averted by the program at one-fourth of what would otherwise have been the case. A figure intermediate between these two estimates gives us about a million averted births.

A million averted births in a period of twelve years may be judged against the size of Taiwan's population, 17 million. This is a reduction of about 6 percent, similar to the achievement in the People's Republic, somewhat differently calculated, during a period of similar length.

There are problems. Abortions are on the increase. Though they are illegal there is one abortion for every three live births. Premarital pregnancies have become more numerous. Thirty percent of the women are pregnant before marriage. Eighty percent of the premarital births are by mothers sixteen to eighteen years of age. A predominantly young population, the result of birthrates that were very high until recently, means that there are many women in or coming into childbearing age with a potential for population increase.

Some traditional values remain. Preference for sons continues and inclines parents to keep having children until the desire for a male offspring is fulfilled. The belief that to be born in the Year of the Dragon inclines one toward a happy and successful life causes parents to schedule births in such years, introducing a disturbing element into the statistics and obscuring trends.

However all this may be, the Taiwan family-planning program is well established. In the first phase, the major objective was to help families limit their offspring to the desired number, that number being essentially as it had long been. Beginning about 1970, says Dr. Sun, families began reducing the desired family size, in part because of social, cultural, and economic trends, and in part because of the educational effect of the family-planning program. In 1965 the women of Taiwan generally preferred 4 children. By 1976 the preferred number was 2.9.

Projections for population numbers have been established for 1989. Comparisons are:

	Actual earlier date	Projection 1989
Total fertility rate per woman	2.9 (1976)	2.0
Birthrate per thousand	24.4 (1979)	18.5
Rate of natural increase per hundred	1.86 (1980)	1.25

Source: *Taiwan Provincal Institute of Family Planning Annual Report, July 1980–June 1981.*

Population researchers speak of the "demographic transition." This is their phrase for that period, counted in decades, during which the death rate is low or falling and the birthrate remains high. This is the condition which yields the "population explosion." In time the birthrate falls to approximately that of the death rate and population plateaus at some level, considerably higher than prior to these changes. Length of the transition varies, as does the degree of population increase while the change is under way. Likewise, the posttransition relationship of death rate and birthrate may vary. Despite its vagaries the demographic transition is a useful concept.

Taiwan apparently is well along in its demographic transition and may accomplish it in record time. The death rate began to fall about 1920. The birthrate began to fall about 1960, forty years later. A period of uncertain length will be required before the two come into something like a new accomodation to one another and total population numbers change at a tolerable rate.

We have looked at three countries in which family planning is, in varying degrees, offered and accepted (United States, India, Taiwan) and at one (China) in which it is required. In each of these countries progress is being made and even in one most threatened by population growth, India, an avowed optimist can find grounds for hope. Despite what favorable assessment one can draw from the "success" stories included in this section, much of the Third World lacks effective family-planning programs. One must conclude with Paul Demeny, director of the Center for Policy Studies and vice-president of the Population Council of New York, that in many areas "the brunt of the population explosion is yet to come."

Perhaps we should be restrained in our expectations. Pronatal attitudes are as old as humanity. The death rate didn't begin to drop until one hundred years ago. The surge in numbers didn't attract the world's attention until about seventy-five years ago. Family-planning programs, as conscious national policy, began only after World War II.

Family planning is long range in its very nature. Generating a birth takes nine months; the length of time required to avert a birth apparently is much longer.

REFERENCES

Bianco, Lucien. 1985. "Family Planning Programs and Fertility Decline in Taiwan and Mainland China: A Comparison." *Issues and Studies* 21, no. 11 (Nov.). Institute of International Relations, Taipei, Taiwan, Republic of China.

Boorman, ed. 1967. "Chiang Mon Lin." *Biographical Dictionary of Republican China.* New York: Columbia Univ. Press.

Demeny, Paul. 1984. "A Perspective on Long Term Population Growth." *Population and Development Review* 10, no. 1 (Mar.):103–26.

Liu, K. G., and T. H. Sun. 1979. "The Determinants of Fertility Transition and Their Implications in Taiwan, ROC." *Industry of Free China* 52, nos. 2, 3 (Aug.–Sept.).

Oshima, Harry T. 1983. "The Industrial and Demographic Transitions in East Asia." *Population and Development Review* 9, no. 4 (Dec.):583–607.

Sun, T. H. 1977. "Demographic Evaluation of Taiwan's Family Planning Program." Mimeographed paper presented at the Eighth Summer Seminar on Population, Population Institute, East-West Center, Honolulu.

———. 1982. Interview with the author, Taichung.

Taiwan Provincial Institue of Family Planning. 1981. *Annual Report, July 1980–June 1981.* Taichung, Taiwan.

V

Summary

CHAPTER 32

The Ancient Enemy in Retreat

IN THE PREVIOUS CHAPTERS we looked at the past, tracing the steps by which the developed countries avoided the Malthusian threat, noting that the developing nations have embarked on their own versions of this path with varying degrees of commitment and success.

In this chapter we look to the future, trying to judge whether those still darkened by the Malthusian shadow can reasonably hope to escape it. Have the agricultural scientists of the past two hundred years put in place or in prospect the needed knowledge base? Will future scientists build adequately thereon? Will the farmers of the developing nations make good use of available and prospective science? Will they have the resources, the incentives, and the institutions to do the job? Will those who work at food aid have public support in alleviating hunger? Can the family planners guide the Third World through the demographic transition without a Malthusian crunch? Is hunger, the ancient enemy, in retreat? Or is our old adversary merely lying in wait, gathering strength for a new assault? In the present chapter we attempt to answer some of these towering questions.

The thesis of this book is that the world is on its way toward overcoming hunger. Already the adversary has been driven from Europe, the United States, Canada, Japan, and parts of Oceania. Ground is being gained on the western rim of the Pacific, particularly in Korea, Taiwan, Hong Kong, Singapore, and Malaysia. Those two enormous nations, the Soviet Union and the People's Republic of China, appear to have won their decisive battles against widespread hunger, though the enemy is still defiant. Even in India hope has replaced resignation. Countries that formerly accepted hunger as inevitable have now challenged it. The initiative has passed from the grim reaper to those who oppose him. Except in a limited number of countries hunger is on the defensive. The trend of the campaign appears to be one-directional. No nation that has overcome hunger has subsequently lost to this enemy. One should not hand down a verdict when the battle is still being waged. But while the casualty lists still are long the crucial period may have been passed. The historian, writing during the twenty-first century, may identify our time as the turning point.

Certainly those nations still in jeopardy will not all escape hunger at the same time. The countries that have already escaped did so severally and gradually over a long period. Liberation from hunger henceforward will follow that same path. Famine will make its last stand in its final stronghold: where agricultural science has not penetrated, where economic development lags, where weather is most erratic, where the food needs of the unfortunate are ignored, where government is unstable, and where birthrates continue at their historic highs. The objective set forth by U.S. Secretary of State Henry Kissinger at the 1974 World Food Conference in Rome, that within the next decade "no child will go to bed hungry," was not achieved, nor will it be. Victory in such absolute terms is not possible. But victory need not be total to be decisive.

A sobering thought is injected at this point. The Four Horsemen of the Apocalypse still ride. As we see the possibility of curbing one, Famine, two others appear as growing threats: War, in the form of nuclear holocaust, and Pestilence, a new deadly disease for which, as this is written, there is no known cure.

Focusing on the hungry nations, we look at the sectors prominent in this book, the salients credited with having freed from hunger the people of the Western world: food production, food aid, and family planning. What can we reasonably expect on these fronts during the next thirty years?

FOOD PRODUCTION

Agricultural science is on the march. It has achieved what the nuclear scientists call "critical mass" and what the economic development people call "takeoff." It now propagates its own next generation. When science broke open the door that had held agriculture within traditional confines, it burst into a new room that in turn had many doors: genetics, pathology, engineering, nutrition. Through these science moved to progressively larger and more complex rooms, each with its own doors. And as science progressed, the doors through which it moved closed behind it. Nothing important that was won was subsequently lost though it was often replaced by something better.

In constant value terms world expenditures on agricultural research appear to have tripled from 1959 to 1974. International support of agricultural development has continued to expand. Resource flows to food and agriculture in the Third World, passing through various conduits of the United Nations, tripled in real terms from 1974 to 1982, totaling $5.2 billion in 1981. To this must be added the bilateral programs of donor countries, the efforts of the great foundations, the investments of international agribusiness firms, and, above all, the efforts of the developing countries themselves. In 1974 the Food and Agriculture Organization estimated financing supplied by the developing countries themselves to be 90 percent of the total. The international research centers partly overlap and partly extend this listing. Despite these impressive statistics, the developing countries typically invest in agriculture a smaller proportion of their gross national product than the proportion that agriculture contributes.

Research in agricultural science is amazingly productive. Estimates of annual rates of return on investment in agricultural research in the United States are indicative rather than definitive. However one may wish to discount them, they fall in the 30 to 60 percent range. Estimated rates of return to public investment in the extension of new information to farmers run even higher. Growing perception of this favorable return is likely to lead to increased investment.

Agricultural knowledge is being internationalized. Discoveries made in the advanced countries are quickly available to the developing nations through literature and exchange of personnel.

Not all of the new findings can be used in the developing nations. The contribution will have to be selective rather than general, more adapted than adopted, and chosen by the recipients rather than prescribed by the suppliers. But it is easier to adapt a technology than to create it wholly new. The agricultural science of the developing nations will be a mix of what is borrowed and what they themselves create. And they create a significant amount, as we have seen to be the case in Mexico, India, China, and the Philippines. All of this will be more efficient in that it now has the advantage of many years' experience in the giving, receiving, and blending of knowledge.

Advancing agricultural science will increase food production in the already developed nations. This will help the hungry countries in two ways. It will permit commercial food shipments from the developed countries to the food-deficit nations in exchange for their exports, and it will make supplies available for food aid.

Agricultural research has become strongly institutionalized, giving it continuity. There now are national and provincial agricultural experiment stations and colleges in most of the developing countries. Some of these are at an elementary level, true enough. But they are serviced by the International Research Network, by the Food and Agriculture Organization of the United Nations, by various foundations, and by the agricultural development agencies of the industrial countries. Agribusiness concerns form technology growth centers from which radiate improved agricultural practices. Most of the food-critical nations have some form of extension service to get information to farmers.

Problems of erosion, depleted forest cover, pollution, desertification, and miniaturized farms are very real. But the doomsday outlook projected by the report to the Club of Rome, so widely accepted a few years back, appears to have been overdrawn. The threat has generated efforts to cope, some promising, some not. That greatest of natural disasters, drought, is as unpredictable and devastating as ever. But through better farming systems and food aid the troubled countries and their helpers are trying to cope.

If they learn about them, farmers of the Third World will adopt new practices that fit into their farming systems and give promise of increasing yield and income. T. W. Schultz was right about that. The opportunity to learn is increasing. Education goes forward in the developing world, contributing to improvement in agricultural production and to declining birthrates. Some of the lowest income countries—Sri Lanka, Tanzania, and Vietnam—have already achieved or are fast approaching universal primary education. For the developing countries as a group, public spending on education increased from 2.3 percent of gross national production in 1960 to 3.9 percent in 1974. The ability to read the instructions on a can of insecticide contributes significantly to agricultural production.

Many Third World governments have policies that hold down the price of food in an effort to help city consumers. These policies have the unfortunate effect of inhibiting agricultural production. A number of countries—the Soviet Union, China, India, and Thailand among them—have modified these policies, giving better promise for food production. More countries are likely to do so.

Despite all the science, the education, and the institutional support, nothing really happens until the farmer puts seed into the ground. What are the new technologies most likely to be applicable in the food-critical nations? We provide a short list, including three of the most promising:

Better germ plasm. Coming both from traditional breeding methods and from gene splicing, better plants and animals will increase Third World yields in the years ahead. Basic work done in the developed countries can be adapted, tested, and modified in accordance with local conditions. This need not require a vast new scientific establishment in the developing countries. To be guarded against is the tendency for a poor nation to set up a sophisticated and expensive agricultural research center not so much to serve its agriculture as to build its reputation for scientific capability.

Pest control. There are new methods, as we have seen, for combatting diseases, insects, and weeds. These stem from basic research done in the developed nations, with coattails available for the Third World to grasp. Adaptation will of course be necessary. Antibiotics and insecticides are not generally capital intensive nor do they displace much human labor. Hence they can, for the better part, be put to use without overstressing social, political, and economic systems in the adopting country.

Plant nutrition. Increased use of fertilizer holds promise for quick increase in yields. For its successful use there must be adaptive research in the country concerned to accommodate local soil, crop, and climatic conditions. There must of course be extension work, transportation, and credit.

There are other promising practices, old and new. Perhaps least useful is the technology so dear to the hearts of farmers in the developed countries – big farming machinery. These machines preempt large amounts of capital, which is limited in the developing countries; they displace labor, which already is underemployed; and they require sophisticated maintenance, which in most developing countries is not available.

During the past thirty years Third World agriculture has fed the largest and fastest-growing population in the world's history. On the average (and admittedly averages mask a great range of individual cases), the typical man in the Third World is better fed than his father or grandfather. Through the past several decades, the most stressful of the demographic transition, agriculture has kept a half-step ahead of population growth. The present and prospective fund of science gives reason for believing that this will continue to be so.

FOOD AID

A number of the developing countries have launched food security systems – India with its fair price shops, Bangladesh with food-for-work, Sri Lanka with its food subsidies, and China with its safety net. All of these are relatively new and testimony that the sharing principle is becoming accepted. The developed countries are acknowledging a role, although they are not yet sure just what the role is, in helping meet the needs of hungry people abroad. Witness American assistance to the people of Ethiopia in 1984–85 despite deep diplomatic differences with the communist government of that country.

Some form of storage is necessary if food aid is to be provided. If international food aid is intended, stocks can be held in the supplying nation or the receiving nation or both. Efforts to set up an international food reserve have been disappointing; some vulnerable countries have provided their own systems. India is an example.

Sometimes food aid is inept and uneven. Always it is costly. There are cases of corruption. The danger of reducing self-reliance is ever present. We have been trading commodities for some thousands of years and have not yet perfected the market mechanisms for doing so. We have been providing food aid outside the market or in a modified market for only a short time and it is not surprising that much remains to be learned. In any case the ethos has changed. Hunger among the unfortunate is no longer tolerated as it once was.

Like agricultural science, food aid has become institutionalized. This is true not only within countries but internationally as well. The World Food Program of the United Nations performs this function. The World Food Council, a United Nations agency, was originally set up in 1948 and was revitalized in 1974. World Food congresses were held in 1963, 1970, and 1974 and no doubt will be held again. Among the active proponents for international food aid are the nongovernment organizations, many of them church related. More than 170 of these were present at the Rome conference. The International Wheat Agreement has a food aid convention, the objective of which is to supply, annually, 10 million tons of cereal in the form of aid to the developing countries. The developed nations have their own international food aid systems; the United States is foremost among them. The International Monetary Fund has a new food-financing facility. Continuity and early response to need are more easily possible because of this institutional structure.

FAMILY PLANNING

In the battle against hunger, food production is the seasoned veteran, food aid a new-fledged fighter, and family planning the raw recruit. But in the long campaign the recruit may be the decisive battler in gaining the victory. At least forty-two developing nations, comprising more than three-fourths of the population of the developing countries, have adopted official policies to reduce the rates of population growth. Geographically, family planning efforts are generally strong in East Asia, less so in South Asia, mixed and moderate in Latin America and the Caribbean, weak in the middle East and North Africa, and very weak in sub-Sahara Africa, precisely the area in which hunger poses the gravest threat (Table 32.1). Family planning has been institutionalized and internationalized, as have agricultural research and food aid, so it, too, has structure and continuity. There have been two World Population Conferences, one in Bucharest in 1974 and one in Mexico City in 1984.

Long-term projections of population numbers have a notoriously poor record. Nevertheless we look at them. Paul Demeny, vice-president of the Population Council of New York, using data from the World Bank and the United Nations, projects a little more than a doubling of the population in

Table 32.1   Population Policy Indicators for Selected Countries with Populations of 15 Million or More

Country	Population Millions 1982	Total Fertility Rate	Per Capita Expenditure on Family Planning Dollars	Percent Decline in Birth Rate 1965–82	Rating of Effort
Sub-Sahara Africa					
Kenya	18	8.0	0.71	0.0	weak
Tanzania	20	6.5	0.18	–	weak
Nigeria	91	6.9	–	0.0	very weak
Zaire	31	6.3	0.06	+3.2	very weak
Sudan	20	6.6	–	1.5	very weak
Ethiopia	33	6.5	–	3.0	very weak
Middle East and North Africa					
Egypt	44	4.6	0.81	22.0	weak
Morocco	20	5.8	0.66	18.3	weak
Turkey	47	4.1	–	30.5	weak
Algeria	20	7.0	–	5.4	weak
Latin America and Caribbean					
Colombia	27	3.6	0.31	30.4	very strong
Mexico	73	4.6	0.58	37.1	very strong
Brazil	127	3.9	0.09	30.4	strong
Venezuela	17	4.3	–	–	weak
Peru	17	4.5	0.32	30.8	weak
South Asia					
Sri Lanka	15	3.4	0.42	30.6	very strong
India	717	4.8	0.34	18.7	very strong
Bangladesh	93	6.3	0.51	14.9	strong
Pakistan	87	5.8	0.30	22.7	strong
Nepal	15	6.3	0.72	–	weak
East Asia					
China	1,008	2.3	1.00	61.3	very strong
Korea, Rep. of	39	2.7	0.71	43.8	very strong
Indonesia	153	4.3	0.59	25.9	very strong
Malaysia	15	3.7	1.18	–	very strong
Thailand	49	3.6	0.60	42.9	strong
Philippines	51	4.2	0.78	38.2	strong

Source: *World Development Report,* 1984, 156, 149, 65, 192–93.

the less-developed regions during the forty-five year period from 1980 to 2025. This increase will occur only if agricultural production validates it. Agriculture holds veto power over any estimate of future population.

One can be frightened at the magnitude of this prospective change. Or one can be reassured by the fact that in the past the developing countries achieved a relative change of like magnitude in a shorter period of time. During the thirty years from 1950 to 1980, modern medicine dropped the death rate while the birthrate continued high and population numbers exploded. Modern agriculture, responding to the challenge, multiplied food production. Population in the developing countries doubled and the people were fed. As testimony to the relative adequacy of the food supply, the real price of food declined during this period.

The forthcoming population doubling, though it is expected to come over a longer period, will be more difficult than the past doubling because it comes on top of the previous surge; it will place an additional burden on physical resources and social institutions, already stressed. On the other hand the problem will be somewhat alleviated by greater awareness, a growing body of agricultural science, the momentum gained by agriculture during the phenomenal performance of the last thirty years, and the development of institutions for coping.

Not surprisingly, the prospective change in numbers of people is viewed with deep concern by many people. The average person has these attitudes toward change: The present, whatever it is, is accepted as the norm. Past changes, which led to the present are considered understandable and generally appropriate. But prospective changes of like magnitude are looked on with apprehension.

The hunger problem is likely to recede for the generations that follow our own. In the long run, well into the twenty-first century, economic development and family planning seem likely to bring the birthrate under control and move the demographic transition toward completion. By the year 2050 the world population is expected to approach stability at somewhere around 10 billion people, 2.25 times the 1980 level. Except for unforeseeable disasters and pockets of poverty that escape the sweep of events, widespread hunger should then be a topic of history. There will be enormous numbers of people but in all probability a smaller percentage of them will be hungry than is now the case. Put simply, the problem is how to utilize the services and meet the needs of people who in former times would have starved to death. I know of no one who, on reflection, would prefer the Malthusian solution.

The ancient enemy is in retreat. Coming into being is a world that will be well fed. We must visualize this better world before it can be achieved. And this we are doing. Ours is the first generation to dare to think in terms of food enough for all.

REFERENCES

Demeny, Paul. 1984. "Bucharest, Mexico City, and Beyond." *Population Notes* 55. Center for Policy Studies, The Population Council, New York.

Evenson, Robert E., and Yoav Kislev. 1975. *Agricultural Research and Productivity.* New Haven: Yale Univ. Press.

Food and Agriculture Organization. 1981. *Agriculture: Toward 2000.* Rome.

Food Policy. 1984. *Butterworth Scientific Journal* 19, no. 4.

Mellor, John W., and Bruce F. Johnston. 1984. "The World Food Equation: Interrelations among Development, Employment, and Food Consumption." *Journal of Economic Literature* 22 (June). Reprinted by International Food Policy Research Institute, Washington, D.C.

Population Council. 1984. *Population and Development Review* 10, no. 1 (Mar.).

Presidential Commissoin on World Hunger. 1980. *Overcoming World Hunger: The Challenge Ahead.* Washington, D.C.

World Bank. 1984. *World Development Report 1984.* New York: Oxford Univ. Press.

INDEX